COUNTRY CUISINE

COUNTRY CUISINE

Cooking with Country Chefs

ELIZABETH KENT

Wines chosen by Jancis Robinson

Special illustrations by Jane Jamieson

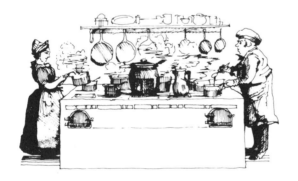

SIDGWICK & JACKSON

LONDON

ISBN 0 283 98636 0

Filmset by Northumberland Press Ltd,
Gateshead, Tyne and Wear
and printed in Great Britain by
Biddles Ltd, Guildford, Surrey
for Sidgwick & Jackson Limited
1 Tavistock Chambers, Bloomsbury Way
London WC1A 2SG

For all the friends who shared my passion for country restaurants – tasting dish after dish with unflagging enthusiasm. Especially the epicurean Doctor.

Contents

Acknowledgements

I have acknowledged elsewhere the enormous debt I owe to the restaurateurs; without them this book could not have been written. I am also grateful for the invaluable help and advice given by my editors and by Jancis Robinson. Special thanks to Duncan and to Ian; to those tireless tasters, Steve, Helen and Jill; and to my parents, who received more recipes than letters for far too long.

For permission to reprint published recipes, I would like to thank Macdonald and Jane's (*Entertaining with John Tovey* by John Tovey and *Four Seasons Cookery Book* by Margaret Costa), Agri-Books (*The Ballymaloe Cookbook* by Myrtle Allen) and Hungry Monk Publications (*The Secrets of The Hungry Monk* by Ian Dowding, Nigel and Sue Mackenzie).

Introduction

Are you old enough to remember whalemeat rissoles? luncheon sausage? Colonel Peron's little portions of elderly Argentine beef? hot sausages made almost wholly of soya bean? custard powder, and desserts made of saccharine and imitation cream? If so, pause to consider how great our progress has been. If not, ask your elders.

Raymond Postgate, *The Good Food Guide* (*1963*)

For centuries, country inns have acted as hospices to weary travellers, providing warmth, sustenance and liquid fortification. They had no gastronomic pretensions and unlike the French *auberges de route* were not equipped to serve five-course feasts to itinerant gourmets. Instead, it was simple, hearty fare (boiled meat, pies and 'sawsidges') and, in early days, guests joined their host at one large table, eating whatever he provided (thus the expression *table d'hôte* for a set meal).

Only in this century has the country restaurant emerged with an identity of its own, with the primary aim of offering superior food and wine in congenial surroundings. Among the first to appear – in the 1920s – was The Spread Eagle at Thame, then run by John Fothergill. At first, his efforts to upgrade the cooking met fierce opposition from the local farmers, content with their pints and 'ploughman's'. In desperation, he finally posted a notice which read:

Wanted – thirty good men to eat the
following dinner on Saturday,
January 20th (1923)

Tomato Soup
Fish–brown stew
Venison
Jugged Hare
Plum Pudding
Toasted Cheese
Filberts

4s a head

Twenty-five people duly booked but when only half that number turned up, Fothergill abandoned all hope of converting the locals and instead set about attracting a new kind of customer. In this he was considerably more successful and the restaurant soon became a popular watering-hole for the Oxford intelligentsia and visiting London epicures. Its wine list, of impressive proportions, undoubtedly added to its attractions. The Spread Eagle presented a gastronomic novelty: a restaurant which customers actually went out of their way to visit.

In the next county, Barry Neame ran a comparable establishment: The Hind's Head at Bray. Here again, the food was not *de luxe* but it was well prepared from first-class ingredients. The cellar was of a standard not often found outside London and its contents attracted many members of the Wine and Food Society, including their mentor, André Simon. In one of his articles on 'Memorable Meals', Mr Simon describes a dinner held at The Hind's Head praising, amongst other things, 'the proper slowness of service'. He also voices a feeling widely held at that time: 'Mine host takes the view, and we all unhesitatingly agreed with him, that it is far better for the English innkeeper to produce plain dishes really well cooked, than attempt elaboration and fail in the attempt.'

Further north, Willie Heptinstall began a more ambitious enterprise in the Highlands. After cooking in several foreign capitals, he bought (in 1929) a hotel in Fortingall, a part of Scotland known for its beauty but not its accessibility. There he cooked as if he were still in the kitchen of the Carlton Hotel in Budapest or the Continental in Paris. His menus were staggering in scope and the cold table, served as a preface to Sunday lunch, became legendary; stretching the length of the entrance hall, it tempted diners with at least forty different hors d'oeuvres. Despite its remoteness, Fortingall became immensely popular, attracting customers from all parts of the country. It achieved a reputation for excellent food which continued until Heptinstall finally retired, thirty-five years later.

The war years were a major setback to the development of country restaurant cooking, especially as chefs continued (even after rationing ended) to improvise with substitutes. It wasn't until the early fifties that a noticeable change took place. Then a totally new breed of restaurateur emerged: the complete amateur. With no professional training whatsoever, his only qualifications were an indomitable enthusiasm for food and an aptitude for hard work. In London, this resulted in the debut of the 'bistro', usually run on a shoestring by an enterprising individual. Restaurants like La Bicyclette, The Ox on the Roof, Chanterelle and Nick's Diner all offered a novel approach to dining out. The food was imaginative, the prices reasonable and the atmosphere immense fun.

In the country, this entrepreneurial spirit was represented with no less verve but in slightly more traditional form. The first of the 'new breed' to appear was Francis Coulson, a young out-of-work actor and recent emigré from London. Helped by a small inheritance and a sanguine bank manager, he bought a large Victorian house overlooking Ullswater, a few miles from Penrith. It was run-down and nondescript but in two years, by 1951, he had made 'Sharrow Bay' a Cumbrian landmark. The teas were spectacular and attracted eighty to a hundred people a day. Everything, from the crusty white bread to the famous 'fatless sponge', was baked in the Sharrow kitchen. Despite the rationing, lunches and dinners were a feast for post-war palates. With a magic touch, Coulson turned lamb, fish and rabbits (pulled seemingly from thin air) into a series of culinary hat-tricks. He was soon joined by Brian Sack (until then a surveyor in London) and together they created a gastronomic paradise. Thirty years later, dripping with stars and accolades, Sharrow Bay is still regarded as one of the best restaurants anywhere.

The next to appear was George Perry-Smith who, after teaching English in Paris, decided to develop other interests and start a country restaurant. When he opened the doors of The Hole in the Wall in 1952, residents of Bath couldn't possibly have anticipated the treats that lay in store. The traditional *table d'hôte* was jettisoned and replaced by a mind-boggling *à la carte*. It was a cosmopolitan collection, from humble spaghetti to more sophisticated Lobster Newburg. Customers could choose from almost a hundred different dishes, under fifteen headings. The range was enormous, the portions generous and, compared to other establishments' offerings – variations of 'meat and two veg' – it must have seemed like Wonderland. As the restaurant grew older, the menu became slimmer and more distinctive. It was divided into 'Hot or Cold Beginnings', then about twenty main courses under the headings 'Always' and 'Sometimes', rounded off with substantial 'Endings'. The quality of the dishes remained consistently high and the *Brandade, Ceviche, Rissoles à la parisienne* and Salmon in pastry with ginger and currants became celebrated favourites.

Sharrow Bay and The Hole in the Wall are significant not simply because of their exceptional food but because they proved that an 'amateur' could run a successful restaurant – without a huge retinue of kitchen staff and without an obligation to serve classical French *cuisine*. Both restaurants were used as models by many young chefs who, encouraged by their success, started similar establishments in the country. (The Wife of Bath, The Carved Angel, White's and Mallet's were all founded by Perry-Smith and Coulson disciples.)

But the greatest single influence in the 1950s was undoubtedly the writing of Elizabeth David. With the publication of her first book, *Mediterranean Food*, in 1950 and then *French Country Cooking* a year later, she introduced food-lovers to a tantalizing new world. It was the birth in this country of *cuisine bourgeoise*. Elizabeth David herself describes this as:

> French regional and peasant cookery, which, at its best, is the most delicious in the world; cookery which uses materials to the greatest advantage without going to the absurd lengths of the complicated and so-called 'Haute Cuisine' . . .

British cookery, sluggish and stodgy, was given a much-needed transfusion. Mrs David provided a goldmine of new recipes and, even more important, showed that they were within easy reach of the ordinary cook: they required neither a costly *batterie de cuisine* nor a chequebook the size of the Ritz. These two books provided inspiration for many talented cooks, some of them restaurateurs or professional chefs already, and gave them the impetus to develop in a different direction. The basic tenets of *cuisine bourgeoise* are so fundamental to the new style of country restaurant that their compatibility must have been seen immediately. Variations of Mrs David's recipes for *Bouillabaisse, Bourride, Tarte à l'oignon, Cassoulet, Piperade* and *Poulet à l'estragon* can still be found on numerous country menus.

Another seminal work of the early fifties was *The Good Food Guide*. The brain-child of Raymond Postgate, it aimed 'to improve British cooking and service' by the creation of a Good Food Club. Its members would have one interest in common – 'the discovery of good inns and their improvement' – and by sending in reports would establish a reliable gastronomic network, nationwide. Postgate was appalled by the depths to which restaurant cooking had sunk after the war and the *Guide* was a rallying call to the British eating public. In the Preface to the first edition (1951) he wrote:

> There is no other way that I can see of bringing the force of public opinion to bear on British catering than some such guide as this. For fifty years now complaints have been made against British cooking, and no improvement has resulted. Indeed, it is quite arguable that worse meals are served today in hotels and restaurants than were in Edwardian days.... British food is sometimes said to be the worst in the world bar American. Yet there is no reason in nature why British cooking should be worse than, say, French.... We have no worse materials than the French have; indeed in some cases our materials are undeniably tastier. It remains worse only because public discontent is unorganized and (it must be admitted) sometimes also ignorant.

Though only slightly bigger than a packet of cigarettes, with a fraction of the entries it has today, the *Guide* quickly attracted a devoted following. Throughout the fifties a secret army of good-food detectors systematically ate their way across the country.

At the tail end of the same decade, another country restaurant, distinguished by its lack of convention and outstandingly good food, began to attract special attention. It was The Elizabeth in Oxford, run by Kenneth Bell. Though Bell had been professionally trained, it is doubtful whether his instructors at the prestigious *Ecole Hôtelière* Lausanne would have recognized many dishes on his menu. Encouraged by Perry-Smith's success at The Hole in the Wall, Kenneth Bell's style was also characterized by its originality. But while Perry-Smith drew inspiration from Elizabeth David and various international sources (including his chef, a former Canadian

16

Mountie), Bell concentrated exclusively on Mediterranean cooking. Recipes such as Taramasalata, Paella, Moussaka and Prawns with rice and *aioli* soon became 'specialities' of the house. Despite the success of The Elizabeth, Kenneth Bell was not entirely happy. The conditions were cramped, there was no proper cellar and he longed to run a restaurant which really *was* in the country. By 1966 he had bought Thornbury Castle, a few miles from the Severn, and began serving meals from its two magnificently panelled dining-rooms. With a menu considerably shorter than the one at The Elizabeth, he continued to provide remarkable food, this time veering towards a French provincial style.

At roughly the same time, in the depths of Somerset, an unusual type of cooking was being done at The Miners' Arms in Priddy. Here, Mr and Mrs Paul Leyton produced a highly original menu. The dishes on it were so mystifyingly described that they must have driven the customers wild with delight or despair. They included Oxford John, Chicken Chamonix and Priddy Oggy, plus sweets like Chewton Cherry, Miners' Delight and Mendip Moonshine. The cooking was consistently good, but it was some time before customers knew what to expect. And *The Good Food Guide* (1961) felt it necessary to draw members' attention to the fact that 'everything is cooked to order; you must wait a quarter of an hour or so ... this is no place for a fast snack.'

During the 1960s, an equally novel approach could be found at The Box Tree in West Yorkshire. Colin Long and Malcolm Reid, retiring prematurely (still in their twenties) from the menswear trade, bought an old tea shop in the quiet town of Ilkley. Here they began serving teas more exciting than a three-act matinée. With a waiter in white tie and tails, a waitress in long dress, and a silver tray brimming with fresh cream cakes, the customers felt like film stars. When the queues threatened to block the traffic outside, they expanded and opened for lunch and dinner. At the start, they knew nothing about cooking or catering and simply lived by their wits and a determina-

17

tion to succeed. Unlike other country restaurateurs at this time, they had little interest in *cuisine bourgeoise*; for them the ultimate was three-star classical French cooking. Their menu, which began modestly, has become progressively more elaborate and sophisticated. They have now established a kitchen which is known for its professionalism and as a prestigious training ground for budding chefs. It has won countless awards (including the Egon Ronay Restaurant of the Year award in 1971) and is now firmly in the realm of *haute cuisine*, with few traces of country cooking on its menu.

The sixties also saw the rise of another exceptional restaurant, this time in the West Country. In 1967, Sonia and Patrick Stevenson, both professional musicians and amateur cooks, opened The Horn of Plenty in Gulworthy. Their menu was eclectic, borrowing recipes from old Cornish cookery books, classic dishes from Escoffier and regional ones from Elizabeth David. But whatever the dish, it was exquisitely prepared and presented by Sonia Stevenson, an intuitive and talented cook. It was like manna in the wilderness and food-lovers flocked to try her Salmon in sorrel sauce, Peruvian duck and Cornish parsley pie. Motorized gourmets made it an obligatory stop en route to the West Country and its success proved unquestionably that this standard of cooking could attract custom from any distance.

By the mid-1960s, the level of British catering had improved dramatically. A decade after the first *Good Food Guide* was published, Raymond Postgate wrote in the Preface of the tenth edition:

> ... food in Britain is nothing like as bad as it was ten or so years ago. But then, it was intolerable in those days. There is still a lot of dreadful food served in this island, but at that time there was practically nothing else at all but dreadful food. One had to single out for praise places where a joint and two veg. were merely edible, and the staff were neither too obviously incompetent nor unbearably rude. ... As for materials, butter was never

used in cooking, it was always marge. Cream was never real cream.... That has changed. Materials are better and more abundant, and though, in roughly half the establishments in this country, the cooking is as bad as it was then, in the other half it isn't.

Still not a paradise isle, but it was progress. Furthermore, this gastronomic 'bug' was obviously infectious. For as the customers revolted, there appeared a rash of outstanding restaurants outside London. The sixties and early seventies saw an unrivalled selection of places to dine at in the country. The Wife of Bath, The Hungry Monk, Gravetye Manor, The Old House, Le Talbooth, Houstoun House, Pool Court and Miller Howe were just a few of those which sprang to life at this time.

By the mid-1970s, it was obvious that the 'new breed' of country restaurant had at last come of age. After a prolonged adolescence, it was recognized as a potent source of original cooking. The 'bumpkin' status had finally gone and it was no longer measured by an urban yardstick. Greater awareness of these restaurants came at a time when the competition was putting up a pretty dismal show. The big brewers were exchanging character for plastic beams and food of roughly the same consistency, while hotel chains served a varied menu of steak and scampi. It is hardly surprising that these small, owner-run establishments were so well received. The fact that every other restaurant was dishing up prawn cocktail, chicken in a basket and jellied trifle made them even more determined to serve anything but.

These country restaurants, all characterized by their individuality, have several traits in common. On the whole, they have abandoned the *à la carte* menu and have substituted a more flexible *table d'hôte*, changing by the day, week or month. This does not feature *fraises de bois* or *escargots* but offers instead imaginative cooking, based on country produce, of an unusually high standard. Dishes are tailored to the season and the menu shrinks or expands according to the availability of ingredients. Frozen foods are as popular as the plague and these restaurateurs wouldn't be caught dead near a packet of frozen peas, sprouts or chips. The *table* reflects the idiosyncrasies of the *hôte* for it is he (in nine cases out of ten) who does the cooking and his ability which determines the success or failure of the restaurant. There is no handing over, as in a city kitchen, to a *sous-chef* when the energy or inspiration run out.

While the atmosphere of a restaurant can be quite distinct from the quality of its cooking, in the country the two become inextricably linked. A warm welcome at the door usually indicates a similar enthusiasm in the kitchen. In a city restaurant, the ambiance is often diluted by its size and the number of business clients. But to most country patrons, dining-out is still primarily a social occasion and however good the food may be, it will be ruined by a long wait, uninterested waiter or hushed silences. As many have had to book several weeks in advance (necessary for the smaller restaurants like Tullythwaite House, La Potinière, White Moss House etc.) and have driven quite a distance, their critical faculties are, understandably, more finely tuned than those of the casual urban diner. If the surroundings are not congenial, then you have not only unhappy customers but incipient indigestion. Here again, the weight lies firmly on the shoulders of the *chef-patron* who must attend to the food *and* its consumers.

There is now such a wealth of excellent restaurants in the country that to do all of them justice would take a book of epic proportions. It would also necessitate, for reasons of space, no more than a cursory glance at each one. Instead, this book takes a sampling of the best to be found in Great Britain and Ireland and looks at them in greater depth. Each represents the new style of country restaurant (though some may be ten or twenty years old) with the characteristics mentioned in previous paragraphs. To dispel any illusion that these are 'country cousins' in relation to their French or continental counterparts, it was decided to trumpet our native talent by featuring restaurants with British chefs. This means, by virtue of this distinction, that a number of outstanding country restaurants have not been included. To redress the balance, these have been incorporated in the complete restaurant listing at the back of the book.

Exceptional cooking was the key criterion used in choosing the restaurants, with an individual menu being a top priority. Size was unimportant and every effort was made to include the smallest as well as the largest, provided the standard in each case was high. The book in no way attempts to be an 'official guide' and limitations of space have made it impossible to cover the recent mushrooming of superb country 'bistros'. Its focus is on the people: the chefs and owners responsible for creating these distinctly individual restaurants. It contains their ideas, their thoughts about food and their own recipes. The latter provide a culinary bonanza and convincing testimony to the superlative cooking now to be found in all parts of the country.

A word about recipes. These have been divided by category rather than by restaurant so that they are easier to find and use. Though chosen because they are imaginative or particularly delicious, you will also find that professional expertise has made them effortless to execute. The results on your plate will be just as mouth-watering as they are in any of the restaurants themselves. To accompany the main courses and the lunch and supper dishes, Jancis Robinson, author of *The Wine Book*, has suggested suitable libations. Peppered throughout the text are notes on outstanding food shops which will undoubtedly prove irresistible to anyone interested in 'country cuisine'.

Even though it is hoped that this book may become floury and grease-stained through frequent use in the kitchen, maps have been added at the back to help the curious gourmet or hungry traveller to find his way to the restaurant featuring Mussels with cider, apple and celery or Chicken with Pernod and tarragon. If taking the book *en route*, I cannot recommend too highly *The Good Food*

21

Guide, *The Egon Ronay Guide* and Susan Campbell's *Guide to Good Food Shops* as aids to further discoveries.

Finally, heartfelt thanks to all the restaurateurs who provided such a warm welcome and patiently suffered my culinary inquisition. Their enthusiasm, infectious love of food and generous hospitality (transmitted, I hope, through these pages) have made the book a very great pleasure to write.

Starters

Lovely Ripe Pears – as Good as Tinned!

Notice outside a village General Stores*

Before dining at any of the restaurants in this book, one should take as apéritif a quiet read of Derek Cooper's *The Bad Food Guide.** For in it, you will find not only a riveting account of modern British catering but convincing proof that you have come to the right place to eat. From his research, it is obvious that 'the age of convenience' has wreaked havoc in most restaurant kitchens, turning chefs into fast food junkies. The effect has been so hypnotic that both chefs and customers now have faint recollection of the genuine article. But in smaller establishments, the gilt is finally wearing off the packet gingerbread. The freshness and quality of the ingredients have become more important than their number or sophistication.

Starters, particularly, have been victims of this

stampede to the store cupboard and deep freeze: pâté, with the ridge marks of the tin still intact; shrimps, well potted in their polythene tubs; and soups, at least 57 varieties from Mr Heinz. But with the cold tables at Fortingall and The Hole in the Wall blazing the trail, starters have blossomed in the past two decades. There is now an imaginative range to choose from, and in the country this is more than ever true, especially at those restaurants which feature a daily changing *table d'hôte*. At Bowlish House, for instance, you can dig into *Champignons 'Café de Paris'*: whole mushrooms, on a granary croûte, grilled for a second with a dollop of garlicky butter. The Toastmaster's Inn serves a creamy Baked avocado, filled with prawns, tomatoes and crisp bacon. The Mushroom brioche at Well House is a speciality, filled with a delicate *duxelles* and topped with a hollandaise sauce. For simplicity, there is nothing to beat the feather-light Courgette soufflé cooked by Hilary Brown at La Potinière.

The advent of the food processor has made way for a new star: the mousseline. The variations are infinite and, with the work of pounding the fish or meat now done by machine, its execution is no longer daunting. Chicken mousseline, *Quenelles de saumon* and Dariole of mushrooms can be produced as easily at home as in the restaurant kitchen.

The chunky terrine has surpassed the smooth liver pâté, which appears to be in forced exile. At Lamb's, Paul Barnard makes a Duck and veal terrine dotted with pistachio nuts and ringed with cold Cumberland sauce. No. 3 at Glastonbury is well known for its pâtés, the hot varieties encased in a thin parchment of pastry, the cold in colourful layers with a contrasting sauce. The *Terrine maison* at Longueville House arrives with a corner of Jane O'Callaghan's homemade gooseberry chutney.

LA POTINIÈRE

Gullane, East Lothian, Scotland

If you are a Mrs Bridges, with a kitchen the size of a
cricket pitch and an army of servants to fill it, then serving
twenty people at once is as easy as whistling. But if you
are a Mrs Brown, in a kitchen a tenth the size with only an
old dear from the village to peel the spuds, then the chances
of cooking (*haute* or otherwise) for that many people seem
extremely remote.

Remote, but not impossible, as Mrs Brown is proving
daily in her unassuming restaurant in Gullane. While her
husband David plays the role of 'Hudson', she cooks an
inspired *table d'hôte* for about twenty people. They arrive
promptly at twelve-thirty, knowing that at one o'clock the
first of four exquisite courses is served and late-comers have
no alternative but to eat the second course first. As this
could easily be Hilary Brown's velvety Courgette soufflé,
your timing, as well as hers, is crucial. To start, there may
be a warming *Crème flamande* or *Potage Crécy*, served with
crusty French bread and unsalted butter. After a soufflé
or perhaps a Mousseline of sole, there might be *Noisettes de
porc vallée d'Auge, Poulet au Pernod* or *Steak au poivre vert*. Each

is presented with fresh vegetables on a generous platter and left, French-style, for guests to help themselves. A bottle from David Brown's superb cellar can be finished off with a wonderfully ripe Brie, then a few mouthfuls of something sweet like *Velour de chocolat, Crème brûlée* or *Tortoni*.

While there always exists the temptation to take more customers (especially when many are disappointed at not being able to get in), the Browns realize that this would be stretching their capacity and capabilities at the moment. But with David's knowledge of wine and Hilary's cooking skill, it would be a pity if they didn't eventually move to somewhere slightly larger which would do full justice to their talents.

Courgette Soufflé

1¼ lb (550g) small, firm
   courgettes
salt
1½ oz (40g) butter
1½ oz (40g) flour
4 fl oz (100ml) milk,
   flavoured as for
   béchamel (page 376)

2 oz (50g) grated cheese
   (ideally half Parmesan,
   half Cheddar)
2 egg yolks
4 egg whites
pepper
oil *or* butter for frying

6 ramekins, 3 inches (7·5 cm) in diameter, well greased

Wash, finely slice and salt 1 lb (450g) of courgettes. Dice the remaining ¼ lb (100g) into ¼-inch (0·50cm) cubes, then salt. Leave all the courgettes for about an hour, then rinse off the salt and pat dry with kitchen paper.

Put the sliced courgettes into a saucepan with a small amount of lightly salted water. Cook until just tender, then drain and liquidize until smooth.

Melt the butter in a heavy pan and stir in the flour to make a roux. Cook for a minute or two, then gradually stir in the milk. Add the courgette purée and whisk until well blended. Cook over a moderate heat, stirring frequently, until the mixture thickens (at least 10 minutes). Allow to cool slightly, then add the cheese, followed by the yolks. Whisk well to make sure that they are evenly mixed. Season to taste with salt and pepper. At this stage the soufflé mixture can be left for an hour or two if necessary.

Preheat the oven to gas mark 5, 375°F (190°C). Fry the cubed courgettes in a small amount of butter or oil until golden. Lift out and drain on kitchen paper. Whisk the whites until stiff. Fold a tablespoon of the whites into the yolk mixture to loosen it slightly, then fold in the remaining whites. Be very gentle but thorough. Ladle the soufflé mixture into the ramekins, half filling each one. Top with a teaspoon of the fried courgettes, then cover with the remaining mixture. Place the ramekins in a large roasting tin. Fill the tin with boiling water until it comes halfway up the sides of the ramekins. Bake in the preheated oven until well risen and golden (20–25 minutes). Take out and serve at once.

Serves 6

Chef: Hilary Brown
Proprietors: Hilary and David Brown

KINCH'S

Chesterton, Oxfordshire

Christopher Greatorex's taste in cooking is eclectic, drawing ideas and inspiration from French, Italian, American and English sources. On the whole, it is closest to the French *cuisine bourgeoise*, an unpretentious style of cooking which makes the best of country produce. Keeping as closely tied to the farm and his own kitchen garden as possible, his repertoire is based on homegrown fruits, vegetables and herbs, local beef, geese, lamb, pork and game. The last is the mainstay of the menu: his Roast pheasant with port wine and redcurrants, Quail pudding and Wood pigeon in red wine sauce all highly praised.

Even before Michel Guérard's ideas became fashionable, the dishes at Kinch's were characterized by their lightness and flour-free sauces. A visit to America last year generated an interest in vegetarian and Japanese cooking, both enjoying a heyday there. Christopher looks forward to experimenting with their techniques, incorporating perhaps a little of the Japanese *tofu*, a soya bean extract.

This recipe, with shades of *cuisine minceur*, adds gelatine to the basic mixture (unusual for a hot soufflé) to keep it from becoming watery and soft.

28

Hot Tomato and Basil Soufflé

2 lb (900g) fresh ripe
  tomatoes
1 14-oz (397g) tin of
  tomatoes
1 teaspoon sugar
½ oz (15g) gelatine
salt and pepper

8 egg whites

1½ slices dried bread
handful of fresh basil *or* 2
  teaspoons dried basil
butter

6 ramekin dishes, 4 inches (10cm) in diameter

Quarter the fresh tomatoes and put into a large saucepan
with the tinned tomatoes (drained of their liquid) and the
sugar. Cover and cook until soft, then remove the lid and
continue cooking, stirring frequently, until the liquid has
reduced by two-thirds, leaving you with about 12 fl oz
(350ml). Press through a sieve into a large bowl. Season
well with salt and freshly ground black pepper (and, if
bitter, add a pinch of sugar). In a small cup, soak the
gelatine in 5 tablespoons of cold water, then dissolve over
gentle heat. Whisk into the tomato purée then allow to cool
slightly.

Preheat the oven to gas mark 7, 425°F (220°C). Put the
bread and basil into a liquidizer or food processor. Blend
until you have fine breadcrumbs. Butter the ramekin
dishes generously, then coat the sides and base of each one
with a layer of breadcrumbs and basil (leaving a thicker
layer on the bottom).

Whisk the egg whites until stiff, then fold into the
tomato purée carefully. Spoon into the prepared dishes
and put straight into the preheated oven for 12–14
minutes. Take out and serve at once.

Serves 6

Chef: Christopher Greatorex
Proprietors: Frances and Christopher Greatorex

THE HORN OF PLENTY

Gulworthy, Devon

The signpost marked 'Chipshop' which you pass en route to The Horn of Plenty is slightly misleading as you're unlikely to get anything so prosaic at the Stevensons' starred restaurant. *Quenelles de saumon à la crème, Sole Colbert* or *Cassoulet de ménage* would be more probable.

For though this restaurant sits a few miles above Tavistock in the heart of Devon, it does, both in décor and style, seem distinctly French. The owners, Sonia and Patrick Stevenson, are former classical musicians who decided thirteen years ago to pack their house with paying customers. Opening with little fanfare, they began as they continued, with a range of beautifully cooked English and international dishes.

They soon attracted a dedicated band of *aficionados* who came regularly to the Stevenson shrine. Accolades from all the guides quickly followed, including the much-coveted Michelin star and, finally, the Egon Ronay Restaurant of the Year award in 1976. Mrs Stevenson's recipes for Lamb's sweetbreads *en brioche* took her to Maxim's, giving her the unusual honour of being the first woman to cook in their kitchens. Patrick Stevenson, an opera-singing Orson Welles, provides the wines to complement his wife's cooking. At this he is excellent, and the force of his recommendations soon quashes any indecision. Guests are bemused by his idiosyncrasies which, undeniably, endow the restaurant with great character.

Quenelles de Saumon

Sauce au Vin Blanc

3 lb (1·5 kilos) white fish bones (preferably turbot *or* sole)
½ oz (15g) butter
1 tablespoon finely chopped onion *or* shallot
¼ pint (150ml) dry white wine
8 fl oz (225ml) double cream
beurre manié (¾ tablespoon flour and ¾ tablespoon butter)
salt and pepper

½ lb (225g) raw salmon flesh
3 egg whites
½ pint (275ml) double cream, lightly whipped
salt, white pepper

Purée the salmon with the egg whites in a liquidizer. Then press through a fine sieve. Add salt and pepper to taste, then fold in the cream. Refrigerate until well chilled.

To make the sauce, start by putting the fish bones into a large saucepan and cover with cold water. Bring to the boil, simmer for 10 minutes, then strain and simmer again until very well reduced and well flavoured.

Melt the butter in a saucepan and cook the onion gently in it until soft and transparent. Pour in the wine and simmer until reduced by half. Add ½ pint (275ml) of the fish stock, then blend in the cream. Bring to the boil, stirring all the time. Make the *beurre manié* by working the flour and butter together to make a smooth paste, then whisk into the sauce, small pieces at a time. Continue simmering until it has dissolved and thickened the sauce. Season to taste with salt and pepper, then leave the sauce to 'mature' for 10 minutes. Taste and adjust the seasoning if necessary. Keep warm until the quenelles are ready.

When ready to serve the quenelles, fill a flat pan with boiling water, then put it on the stove and leave to simmer gently. Fill a warm dessertspoon with the chilled salmon mixture. Dip another warm dessertspoon in the simmering water, then invert it over the first spoon to mould an oval-shaped quenelle. Poach gently for 8–10 minutes until firm but still slightly creamy in the centre. Lift out with a slotted spoon and serve with the *sauce au vin blanc*.

Serves 4–6

Chef: Sonia Stevenson
Proprietors: Sonia and Patrick Stevenson

CREBER'S

Many of the supplies for The Horn of Plenty come from Creber's in Tavistock. Started in 1881 and now run by the founder's grandson, this is a grocery shop 'par excellence'. Besides a dazzling selection of fresh, frozen and tinned foods, it offers five types of cured ham, twenty kinds of Continental sausage, various pâtés and cold meats, sixty European and English cheeses, an extensive wine list and a full range of gift boxes and hampers. The Creber's take pride in upholding family traditions, now almost a century old, and their motto 'Creber's for quality' is just as true as it ever was. A catalogue listing all their stock is available on request and they will happily send goods by post (charging for postage but not packing).

THE PLOUGH INN

Fadmoor, North Yorkshire

Despite the fact that the owners of The Plough spend every day in the kitchen, their holidays inevitably take them to a cookery course in Dieppe, a tour of restaurants in the British Isles or a gastronomic pilgrimage to favourite spots in France. The rest of the year they run the pub and serve dinners Tuesday to Saturday, with an average of twenty-five people each night.

While Kath Brown does most of the cooking, her husband Don does all the butchering, makes the bread, a few of the starters and the sorbets. Considering the pub's size and remoteness, their menu is staggering. To offer a *table d'hôte* plus an extensive *à la carte*, featuring delicacies like Chicken mousseline, *Soupe de poisson* and Pheasant with apples and Calvados, in a tiny moorside village, takes courage and devotion.

Inspiration for their cooking is drawn mainly from France and each trip brings fodder for future menus. The repertoire is now so speckled with recipes from all parts of France that their regular customers are wondering if they ever need go there. Presentation is done with professional flair, and vegetables, in particular, are treated with great originality. Everything is cooked to order but Mrs Brown manages the fine timing with remarkable calm. Two local girls help to ease the pressure, and with her husband out front to synchronize the orders, the dinners have unusually few hiccups.

Chicken Mousseline
with Curry Cream Sauce

½ lb |(225g) raw chicken breast (skinned and boned weight)
1 large egg, beaten
8 fl oz (225 ml) double cream
salt and white pepper

Garnish
6 tablespoons cooked, long grain rice
6 cubes of pineapple, chopped
a few flaked almonds
chopped parsley

Curry Cream Sauce

1 oz (25g) butter
¾ oz (20g) flour
¼ pint (150ml) hot chicken stock
½ level teaspoon Vindaloo curry paste
¼ pint (150ml) double cream
2 teaspoons clear honey
a little pineapple juice (if needed)
salt and pepper

6 dariole moulds *or* straight-sided coffee cups

Start by making the sauce. Melt the butter in a saucepan, stir in the flour and cook for a minute or two to make a light roux. Blend in the hot stock and Vindaloo paste, stirring well to keep the mixture smooth, and cook over a very low heat for about 5 minutes (stirring from time to time). Mix in the cream, honey and a little pineapple juice if the sauce is too thick. Season to taste with salt and pepper. Cover until needed.

The mousselines: well butter the moulds or coffee cups, making sure that the base of each one is generously coated. Have ready a roasting tin which can hold the moulds and boiling water that reaches three-quarters of the way up the moulds when they are set in it. Preheat the oven to gas mark 5, 375°F (190°C). The water-filled roasting tin can be kept hot in the oven until needed.

Roughly chop the chicken breast, then purée in a liquidizer or food processor. Add the beaten egg and blend well together. Add the cream and a light seasoning of salt and white pepper, and mix together just long enough to thicken to a soft dropping consistency (the mixture will become grainy if over-mixed). Fill the moulds three-quarters full and place them in the water-filled roasting tin. Cover each mould with a circle of buttered foil to prevent them browning and hardening during cooking. Bake just above the centre of the oven for 20 minutes.

Meanwhile, heat the sauce gently. Combine the rice and pineapple and heat in a bowl over hot water. The flaked almonds can be lightly browned in the oven while the mousselines are cooking, then roughly chopped (not too finely). Have warm plates ready. Let the chicken 'settle' for a minute or two after removing the moulds from the oven. Run the blade of a small sharp knife round the inside of the moulds then reverse out on to the warm plates. Put a ring of pineapple and rice round each one. Spoon over the sauce to coat the mousseline and the rice lightly, then garnish with the flaked almonds and parsley. Serve at once.

Serves 6

Chef: Kath Brown *Proprietors:* Kath and Don Brown

THE OLD HOUSE

Wickham, Hampshire

The Old House in Wickham could, with no false pretensions, also be called *La Vieille Auberge*. Despite its situation in a Hampshire market town, it has all the atmosphere and style of a French inn. It differs from its English counterparts in several respects, one being a certain lack of traditional fixtures. For instance, there is no reception desk. After a dizzying tour of the ground floor, it becomes patently clear that you have got either the place or the day wrong.

It is worth fighting the impulse to restore your spirits in the pub opposite, as salvation arrives in the form of Annie Skipwith. She is the attractive and extremely chic *patronne* who speaks perfect English with a perfectly gorgeous French accent. Ever since she and her husband Richard bought the hotel in 1971 it has steadily gained a reputation for excellent food and wine.

Though the house is a classic example of early Georgian architecture, there is an unmistakably French influence in the kitchen and dining-room. The menu, composed by Annie Skipwith and her chef, Colin Wood, is based almost entirely on her vast collection of French recipes. It changes every Wednesday and offers a choice of four starters and an equal number of main courses, vegetables and puddings (including homemade ice-creams and sorbets).

36

Mousseline de Sole au Beurre Blanc

½ lb (225g) lemon sole
    fillets
2 large eggs
½ pint (275ml) double
    cream
salt and white pepper
milk for poaching

1 small carrot,
    stick of celery and
    chopped parsley to
    garnish

Beurre Blanc Sauce

¼ pint (150ml) dry white
    wine
¼ pint (150ml) white wine
    vinegar
1 button onion, peeled
    and finely chopped
2 small bay leaves
½ pint (275ml) double
    cream
Aromat *or* salt and pepper
1 oz (25g) butter

Skin the fillets of sole and cut into small pieces. Put into a liquidizer or food processor with the eggs and blend until smooth. Add the cream and whizz again for several seconds until thick and well blended. Season well with salt and pepper. Chill slightly to allow the mixture to firm up.

To make the sauce: put the wine, vinegar, onion and bay leaves into a saucepan and boil to reduce by three-quarters. Add the cream and boil quickly for 3–4 minutes. Season to taste, then whisk in the butter. Put through a strainer, then return to the pan. Keep warm.

Using two dessertspoons, mould the mousseline into egg shapes. Poach these in gently simmering milk for 10 minutes, then lift out carefully with a slotted spoon. Meanwhile, peel the carrot and cut, with the celery, into thin julienne strips. Blanch quickly, drain well, then add to the sauce. Arrange the mousselines on individual plates, coat with the sauce and top with a sprinkling of finely chopped parsley.

Serves 4

Chef: Colin Wood
Proprietors: Annie and Richard Skipwith

LOAVES AND FISHES

Wootton Bassett, Wiltshire

There is no question of feeding five thousand or even fifty in this tiny restaurant, sandwiched into one corner of a modern housing estate in Wootton Bassett.

Before visions of a crowded bungalow spring to mind, the restaurant itself is in The Old Lime Kiln, a house which bears little resemblance to recent architecture. Built during the sixteenth century, it is now cocooned from the twentieth by a thick palisade of conifers. Loaves and Fishes occupies one wing and is run by Nikki Kedge and Angela Rawson (whose family owns the house). They serve dinner to a maximum of twenty people every night except Sunday in a dining-room lit only by candles and a log fire. There are only four tables, all gleaming mahogany and set a discreet distance apart.

Dinner is prefaced by a general toast in front of the sitting-room fire, guests either standing or squeezed into the narrow rockers (more difficult afterwards) beside it. Orders taken by Nikki (for starter and pudding, as there is only one dish for the main course) are transmitted to Angela in the kitchen. When the cooking permits, she occasionally ventures forth, delivering a main course to the dining-room or a pot of coffee to the fireside. This Crab mousse, with colours which are as exquisite as its flavour, is one of her own favourites.

Crab Mousse with Avocado Sauce

1 15-fl oz (425ml) tin
  good-quality crab soup
2 tablespoons mayonnaise
juice of 2 small lemons
$\frac{3}{4}$ lb (350g) Philadelphia
  cream cheese
salt and pepper
4 teaspoons gelatine
$\frac{1}{2}$ pint (275ml) double
  cream
1 lb (450g) crab meat
  (white and brown), well
  picked over

Avocado Sauce

1 large ripe avocado,
  peeled and chopped
juice of $1\frac{1}{2}$ lemons
$\frac{1}{2}$ pint (275ml) double
  cream
salt and white pepper
a little sugar (about 2
  teaspoons)

lemon, cucumber and
  parsley *or* fennel to
  garnish

Put the crab soup, mayonnaise, lemon juice, cream cheese and a good seasoning of salt and pepper into a liquidizer and blend until smooth. Pour into a large bowl.

In a small cup blend the gelatine with 4 tablespoons of cold water and stand in a pan of hot water. When the gelatine has completely dissolved, pour it in a steady stream into the cream cheese mixture, whisking as you do so. Whip the cream until just thick and fold in lightly. Blend in the crab meat and check the seasoning. Pour into a lightly oiled mould and leave in a cool place to set.

Put all the sauce ingredients into a liquidizer and blend until smooth. (This should be done at the last minute so that it stays a clear green colour.) Check the seasoning.

Unmould the mousse on to a serving plate and coat with the sauce (or serve this separately). Garnish with slices of lemon and cucumber and sprigs of parsley or fennel.

Serves 8

Chef: Angela Rawson
Proprietors: Nikki Kedge and Angela Rawson

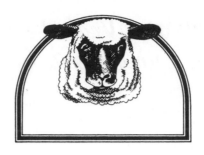

LAMB'S

Moreton-in-Marsh, Gloucestershire

The menu at Lamb's is now a patchwork of well-tried favourites and recent emigrés from the kitchen. As well as the typed menu which changes every few weeks, there is a selection of *plats du jour* (usually based on seasonal game or fish) chalked up on a blackboard beside the bar.

All the starters (eight to ten) can also be eaten as a main course. This further increases the choice and is no doubt much loved by ladies on a diet. In this section, you might find Ham, mushroom and Stilton crêpe, Spicy lamb *quenelles*, Hot curried fruits, Chicken and pheasant terrine with cold Cumberland sauce or *Schwabische Schnecker* (easier to eat than pronounce): snails baked with fresh herb butter and red wine.

Lamb's is fortunate in having a chef, Paul Barnard, whose cooking is as imaginative as it is delicious. Despite his tender years (he is twenty-four), he has built up an impressive repertoire of innovative and traditional dishes. He has little time for cookery books and prefers to rely on taste and experience. Consequently, he is not an easy man to get a recipe from, but when tied to a kitchen chair, the fruits of his labour are more easily transcribed.

Duck and Veal Terrine
with Cumberland Sauce

¾ lb (350g) duck meat
¾ lb (350g) veal
1 large onion, peeled and
   chopped
3 rashers of streaky
   rindless bacon (smoked
   is best)
2 teaspoons freshly
   chopped sage *or* 1
   teaspoon dried sage
2 teaspoons freshly
   chopped parsley *or*
   1 teaspoon dried parsley
juice and rind of 1 orange
2½ fl oz (65ml) port
2½ fl oz (65ml) orange
   Curaçao *or* other

orange-flavoured
   liqueur
splash of Noilly Prat
salt and black pepper
1 egg, beaten
extra veal *or* duck meat
   (optional)
3–4 tablespoons chopped
   cashew *or* pistachio nuts
   (optional)

streaky rindless bacon to
   line the tin
clarified butter

Cumberland sauce (page
   382)

1½-lb (675g) loaf tin *or* terrine dish

Using the coarse blade of the mincer, mince the duck and
veal with the onion and bacon. Put into a bowl and mix
in the herbs, orange rind and juice, port, orange Curaçao
and Noilly Prat. Blend well and season generously with salt
and freshly ground black pepper. Cover and leave overnight in the refrigerator.

The following day, preheat the oven to gas mark 3,
325°F (170°C). Line the loaf tin with rashers of streaky
bacon which have been stretched with the back of a knife.
Add enough beaten egg to the meat mixture to bind it
together and place in the tin. To make the finished appearance of the terrine particularly attractive (and tasty), strips
of tender duck and veal meat may be placed in horizontal
layers in the tin. Chopped pistachio or cashew nuts (but

41

not walnuts as they turn black during the cooking) may be added as well. Cover with greaseproof paper then foil or a lid and bake in a bain-marie half-filled with water in the preheated oven for about $1\frac{1}{2}$ hours or until cooked (when pierced with a sharp knife, no blood should run out). Take the tin out of the oven, cover with a baking sheet and weigh down with heavy weights (sugar or flour bags) for at least 4 hours. Remove the weights and coat the top of the terrine with a layer of clarified butter. Chill and serve the next day with cold Cumberland sauce.

Serves 8

Chef: Paul Barnard *Proprietor:* Ian MacKenzie

WILLIAM'S KITCHEN

Close to Lamb's, in the village of Nailsworth, is another source of good eating: William's Kitchen. Here, Mr and Mrs William Beeston run a shop which, on occasion, seems more like a meeting-place. They stock fresh ducks and chickens and, in season, pheasant, venison, hare, grouse and partridge. A large marble fish-slab holds fresh wet, smoked and shell fish. Cheeses number about eighty (from England and Europe) and there is an impressive range of salamis, cooked meats, homemade pâtés, terrines, pies and quiches. Shop early for their now-famous granary bread – otherwise it might be sold out! Wines and beers from Raffles Wine Co. occupy one corner of the shop floor and wine and cheese tastings are frequently held on Saturday mornings. The Beestons also run an outside catering service; a catalogue giving full details can be sent on request.

McCOY'S

Staddle Bridge, North Yorkshire

The cooking at McCoy's is done in tandem by two brothers, Tom and Peter McCoy. Tom is usually the protagonist and it is he who cooks the lion's share of the menu. He has an intuitive flair for cooking, untrammelled by formal training, which is given free rein in their kitchen. Most of his best dishes seem to have been created in a matter of minutes, by a simple flash of inspiration. Usually they go through an evolutionary process before they reach the restaurant, but often they are 'spot on' from the beginning.

The menu, handwritten on an old piece of pink cardboard, changes every few weeks, with verbal additions of daily 'specials'. These are recited by their two emissaries out front, Eugene and Alison, who, with crumpled crib notes in their pockets, attempt to give accurate descriptions of the latest McCoy creations.

There are always a few runaway successes and Peter's Pâté of chicken livers and pork is one of them. A rough, chunky mixture, it is served with a compote of apricot and onion. Chicken wings, quickly fried, then tossed in a piquant chili sauce is another (accompanied by a 'very spicy' tag on the menu). The *gravlax* is spelled out in no uncertain terms as RAW, FRESH, FARM SALMON (underlined three times) and comes dressed with a mayonnaise and mustard sauce. A Champagne sorbet, made not from champagne but champagne cognac, is a speciality of the house and sensationally good. There are about ten different starters and main courses, all with bikini-sized descriptions. Though tantalizing, these give little inkling of the culinary delectations which await.

Pork and Chicken Liver Pâté with Apricot Relish

1 lb (450g) chicken livers
½ lb (225g) belly pork
½ lb (225g) sausage meat
½ lb (225g) streaky
   rindless bacon rashers
2 bay leaves
4 sprigs of thyme

Marinade

7 tablespoons Armagnac
   or brandy
3 tablespoons port
3 tablespoons sherry
4 large cloves of garlic,
   peeled and finely
   chopped
½ teaspoon dried thyme
pinch of freshly grated
   nutmeg
1 teaspoon sugar

2 teaspoons salt
12 turns of the pepper mill

Apricot Relish

¾ lb (350g) onions
2 oz (50g) butter
¾ teaspoon salt
½ teaspoon white pepper
2½ oz (65g) castor sugar
¾ lb (350g) dried
   apricots, soaked over-
   night then roughly
   chopped
3½ tablespoons sherry *or*
   wine vinegar
1 tablespoon grenadine
¼ pint (150ml) red wine

watercress to garnish

terrine dish *or* 1½-lb (675g) loaf tin

To make the pâté, start by removing any greenish patches from the livers and chop roughly. Cut the belly pork into cubes approximately $\frac{1}{2} \times 1$ inch ($1 \times 2 \cdot 5$cm). Put the livers, pork and sausage meat into a large bowl. Mix all the ingredients for the marinade together and pour over the meats. Cover and leave to marinate overnight in the refrigerator.

Preheat the oven to gas mark 6, 400°F (200°C). Line the terrine dish with the bacon rashers. Mix the pâté well, incorporating any juices from the marinade, then use to fill the terrine dish. Cover with any remaining bacon rashers and put the bay leaves and thyme on top. Place the terrine in a roasting dish half-filled with hot water and cook for $1\frac{1}{2}$ hours uncovered (the top will be pleasantly browned). Take out of the oven and leave to cool (about 3 hours). Then refrigerate until needed.

To make the relish, peel and slice the onions thinly. Heat the butter in a sauté pan until it becomes *beurre noisette* (deep nut brown) but do not let it blacken. Add the onions, salt, pepper and sugar. Cover and let it simmer and soften gently for 30 minutes over a low heat. Then add the apricots, sherry vinegar, grenadine and wine. Cook for a further 30 minutes *uncovered*. It must cook *very gently*. Remove from the heat and allow to cool.

When ready to serve, put a slice of the terrine on each plate with a dollop of apricot relish on one side. Add a sprig of watercress for colour.

Serves 8

Chefs: Tom and Peter McCoy
Proprietors: Eugene, Tom and Peter McCoy

LONGUEVILLE HOUSE

Mallow, Co. Cork, Eire

Set in four hundred acres of rolling parkland, Longueville House enjoys a seclusion which belies its proximity to the town of Mallow. A stately Georgian mansion overlooking the Blackwater valley, it has French connections which date back to the eighteenth century. It was built in 1720 by the Longfield family and renamed in 1795 when Richard Longfield became Baron Longueville (the Longfields claimed they were of French extraction and not Cromwellians). A subtle switch in loyalty can be traced a few years later when oak trees in front of the house were planted in the formation of the English and French battle lines at Waterloo!

Senator William O'Callaghan bought the house in 1938, claiming back the land of which his forbears had been robbed by Cromwell. His son Michael and daughter-in-law Jane have restored the house to its former splendour and, in an effort to defray running costs, began to do bed and breakfast ten years ago. The Longueville breakfast, with its huge bowls of fresh raspberries, porridge, grilled river trout, eggs, butter, ham and bacon from the farm, homemade bread and preserves, acquired such a reputation that Jane O'Callaghan was persuaded to do dinners as well.

Terrine Maison

6 rashers streaky bacon
½ lb (225g) lambs' liver
1 small onion, peeled
clove of garlic, peeled
½ lb (225g) sausage meat
½ lb (225g) minced veal *or* pork
salt and pepper

2 finely chopped hard-boiled eggs
1 teaspoon finely chopped parsley
½ lb (225g) veal *or* pork
4 bay leaves
flour and water for paste

earthenware terrine *or* small pyrex dish with lid

Preheat the oven to gas mark 4, 350°F (180°C). Line the bottom and sides of the terrine with the streaky rashers (remove any rind or bone before doing so). Mince the liver with the onion and garlic and add to the sausage meat and minced pork or veal. Season well with salt and pepper, then add the eggs and parsley. Put a layer of this farce in the bottom of the dish.

Cut the veal or pork into fine strips. Arrange in layers with the rest of the farce until the dish is full, making sure that the top layer is one of farce. Put the bay leaves on top and seal the lid with a flour and water paste. Stand the dish in a roasting tin full of hot water and cook in the preheated oven for 1½ hours.

Take out and remove the lid. Cover with foil and put a heavy weight on top. Leave in the refrigerator or cold room for 24 hours before serving. Serve as a starter or luncheon dish with lots of wholemeal bread and homemade gooseberry chutney (see page 388).

Serves 8

Chef: Jane O'Callaghan
Proprietors: Jane and Michael O'Callaghan

LE TALBOOTH

Dedham, Essex

The menu at Le Talbooth is a curious hybrid, blending modern French and traditional English dishes.

For the first sixteen years of the restaurant's life, the menu offered a daily *table d'hôte* and a limited *à la carte*. As only fifteen per cent of the customers ever ordered the former, it was decided with the arrival (in 1976) of a new chef, Sam Chalmers, to switch completely to *à la carte*. Now there is a printed menu which changes every few months, supplemented by various *plats du jour*.

Though a good proportion of French dishes (with a strong bias towards *nouvelle cuisine*) are represented, they are balanced by a fair share of hearty English ones. Steak and kidney pudding, Jugged hare and Game pie feature regularly. In addition, Sam Chalmers has injected a spirited selection of new dishes and now Yarmouth herrings with cream cheese and apple, Mousse of York ham and Stilton croquettes all beckon invitingly.

This pâté, combining divinely suited partners, is another Chalmers creation. It is at its best when served chilled (but not icy cold) with hot, buttered wholemeal toast.

Stilton, Port and Celery Pâté

$\frac{1}{2}$ oz (15g) butter
$\frac{1}{2}$ oz (15g) plain flour
clove of garlic, crushed
3 oz (75g) mayonnaise
4 fl oz (100ml) double
   cream, lightly whipped
$2\frac{1}{2}$ fl oz (65ml) port

$\frac{1}{4}$ lb (100g) chopped celery
$\frac{1}{2}$ lb (225g) Stilton
salt and pepper

celery hearts and hot toast
   to serve

pâte dish *or* 4–6 ramekins

Melt the butter in a small saucepan and stir in the flour.
Cook for a minute or two, then take off the heat and put
into a medium mixing bowl. Mix in the garlic, mayonnaise
and cream. Gradually blend in the port, then add the
celery. Grate the Stilton and fold into the mixture slowly.
Season to taste with salt and pepper. Pour into a pâté dish
or individual ramekin dishes and leave to set in a refrigerator. Serve with raw celery hearts and hot toast handed
round separately.

Serves 4–6

Chef: Sam Chalmers *Proprietor:* Gerald Milsom

PENLAN OLEU

Llanychaer Bridge, Dyfed, Wales

Penlan Oleu could equally be a writer's retreat, traveller's refuge or gourmet's paradise. It sits high up in the Preseli hills, with a privileged view of the Pembrokeshire coast.

It is run in much the same style as a French *auberge* where standards of comfort and cuisine belie its remote setting. The personal stamp of the proprietor is more than evident and at Penlan Oleu this adds to its attraction. Whereas many would find that running a farm, supervising various breeds of livestock and organizing six children more than fills the day, Ann and Martin MacKeown manage to do all this in addition to their 'restaurant with rooms'.

The farmhouse is a hotch-potch of rooms, brilliantly knit together with warm colours, striking fabrics and water-colours on every wall. The two sitting-rooms, with yawning armchairs and crackling fires, make idyllic spots for a quiet read or cosy drink before dinner. A glass conservatory provides breathtaking views of the surrounding countryside; and the restaurant, which seats only twelve, is informal and friendly.

While Ann cooks, her husband Martin acts as host, keeping the glasses filled, taking the wine orders and serving in the dining-room. Their eldest sons have inherited the same interest in food and wine and take their turn in the kitchen and restaurant. They will, upon gentle prompting, give mouth-watering descriptions of how each dish is made and are delighted to be quizzed on any culinary subject.

Prawn Pâté

$\frac{1}{2}$ lb (225g) peeled prawns
$\frac{1}{4}$ lb (100g) butter
1–2 tablespoons
   homemade mayonnaise
   (page 383)
1 dessertspoon chopped
   chives
1 dessertspoon finely
   chopped green pepper

good pinch of cayenne
   pepper
salt and black pepper

lemon slices and parsley
   sprigs to garnish
hot toast to serve

4 small ramekin dishes

If fresh prawns are used, boil in the usual way, then shell and de-vein. Frozen prawns are best thawed out slowly overnight. Reserve a few for decoration.

Cream the butter until really light and fluffy. Gradually add as much mayonnaise as the butter will absorb. Blend in the chives, green pepper, cayenne and a good seasoning of salt and black pepper. Fold in the prawns. Pot in small ramekin dishes and leave in the refrigerator for several hours to set. Just before serving, garnish each one with a few prawns, a thin slice of lemon and a small sprig of parsley. Serve with lots of hot toast.

Serves 4

Chef: Ann Carr
Proprietors: Ann Carr and Martin MacKeown

NO. 3

Glastonbury, Somerset

George Atkinson, the chef-proprietor of No. 3, came to cooking via a roundabout route, after a successful career as an interior designer. Having commuted to the South of France on various business ventures for ten years, he decided to develop an interest which would involve neither travel nor baggage.

He went into partnership with a friend eager to do the same thing and eventually found a large Victorian house in Hampshire which could be converted to a restaurant. With a perfectionist's eye for detail (and a local builder's marked inattention to same), the conversion took far longer than anticipated and it wasn't until 1971 that Faringdon Dining Rooms opened to the public. Within a year, Mr Atkinson's cooking had won the restaurant a place in *The Good Food Guide* and a devoted clientele. Emboldened now to take a further step, he and his partner Charles Foden (a vet by training), searched for and found an old watermill in Somerset. Its situation was idyllic, its potential enormous and its condition nightmarish. Complete restoration took almost two years and then, at the last minute, the local council refused to grant them a restaurant licence.

Forced to sell, they found their present house in Glastonbury shortly afterwards and have now been running it as a restaurant for six years. Though neither partner has been trained professionally in wine or food, the cuisine offered at No. 3 is far from amateurish. Each dish is cooked to perfection and served with tremendous style. The menu is a select *table d'hôte* (half a dozen starters, with the same number of main courses and puddings), always providing top quality as well as a tempting choice. Considering that both men are now in their mid-seventies, their energy and prodigious output is all the more laudable.

The menu at No. 3 features an outstanding range of hot and cold terrines. The fish variety given below is flavoured with herbs from the garden and served with a steaming sash of hot chive sauce.

Chilled Fish Pâté with Hot Chive Sauce

2 lb (900g) white fish
    fillets (plaice and
    haddock are good),
    cooked, giving 1½ lb
    (675g)
¾ pint (425ml) well-
    flavoured béchamel
    sauce (page 377)
1 level dessertspoon
    gelatine

2 tablespoons fish stock *or*
    white wine
4 tablespoons double
    cream, lightly whipped
large pinch of nutmeg
salt and pepper
½ lb (225g) cooked salmon
    or fish fillets

1½-lb (675g) loaf tin, lightly greased or lined with foil

Put the fish into a large bowl and pound until smooth. Gradually blend in the béchamel sauce. Dissolve the gelatine in the fish stock and stir into the béchamel mixture. Blend in the double cream and the nutmeg, then season to taste with salt and pepper.

Place half this mixture in the prepared tin and cover with a layer of cooked salmon or fish fillets. Fill the tin with the remaining fish mixture and cover with foil. Leave to set for several hours in a refrigerator. Then turn out, slice and serve with hot chive sauce.

Serves 8

Hot Chive Sauce

This sauce must be made just before serving the pâté. It must be very hot and only poured over half the slice of pâté so that the middle layer of salmon can be seen.

5 oz (150g) unsalted butter	1 tablespoon chopped chives
$\frac{1}{2}$ pint (275ml) double cream	1 teaspoon lemon juice salt and pepper

Melt the butter in a small heavy saucepan. When it starts to bubble, pour in the cream. Stir over a gentle heat until thick. Add the chopped chives and lemon juice, then season to taste.

Chef: George Atkinson
Proprietors: George Atkinson and Charles Foden

WELL HOUSE

Poundisford, Somerset

Graham Cornish (who, incidentally, isn't) came to Well House from The Horn of Plenty where he trained under the watchful eye of Sonia Stevenson. He has dogmatic ideas about food and refuses to put anything on the menu that isn't based on the best and freshest ingredients.

Thus, the bill of fare varies in size from one evening to the next, but usually has five starters and five main courses, including one *plat du jour*. You could start off with the soup of the day, a terrine of tongue or the *Brioche farcie aux champignons* given below. Amongst the main courses, there might be *Poulet sauté aux poivres verts*, a Ham and fruit pie or Grilled mackerel with fresh gooseberry sauce. Vegetables and potatoes are brought steaming to the table in their own earthenware pots. To finish, sweet-lovers might sample a Champagne sorbet (Graham insists that only real champagne can be used), chilled Chocolate loaf or crunchy Brown-bread ice-cream, served with homemade biscuits. A cheeseboard groans under the weight of a local farmhouse Cheddar, a ripe Brie and a Stilton. It is accompanied by wholemeal bread, oatmeal biscuits and a cornucopia of fresh fruit. Coffee arrives in its own pot which is kept topped up with piping hot brew and accompanied by a plate of rich fudge.

Being in the wilds of Somerset, Graham depends very much on local help. When the studying for school exams begins, he is left to cope single-handed. Reliable suppliers become crucial as it is then impossible for him to do both the cooking and the marketing. He has shrewdly encouraged a nearby famer to expand his vegetable patch and now has a captive supply of *mange-touts*, courgettes, spinach, sorrel and salsify. Getting fresh fish was practically impossible until a year ago when a small firm offered to deliver direct from the coast and a trout farm opened a few miles away.

Mushroom Brioche

Brioche
½ oz (15g) fresh yeast
1 teaspoon sugar
1 tablespoon warm water
½ lb (225g) strong white
   flour
½ teaspoon salt
3 oz (75g) butter
2 medium eggs, lightly
   beaten
1½–2 fl oz (40–50ml)
   warm milk

Mushroom Stuffing
1 large onion, peeled
6 oz (175g) butter
1 lb (450g) mushrooms
zest of 1 lemon
pinch of ground nutmeg
pinch of lemon thyme
salt and pepper

hollandaise sauce (page
   379) to serve

10–12 small brioche tins, greased and floured

Mix the yeast, the sugar and the warm water together in a small bowl and leave in a warm place until it becomes frothy. Sift the flour and salt into a large bowl and rub in the butter. Make a well in the centre and pour in the frothy yeast mixture and the eggs. Draw in the dry

56

ingredients from around the sides and add just enough warm (but not hot) milk to make a loose paste. Cover the bowl with cling film and leave in a warm place until the dough has doubled in size.

Preheat the oven to gas mark 6, 400°F (200°C). Knock the dough down well, then divide the mixture amongst the tins (filling them about half full). Let the dough prove again until it reaches the tops of the tins, then put the tins straight into the preheated oven. Bake for 10–12 minutes or until golden brown.

While the brioches are in the oven, prepare the stuffing. Chop the onion finely and sauté in the butter until soft but not coloured. Dice the mushrooms and add to the pan with the lemon zest, nutmeg, thyme and a good seasoning of salt and pepper. Continue cooking for 5–10 minutes until the mushrooms have darkened in colour. Keep warm until needed.

When ready, take the brioches out of the oven and carefully remove from their tins. When cool enough to handle, slice the tops off and scoop out the inside of each brioche. Fill the cavities with a generous dollop of mushroom stuffing and replace the lids. Serve with hollandaise sauce and garnish with fresh bay leaves, or sprigs of watercress or parsley.

Makes 10–12 brioches

Chef: Graham Cornish *Proprietor:* Ralph Vivian Neal

FINDON MANOR

Findon, Sussex

Adrian Bannister is a perfectionist and every dish that comes out of his kitchen bears the stamp of a professional. Though now in the country, his training with Trompetto in the kitchen at the Savoy is still very evident. Whether cooking for six or six times that number, the results are always remarkably high.

He refuses to yield to certain local customers who yearn for prawn cocktail and steak with chips. As starters, they are offered instead *Les asperges – beurre fondu* (fresh local asparagus with melted butter sauce), *Le bisque de crabe* (made from scratch to Adrian's own recipe) or *Les nouilles fraîches* (homemade pasta, with separate garnishes of deep-fried squid, Scottish beef flavoured with sage and served with a fresh tomato sauce). How disheartening it must be to make all your pasta and then have it turned down by ladies on a diet or gentlemen too conservative to try it. Yet he battles on and each day produces a menu which would provide delicious thoughts for any epicure.

Brioche with Smoked Trout Mousse

Brioche

½ lb (225g) strong white
  flour
good pinch of salt
½ oz (15g) fresh yeast
1¾ fl oz (45ml) warm
  water
½ oz (15g) sugar
2 eggs, lightly beaten
¼ lb (100g) butter

6 thin strips of smoked
  salmon (optional)

watercress and lemon
  wedges to garnish

Smoked Trout Mousse

2 ½-lb (225g) smoked
  trout
juice of 1 lemon
a little grated fresh
  horseradish *or*
  ½ teaspoon horseradish
  sauce
pinch of cayenne
1 oz (25g) butter, melted
salt and pepper
½ pint (275ml) double
  cream

10–12 small brioche moulds, well greased and floured

Sift the flour and salt into a large mixing bowl and put
in a warm place. In a small bowl, mix together the yeast,
warm (but not hot) water, sugar and a little of the warmed
flour to make a slack batter. Set aside in a warm place
until it starts to froth. Add this and the eggs to the flour
and mix thoroughly. Break the butter into small pieces
over the dough and set aside in a warm place until doubled
in size.

Preheat the oven to gas mark 6, 400°F (200°C). Knock
back the dough, incorporating the butter. Then divide
amongst the brioche moulds, filling them about half full.
Leave to prove until they fill the moulds. Then bake in
the preheated oven for 10–12 minutes until well risen and
golden. Take out and remove carefully from the moulds.

While the brioches are proving or baking, prepare the
filling. Remove the skin and bones from the trout and place
the flesh in a mixing bowl. Flake well with a fork, then

blend in the lemon juice, horseradish, cayenne, melted butter and a good seasoning of salt and pepper. Whisk the cream until thick, then fold in gently. Check the seasoning again and adjust if necessary.

Slice the top off each brioche and then cut each top in half. Pipe the trout mousse (or place a moulded spoonful of it) into the brioche. Replace the tops at an angle and, if possible, place a slice of rolled smoked salmon in the centre. Garnish with watercress and a wedge of lemon.

Serves 10–12

Chef: Adrian Bannister
Proprietors: Mary and Adrian Bannister

LANHYDROCK HOUSE

Anyone interested in cooking should stop off at Lanhydrock House, near Bodmin, on their way to the Riverside. Here they will find one of the most stunning Victorian kitchens in the country. The main kitchen, built like a college hall with high-gabled roof and clerestory windows, has elaborate roasting spits along the far wall, with a 'close range' at right-angles to it. A mahogany cabinet houses a dazzling copper *batterie de cuisine*, porcelain moulds and period china. A scullery fitted with slate-lined sinks for the preparation of vegetables and for washing-up is reached by a door at one end. Directly opposite, another door leads to the 'dairy passage' which connects the dairy, dairy scullery, meat larder, fish larder, dry larder and bakehouse. Equally Victorian teas are served to visitors in the servants' hall and offer freshly baked splits and scones with clotted cream and jams, homemade Banbury, fruit and banana cakes, gingerbread and butter biscuits.

RIVERSIDE

Helford, Cornwall

George Perry-Smith, as mentioned in the Introduction, has played an influential role in the genesis of country restaurant cooking. With the opening of The Hole in the Wall in 1952, he provided a new experience in dining out.

Having only his knowledge of eating in French restaurants (while teaching in Paris) to guide him, he felt no compunction to follow an established pattern. Instead, he pulled together dishes from international sources to create a menu that was original, extensive and, for its time, breathtakingly bold. Instead of offering the customary Cream of tomato or Oxtail soup, he provided eleven different kinds. Not only was he dishing up Pea ('navy fashion') and Game soups but also *Bouillabaisse*, Bisques, Fish chowders and Borstch.

For anyone used to the simple fare of country inns – Steak and kidney pie, Boiled beef with dumplings or Fish with white sauce – a first glimpse of The Hole menu might well have caused a coronary. Under the modest heading of Fish, there were fifteen dishes to choose from, including Koulibac, Dressed crab and Casserole of fish. As well as Omelettes and Eggs 'whenever we are allowed to serve them' (rationing still in effect) and Mixed grills, there was a rambling list of Entrées. Long before package tours made paella and lasagna fashionable, Perry-Smith was serving an ambitious range of continental and American specialities. Ravioli, Hungarian goulash and Vienna schnitzel kept company with the more traditional Jugged hare and Game pie. These were followed by Roasts, Cold buffet (which became a speciality of the house), Vegetables, Salads, Cheeses (twelve at least), Sweets (including Rum omelette, Sundaes and Waffles with syrup!), Savouries and a choice of seven different coffees and teas.

As the years progressed, the restaurant expanded and the number of dishes decreased but the quality and style remained the same. When Perry-Smith left in 1974 to start the Riverside, it soon achieved similar acclaim. The menu, a quarter the size of the one at The Hole, now represents the distilled essence of Perry-Smith's cooking, and with it he has unwittingly created another gastronomic landmark.

Brandade of Smoked Mackerel in Pastry

Filling
2 cloves of garlic, peeled
salt
½ lb (225g) smoked mackerel, skinned and boned
2–3 fl oz (50–75ml) milk
2–3 fl oz (50–75ml) *good* olive oil
pepper
a little lemon juice

¾ lb (350g) puff pastry (for homemade see page 386)
1 egg yolk
dill cream and cucumber sambal to serve (see below)

Pound the garlic in a mortar with just enough salt to melt the garlic. Add the smoked mackerel and pound energetically until the resultant paste is smoother than you believed possible, checking for escaped bones as you go.

Prepare a bain-marie and in it warm the mackerel paste in a decent-sized pudding basin, and the milk and oil in two jugs; don't let them get hot, just warm. Add the oil and milk to the mackerel alternately, a little at a time. The more you can work in without making the mixture sloppy, as opposed to soft and light, the more interesting will be the contrast between crisp pastry and moist, light filling. Season to taste with pepper and lemon juice, with perhaps a little more salt. Chill.

Roll out the puff pastry fairly thinly and stamp out rounds with a 3-inch (7·5cm) cutter. Put a generous teaspoonful of mackerel mixture on each, brush the edges with water, fold over and seal; get as much mixture in as you possibly can, but seal tightly. Keep the patties on a lightly floured tray in the refrigerator until the meal. Then bake three per person, brushed with egg yolk, and pricked lightly with a fork, in a pre-heated oven – gas mark 8, 475°F (240°C) – for about 12 minutes. Serve with a generous tablespoonful of dill cream and cucumber sambal per person. For the dill cream: season lightly whipped double cream with salt, pepper, a little lemon juice and pounded dill seed. For the sambal: dice a peeled cucumber fairly small and mix with a little finely chopped onion, celery, red pepper and parsley. Dress with oil and lemon, salt and pepper.

Serves 6

Chef: George Perry-Smith
Proprietors: Heather Crosbie and George Perry-Smith

THE OLD BAKEHOUSE

Colyton, Devon

Susan Keen differs from the majority of chefs in this book by specializing exclusively in French provincial cooking. All the recipes she uses are drawn from various districts, with the favourite perhaps being the Périgord. Her menu now represents a colourful cross-section of country dishes; from the simplest to the most esoteric.

The daily *table d'hôte* revolves around seasonal produce, offering five starters and five main courses, with a varied selection of fresh vegetables. Amongst the starters, you might find *Moules bordelaise* (cooked in white wine, parsley and tomatoes), Walnut soup or *Salade cauchoise*.

Everything is done with the same attention to detail that one would find in France. The *friands*, for instance, arrive on a piping hot white enamel dish, garnished with gherkin fans and accompanied by a glass of Marsala. The vegetables taste as if they had been picked five minutes earlier. The leeks, a brilliant green, are as wide and as long as your smallest finger; the carrots, cut into matchstick lengths, still have a hint of crunch to them; the potatoes, a choice between a creamy *dauphinois* or miniature *nouvelles*. The waitresses are from the village and, though lacking the solemnity of their French counterparts, take such obvious interest in the food and your enjoyment of it that you are more than ever inclined to do so.

Friand Provençal

½ lb (225g) plain flour
pinch of salt
6 oz (175g) butter
4 tablespoons iced water

2 oz (50g) lean pork
2 oz (50g) lean veal
1 shallot, peeled
1 clove of garlic, peeled
1 tablespoon chopped
  parsley

1 tablespoon chopped
  chives
1 tablespoon brandy
salt and pepper
1 egg, beaten

gherkins and black olives
  to garnish
Marsala (optional)

Start by making the pastry. Sift the flour and salt into a large bowl and rub in the butter until the mixture resembles breadcrumbs. Add enough water to bind the mixture, then knead lightly into a ball. Put into a polythene bag and leave in a cool place for 30 minutes.

In the meantime, roughly chop the meats and simmer in a small amount of water for about 10 minutes or until cooked. Leave to cool, then drain off any excess water and put the meats through a fine mincer. Finely chop the shallot and garlic and mix into the meat with the herbs and brandy. Add a generous seasoning of salt and pepper and enough beaten egg to bind the mixture together.

Preheat the oven to gas mark 6, 400°F (200°C). Bring the pastry to room temperature, then roll out to an ⅛-inch (0·25cm) thickness and stamp out 2-inch (5cm) rounds. Place a spoonful of the meat mixture in the centre of half the rounds. Dampen the edges with water or beaten egg and cover with the remaining rounds, pinching the edges well to seal. Mould them to form small patties. Brush with beaten egg, prick lightly with a fork and place on a greased baking tray. Bake for 10 minutes or until golden. Serve hot, with gherkin fans and black olives.

Serves 8 (allowing 2 per person)

Chef: Susan Keen *Proprietors:* Susan and Stephen Keen

WHITE MOSS HOUSE

Rydal Water, Cumbria

'The only thing that can be said against eating is that it takes away the appetite' – *The Greedy Book*

The art lies in sating the appetite without rendering it unconscious. The diner should rise from the table feeling contented, but not so full that he never wants to eat again. For too long, restaurateurs have laboured under the illusion that if they piled the plates high with food, no one would have the strength to examine the contents closely. But customers have proved more discerning and mountainous portions are now being replaced by ones which are smaller and more quality-conscious.

Lessons on how to satisfy the appetite without knocking it sideways should begin with a visit to White Moss House. Here Mrs Butterworth succeeds in serving a five-course dinner without making it seem like a marathon event. The secret lies in her precision tailoring. No single course is dominant and each one seems to whet the appetite for those that follow. The delicate portions may be viewed with dismay by some guests, ravenous after a day on the fells, but their gradual progression will produce contented sighs and a smooth digestion.

Smoked Mackerel Hot Pots

2 smoked mackerel *or*
    Arbroath smokies
¼ lb (100g) mushrooms
3 oz (75g) butter
1 level tablespoon flour
½ pint (275ml) milk
salt and pepper

clove of garlic
4–6 tablespoons dried
    breadcrumbs

tomato and sprigs of
    parsley to garnish

4–6 ramekins

Skin and flake the mackerel, removing any bones, and divide amongst the ramekins. (You can put a smoked oyster in the middle to add to the flavour.) Slice the mushrooms and fry gently in half the butter. Add the flour and cook for 1 minute. Blend in the milk and cook (stirring all the time) until it has thickened to make a mushroom sauce. Season with salt and pepper, then pour over the mackerel.

Crush a clove of garlic and sauté in the remaining butter over low heat. Add the breadcrumbs and continue cooking until they are light brown and crisp, adding more butter and a little oil if necessary. Put a layer of this mixture over the mushroom sauce in each ramekin.

The hot pots can be prepared to this stage in advance and then reheated in a moderate oven – gas mark 4, 350°F (180°C) – for 10–15 minutes before serving. Top each one with a slice of cold, skinned tomato (cut in three to make it easier to eat) and a sprig of parsley.

Serves 4–6, depending on size of mackerel

Chef: Jean Butterworth
Proprietors: Jean and Arthur Butterworth

PLUMBER MANOR

Sturminster Newton, Dorset

Plumber Manor is run by a triumvirate of Richard, Alison and Brian Prideaux-Brune. They have discreetly converted this stone-built Jacobean manor house, the family home of the Prideaux-Brunes since the seventeenth century, into a 'restaurant with bedrooms'. To preserve the feeling of a country home, they have tried to keep the house very much as it's always been. With the exception of the drawing-room, which is now the main dining-room overlooking the garden, few changes have been made. The library is stacked with leather tomes, portraits line the walls and the family hound still rushes out to greet you. With a different Prideaux-Brune (brothers and sisters-in-law have now been co-opted) to pour you a drink, take your order, cook the dinner, uncork the wine and serve the coffee, there can be little doubt by the end of the meal that the place is 'owner-run'.

The chef is Brian Prideaux-Brune and he commands a kitchen of Olympian proportions, with a labyrinth of larders, cold rooms and cellars leading off it. From this spacious station, he cooks dinner five nights a week for forty to sixty people, tempting them with such delicacies as Smoked salmon paupiettes with avocado *fromage*, Chicken and almond pancakes with spinach sauce, Kidneys with mint and anchovy, or Lamb Shrewsbury.

68

Paupiettes of Smoked Salmon with Avocado Fromage

2 ripe medium avocados
juice of 1 lemon
¼ lb (100g) Philadelphia
cream cheese
dash of Worcestershire
sauce
1 teaspoon finely grated
onion
salt and pepper

½ pint (275ml) double
cream
24 slices of smoked
salmon, each 3 × 4 in
(7·5 × 10cm)

watercress and lemon to
garnish

Peel and stone the avocados, then chop roughly. Purée with the lemon juice until smooth. Add the cream cheese gradually and blend until smooth. Transfer to a large bowl, then add a generous dash of Worcestershire sauce, the grated onion and a good seasoning of salt and pepper. Whisk the cream until thick, then fold in. Check the seasoning again and adjust if necessary. Cover the bowl with cling film and chill for 15–20 minutes.

Put a dollop of the avocado *fromage* in the centre of each slice of smoked salmon and roll up carefully. Place three paupiettes on each plate, garnish with a sprig of watercress and wedge of lemon and serve.

Serves 8

Chef: Brian Prideaux-Brune
Proprietors: Alison, Richard and Brian Prideaux-Brune

FISHES'

Burnham Market, Norfolk

Though the north coast of Norfolk is blessed with beautiful beaches and scenery, there is a marked absence of good restaurants. This must be why residents and visitors fall with delight into Fishes', Gillian Cape's *poissonerie* in Burnham Market. It is typically French in the sense that the food comes first and everything else (except perhaps the customers) takes second place. The décor is unsophisticated, with spindly chairs and cork-topped tables, and seems to emphasize that this is a place where the food and the customers create their own atmosphere.

Because there is only Mrs Cape or her assistant in the kitchen, cooking everything to order, customers must be prepared for a leisurely meal. There are rarely complaints as the nutty wholemeal rolls, pots of unsalted butter and chilled bottles of white wine make the wait extremely bearable. The smells wafting from the kitchen trigger off the appetite and every dish arriving at nearby tables looks better than the last. The daily changing *table d'hôte* might feature Crab soup, Stilton pâté or Moules (done provençale, marinière or, as below, with apple, cider and celery) to start.

70

Mussels in Cider
with Celery and Apple

4 pints (2 litres) mussels
2 oz (50g) butter
1 oz (25g) finely chopped
  onion
1 oz (25g) finely chopped
  leeks
2–3 sticks of celery,
  chopped

2 small eating apples,
  chopped
8 fl oz (225ml) dry cider

coarsely chopped parsley
  to garnish

Clean the mussels: scrub, scrape and pull off the 'beards', then wash in lots of cold water. Discard any that remain open or that are cracked.

Melt the butter in a large, fairly deep pan and gently soften the chopped onion and leeks in it. Add all the other ingredients (except the mussels) and when bubbling, add the mussels. Cover the pan with a lid.

Shake the pan vigorously every few minutes. After 5 minutes, all the mussels will be open (discard any that are still closed) and ready to serve (do not overcook). Transfer the mussels to warmed bowls. Reduce the liquid if there appears to be too much (but the apple and celery are better if still a bit crunchy) and pour over the mussels. Sprinkle with the chopped parsley. (Don't add salt.)

NB. If cooking larger quantities, use two pans or the weight of the mussels on top will prevent those underneath opening properly.

Serves 4

Chef and proprietor: Gillian Cape

THE BEAR

Nayland, Suffolk

The village of Nayland, nestling into a corner of England made famous by Constable's paintings, is now achieving notability for another reason. To the *cognoscenti*, it is known as the home of The Bear restaurant, a den of gastronomic pleasure.

For almost four years, Jane and Gerry Ford have been providing considerably better-than-bistro food in this tiny Suffolk town. They started with high standards, making everything (including all their own pasta, pastry and bread) themselves, and these have not faltered. In the kitchen, there is a distinct division of labour (though in the restaurant, the customers would be hard pushed to discern it) with Jane doing all the starters and puddings, while Gerry concentrates on the main courses. It is a generous country menu, with no false pretensions. Starters might be *Moules provençales*, Artichoke, tomato and fresh basil salad, or a hot *Bourride*. Of the six main dishes which follow, *Boeuf en croûte*, *Lasagna verde* (with delicious homemade pasta), Wild rabbit and mushroom or Pheasant pie would probably be the most popular. All come with a selection of three fresh vegetables. Puddings are mainly 'true Brit': Winchester ice-cream, Crème brûlée, Mulberry pie, Eton mess or Loganberry fool, though a few sound distinctly Gallic: *St Emilion au chocolat* and *Sorbet cassis*.

Sunday lunch is a family favourite at The Bear and then even the two younger Fords help, taking orders and serving. Catering for all ages and appetites, the menu is a fixed price for three courses, with a joint, Suffolk baked ham and a meat or game pie as the middle choices. It is outstandingly good value and, consequently, a popular Sunday outing for locals and visitors.

Stuffed Mussels 'Provençal'

Garlic Butter

½ dessertspoon green
  peppercorns
2 medium-sized cloves of
  garlic
salt
¼ lb (100g) good butter
½ tablespoon parsley,
  finely chopped

5 pints (2·5 litres) mussels
  (allow 7–10 per person)
1 glass of white wine
2 oz (50 g) soft white
  breadcrumbs

Start by making the garlic butter (this can be made in advance and kept wrapped in cling film or slightly dampened greaseproof paper in the refrigerator until needed). Crush the peppercorns. Crush the garlic with a little salt. Soften the butter, then mix in the crushed garlic, peppercorns and chopped parsley. When well blended, put to one side.

To prepare the mussels: keep the mussels in fresh cold water until ready to use. Scrape the mussel shells and pull out the beard. Discard any which stay open while scraping and any that are unnaturally heavy or cracked.

To cook the mussels: pour the wine into a large saucepan. Add the mussels, taking care NOT to include any grit. Place on a hot stove, put the lid on and shake occasionally until all the mussels have opened (about 5 minutes). Removing one at a time, discard top shells (and any that have not opened) and lay mussels on a tray in their half shells.

To stuff the mussels: make up a mixture of the softened garlic butter and soft white breadcrumbs. Cover each mussel with a teaspoon of this mixture. (If covered with cling film, these will keep in a fridge for several days.) When required, put the mussels on a baking tray under a hot grill until they are golden brown. Spoon over any buttery juices which escape during the cooking. Serve at once.

Serves 5

Chefs and proprietors: Jane and Gerry Ford

THE OLD BAKERY

When in Suffolk, a detour to Woolpit (near Bury St Edmunds) is well worth the effort. Here you'll find, besides a charming town, The Old Bakery. This building, originally medieval, has been faithfully restored by its owner, Mrs Eileen Gorman. It is a combined restaurant and shop, with the girls who serve dressed in long skirts and mob caps. Lunches offer homemade soups, pies, pâtés, roast Suffolk ham, baked potatoes, tarts, puddings and cakes and, in the summer, a varied cold table. Dinners are based on old English recipes, mainly taken from eighteenth- and nineteenth-century sources. The shop sells breads from an old-established village baker (still using the original oven) and Mrs Gorman's cakes and biscuits.

POOL COURT

Pool-in-Wharfedale, West Yorkshire

Roger Grime, the head chef at Pool Court, decided a few years ago that he and his chefs were being a bit too clever, trying too hard to make every dish an 'original'. Though no deliberate policy was made, they began to rely less on their own ingenuity and pay closer attention to cookery books.

Instead of making up a recipe, they would religiously follow one from, for instance, *Secrets of Great French Restaurants*. By following it to the letter, they could see if the techniques differed from their own, picking up new methods and ideas. For a professional chef, it is often far more difficult to be so precise than to adapt the recipe as he thinks it should be done. But it paid dividends in the end, for they found that by drawing on diverse sources, the range of their repertoire improved considerably. 'Cooking by the book' has now become a frequent exercise and several new dishes are tested each week; first by the book, then, if not exactly right, adapted for the restaurant.

This is a good example of a recipe, borrowed from Michel Guérard's *Cuisine Minceur*, which has been tailored to the Pool Court restaurant. It is a vegetable *tour de force* and will delight both slimmers and *gourmands*.

75

Carrot and Chervil Gâteau

1½ lb (675g) carrots
1½ oz (40g) unsalted butter
1 teaspoon sugar
1 teaspoon salt
pinch of pepper
½ pint (275ml) jellied *or*
 strong liquid chicken
 stock
¼ lb (100g) button
 mushrooms

1 shallot, peeled
a little olive oil
¾ oz (20g) Gruyère cheese,
 grated
½ oz (15g) fresh chervil,
 finely chopped, *or* 3
 rounded teaspoons dried
 chervil
2 eggs

small soufflé dish *or* 4 ramekins, 3 inches (7·5cm) in diameter

Wash and peel the carrots, then slice into rounds ¼ inch (0·50cm) thick. Heat 1 oz (25g) of the butter in a heavy saucepan and cook the carrots in it, stirring frequently, until lightly browned. Add the sugar, salt, pepper and stock. Cover the pan and cook over moderate heat for about 20 minutes or until all the liquid has evaporated. Dice the mushrooms and chop the shallot finely, then sauté in a small frying pan with a little olive oil.

Preheat the oven to gas mark 7, 425°F (220°C). Take the carrots out of the pan and chop coarsely. Put into a bowl with the softened shallot, mushrooms, grated Gruyère and chervil and mix together carefully. Beat the eggs until frothy, then pour over the other ingredients, and fold in until completely blended. Grease a soufflé dish or ramekins with the remaining butter and pour in the mixture. Place in a roasting tin half-filled with warm water and bake for approximately 20 minutes. Turn out on to a warm serving dish and serve with Spinach and mushroom sauce or with a hollandaise sauce (page 378).

Serves 4

Chefs: Roger Grime and Melvin Jordan
Proprietors: Michael, Kenneth and Hanni Gill

Spinach and Mushroom Sauce

8 fl oz (225ml) jellied *or*
strong liquid chicken
stock
½ oz (15g) butter
½ lb (225g) spinach,
washed and finely
chopped

2 oz (50g) flat
mushrooms, finely
chopped
½ oz (15g) flour
salt and pepper
¼ pint (150ml) double
cream

Put the stock on to boil. Melt the butter in a heavy saucepan, then add the spinach and mushrooms. Toss well in the
butter and cook for several minutes, then stir in the flour.
Blend thoroughly, then cook for 2 minutes. Gradually pour
in the stock, stirring all the time. Simmer gently for 10–15
minutes. Cool slightly, then liquidize until smooth. Pour
into a clean pan and season to taste with salt and pepper.
Just before serving, lightly whip the cream, fold in lightly
and pour round the Carrot and chervil gâteau.

FARNLEY SHOP

In Farnley, you will find one of the most unusual and
outstanding shops that West Yorkshire has to offer.
Run by Alan Porter, it is an Aladdin's cave of farm
produce and country cooking, brimming with delicious homemade breads, cakes, biscuits, ice-creams,
jams, chutneys, 'vintage pickled shallots', pâtés, meat
pies, and pizzas. As well as regional specialities
(Farnley sausage, gingerbread and Eccles cakes)
there are exotic foods from all over the world. The
cheese counter alone boasts over a hundred English
and Continental varieties. Local farm-cured bacon
and hams are also stocked, plus a wide range of wines,
beers, ciders (including Devon Farm scrumpy) and
mead. Herbs and spices are sold from tall glass jars.

BOWLISH HOUSE

Shepton Mallet, Somerset

The wine used in this recipe might come from any one of a dazzling number of bottles dotted round Martin Schwaller's kitchen. This is not due to a fondness for the bottle but to the owner's interest in the grape. When Brian Jordan bought Bowlish House in 1977, it came with a 'dry' cellar. Consequently, he was forced to acquire a knowledge and a supply of wine quickly.

At Bowlish House guests can now choose from two wine lists, one containing over 136 bins of wines from every major production area, with the most expensive bottle costing £8.30, and another which provides a selection of 'fine wines'. The *patron* has also started a 'Why buy a bottle?' scheme which offers various wines by the glass. The house wines change frequently and always include a Bordeaux Sauvignon, a Hock, a red Rioja and a Claret. A classed growth claret is also decanted every day and sold by the glass, in addition to two dessert wines, either a Setubal, a Beaumes de Venise or classed growth Sauternes and a 1960 or '63 vintage port. This enthusiasm for wine is now shared equally by the customers, the chef and the owner. With all three in mind, wine evenings which match dishes and wines of a particular region are held several times a year.

Champignons 'Café de Paris'

'Café de Paris' Butter

4 button onions
3 cloves of garlic
2½ fl oz (65ml) dry white wine
½ lb (225g) unsalted butter
pinch each of chopped tarragon, chives, marjoram, thyme, chervil
2 pinches of chopped parsley
2 teaspoons German mustard
1 teaspoon English mustard
salt and pepper

4 slices granary bread, buttered on one side
2 oz (50g) Cheddar *or* Gruyère cheese, grated
32 good open button mushrooms

tomato slices and lemon twists to garnish

4 small shallow ovenproof dishes

Start by making the *Café de Paris* butter. Peel and chop the onion and garlic very finely. Put into a saucepan with the wine and heat until the wine has reduced completely. Leave to cool. Cream the butter until light, then blend in the onion, garlic, herbs and mustards. Season to taste with salt and pepper.

Gently fry the buttered side of the bread slices until nicely browned. Take out and press the grated cheese on the other side, then grill until golden brown. Dice into small croûtons and arrange in the bottom of the four oven-proof dishes. Place eight mushrooms in each dish, hollow side up with the stem removed. Place a teaspoon of *Café de Paris* butter in each mushroom and grill until cooked through (about 4 minutes). Garnish with tomato slices and a twist of lemon. Serve immediately.

Serves 4

Chef: Martin Schwaller *Proprietors:* Pat and Brian Jordan

PLUMBER MANOR

Sturminster Newton, Dorset

You could count on one hand the number of gastronomes who return from Italy without a taste for the incomparable *Pasta alla genovese*. It may be *linguine, fettucini* or *tagliatelle* but the sauce will always have *pesto*. This blend of basil, garlic, oil, pine nuts and cheese makes an Elysian partner for any pasta. It is served *con amore* by all the Northern Italians, particularly the Genoese who will eat it any time of the day or night. In London, a dedicated search will find it in an Italian restaurant or good delicatessen, but in the country, it becomes decidedly more elusive. This makes the sight of Mushrooms with basil and cream on the menu at Plumber Manor all the more pleasurable. It must be the particular weakness (and consequent strength) of the chef, Brian Prideaux-Brune, for he uses pesto sauce not only with pasta but also with loin of veal and in this mushroom starter.

A recipe which will console expatriate Italians and delight pesto addicts of any nationality. Highly recommended as an easy and unusual first course or supper dish.

Mushrooms with Basil and Cream

1½ lb (675g) mushrooms
3 oz (75g) butter
2–3 tablespoons brandy
½ pint (275ml) double
  cream
1–2 tablespoons pesto
  sauce (for homemade,
  see page 384)

salt and white pepper

finely chopped parsley to
  garnish
croûtes of toasted brown
  bread (optional)

Wipe the mushrooms and slice thickly. Melt the butter in a large pan and sauté the mushrooms quickly until soft and dark in colour. Pour off any excess liquid. Warm the brandy, then pour over the mushrooms and flame. Mix the pesto sauce (as much or as little as you like) with a little of the cream in a small cup, then pour into the pan and blend into the pan juices. Add the remaining cream and simmer until slightly thickened. Season to taste with salt and white pepper. Sprinkle lightly with finely chopped parsley and serve the mushrooms as they are or on croûtes of toasted brown bread.

Serves 4–6

Chef: Brian Prideaux-Brune
Proprietors: Alison, Richard and Brian Prideaux-Brune

MOULD AND EDWARDS

A short distance from Plumber Manor is the cobbled town of Sherborne. Walking down Cheap Street, it is difficult to resist the homemade pies displayed temptingly in the windows of Mould and Edwards. Inside, marble slabs hold waxy rounds of farmhouse Cheddar, strings of sausages, charcuterie, fresh game and poultry. Shelves at the back hold jams and special biscuits, including the famous 'Dorset Knobs'.

THE TOASTMASTER'S INN

Burham, Kent

You might find it necessary to retrace your steps to The Toastmaster's Inn to do full justice to the menu. Its situation in the sleepy town of Burham, a mile or two from Snodland, gives no hint of the remarkably high standard of cooking to be found there.

It has long been known to wine-lovers, appreciative of the staggering list built up by Sydney Ward, a former toastmaster at the Guildhall. The cellar is still one of the best in the country and the wine list, with a tempting 500 bins to choose from, almost needs a Heath Robinson crane to lift it. His son Gregory and daughter-in-law Judith are now in charge and it was Gregory who, in the early 1970s, breathed life into the restaurant.

As much as possible is 'homemade' at The Toastmaster's and this includes 'home-smoked' as well. Their pride and joy is the smokehouse (referred to lovingly as 'the shed') at the bottom of the garden. In it, they smoke all kinds of fish, some game (venison and quail) and occasionally chicken. Sausages have become a speciality and the Daglish/Duval team make one of venison, also a *boudin blanc* and a *boudin aux fruits de mer*.

The Toastmaster's two most popular starters are both avocado: one is filled with a poached egg and topped with hollandaise; the other is the devastating combination opposite.

Toastmaster's Baked Avocado

2 rashers rindless back
  bacon
1 tomato
1 oz (25g) onion, finely
  chopped
3 oz (75g) peeled prawns
2 soupspoons thick
  mayonnaise (for
  homemade, see page
  383)

pinch of allspice
salt and pepper
2 avocado pears
2–3 oz (50–75g) mild
  Cheddar

sprigs of parsley and
  lemon wedges to garnish

Start by frying the bacon rashers until crisp. Drain on kitchen paper, then chop into small pieces. Blanch the tomato quickly in boiling water, remove the skin and chop the flesh coarsely. Put the bacon, onion, tomato, prawns and mayonnaise into a bowl and mix together. Add a pinch of allspice and season to taste with salt and pepper.

Preheat the oven to gas mark 5, 375°F (190°C). Halve the avocados and remove the stones. Scoop out the flesh and roughly chop it, leaving about $\frac{1}{4}$ inch (0·50cm) all the way round. Carefully fold into the mayonnaise mixture. Check the seasoning and adjust if necessary. Put this filling back into the shells, mounding it up slightly in the centre. Grate the cheese and scatter evenly over the top. Place the avocados in a shallow ovenproof dish (or individual ones) and bake in the preheated oven for 10 minutes. Put under a hot grill for several minutes to brown slightly, then garnish with a sprig of parsley and wedge of lemon. Serve at once. If preparing in advance, brush the inside of the shells with lemon juice to prevent discolouring.)

Serves 4

Chefs: Tim Daglish and Paul Duval
Proprietors: Judith and Gregory Ward

MALLORY COURT

Tachbrook Mallory, Warwickshire

You could be forgiven for thinking, on the doorstep of Mallory Court, that you were about to enter an Elizabethan manor house. But inside, once you've settled into a comfortable sofa, it becomes obvious that all is not Elizabethan here. There is not a single draught to speak of and the oak panelling shows no signs of several centuries' wear and tear. It is not, in fact, historic at all but a fine example of early twentieth-century 'mock Elizabethan' architecture.

There are many country house hotels where the proprietor is willing but the staff, alas, is weak. This is not true of Mallory Court where, upon crossing the threshold, you will be met by a young lad whose welcome is absolutely genuine. He will, unprompted, offer to spirit away the 'wellies', dry your coat before the fire, make a pot of tea or pour you a stiff whisky and soda. Further interest in your welfare is found in the bedrooms, kitted out with recent books, magazines, towelling bath robes, colour television and medium dry sherries. The combination of luxurious surroundings and relaxed atmosphere is further enhanced by a *cuisine* of the same high standard. It is prepared by Allan Holland, one of the two *patrons*, whose professionalism is all the more astonishing considering this is his first restaurant venture.

Poire d'Avocat 'Mallory Court'

1 ripe avocado pear
1 small ripe Ogen melon
6 oz (175g) crabmeat,
   shredded and well
   picked over
¼ lb (100g) peeled prawns
½ pint (275ml) homemade
   mayonnaise (page 383)

salt and pepper
a little lemon juice
a little tomato purée
a little double cream
two 5-fl oz (150ml) cartons
   soured cream

sprigs of parsley to garnish

Peel the avocado, remove the stone and cut into quarters lengthwise. Peel the melon, cut into quarters (lengthwise) and remove the seeds.

Mix the crabmeat and prawns together with 3 or 4 tablespoons of the mayonnaise. Season to taste with salt and pepper and a little lemon juice if necessary.

Place one piece of the avocado pear on a serving plate and put a quarter of the crab and prawn filling along the inside length of the pear. Place a melon quarter on the other side of the filling and gently push the avocado and melon together, so enclosing the filling and forming an oval shape.

Add a little tomato purée to the remaining mayonnaise and mix well together so that the mayonnaise is a pale pink. If necessary, add a little double cream in order to obtain a nice coating consistency. Stir the soured cream until smooth and if necessary add a little lightly whipped double cream to obtain the same consistency as the mayonnaise.

Coat the avocado half of the oval with the mayonnaise and the melon half with the soured cream. Garnish the top of each oval with a sprig of parsley.

Serves 4

Chef: Allan Holland
Proprietors: Allan Holland and Jeremy Mort

GRAVETYE MANOR

East Grinstead, West Sussex

From strictly classical dishes, Michael Quinn and his kitchen team at Gravetye have been moving, during the last two years, towards a more individual style. It has been inspired by the culinary vogue now current in France and to a certain extent in this country for lighter, less rich food.

Their cooking now seems to be based in equal parts on tradition and innovation, a blend which is clearly reflected on the menu. You could, for instance, start with a classic *Terrine de foie gras* or the more inventive *Soupe froide au poivre vert et ananas frais*. Recognizing that customers are happiest if they rise from the table satisfied but not over-full, Michael also offers a selection of starters which can be eaten as a main course. Perhaps a Roulade of fresh salmon mousse wrapped in puff pastry and served with a light shellfish sauce or an Egg *en cocotte à la Reine*, with dice of chicken, Noilly Prat and fresh cream. The main courses veer slightly more to the *nouvelle cuisine* and it is here that the influence of Michael Quinn becomes more obvious. His *Sole de Douvres aux avocats*, a grilled Dover sole with sliced avocado and creamed sorrel, is a stunning blend of colour and taste. The *Carré d'agneau Hilda*, roasted with fresh rosemary and served with baby carrots and broccoli hollandaise, has a flavour which belies its simplicity.

The *Poire fraîche vinaigrette* could never have appeared on the Gravetye menu five years ago. It illustrates not only the impact of *cuisine minceur* but also a new interest by customers and chefs in clean, unadulterated flavours.

Poire Fraîche Vinaigrette

6 good-sized Comice pears
¼ pint (150ml) white wine
vinegar
10 fresh mint leaves
10 fresh tarragon leaves

6 fresh mint leaves to
garnish
homemade mayonnaise

Dressing
2½ fl oz (65ml) white wine
vinegar
½ oz (15g) fresh mint and
tarragon, finely chopped
juice of 2 lemons
salt, pepper and castor
sugar to taste
¼ lb (100g) smoked ham

Peel the pears, using a vegetable peeler, leaving the stalk attached. Place in a saucepan and add the vinegar, mint and tarragon leaves. Pour in just enough water to cover, then poach gently until the pears are tender. Drain off the liquid and leave the pears to cool.

To make the dressing, mix together the vinegar, mint, tarragon and lemon juice, then add salt, pepper and castor sugar to taste. Cut the ham into thin julienne strips and blend in.

Slice the top off each pear and put to one side. Carefully scoop out the core, then fill the centre with the smoked ham dressing. Replace the top of the pear, pull the stalk out and put a fresh mint leaf in its place. Serve with the remaining dressing or with a lightly creamed fresh mayonnaise flavoured with fresh mint and tarragon.

Serves 6

Chef: Michael Quinn *Proprietor:* Peter Herbert

POOL COURT

Pool-in-Wharfedale, West Yorkshire

In France, as you sit sipping a *kir* or Pernod and musing over an incomprehensible menu, a waiter is likely to glide over with a plate of *amuse-gueule*.

This is a little *quelquechose* to tickle your tastebuds before the meal. Perhaps a few thimble-sized vol-au-vents, slivers of smoked salmon on toast or finger-lengths of fried fish. They must, above all, be small. The objective is not to stimulate the appetite but merely to trim its rough edges, thus removing the urge to gallop through four courses. In this country, a similar practice produces dismal uniformity: bowls of salted nuts and crisps sprout like mushrooms from every table. When a restaurateur is balmy enough to provide nibbles of a different nature, his guests are likely to regard him and them with some suspicion.

At Pool Court, they succeed in serving an *amuse-gueule* which is as pleasing to the eye as it is to the customers. A small plate is filled with coins of Gruyère shortbread and a delicate swan of choux pastry, with feathers of home-made cream cheese. Only a sparrow-like appetite could be ruined by these offerings.

Gruyère Shortbread

½ lb (225g) plain flour
½ teaspoon salt
6 oz (175g) butter, at
room temperature
2 egg yolks
3 oz (75g) Gruyère cheese,
grated

½ oz (15g) Parmesan
cheese, grated, *or* finely
chopped hazelnuts

1 small egg (for egg wash)

Sift the flour and salt on to a plate. Put the butter into a large mixing bowl and cream until light. Beat in the egg yolks, alternately with a small amount of flour. Then beat in the remaining flour. Blend in the grated Gruyère cheese, then gather the dough up into a ball. Put it into a polythene bag and allow to rest for an hour.

Preheat the oven to gas mark 3, 325°F (170°C). Bring the dough to room temperature, then roll out on a lightly floured surface until about ¼ inch (0·50cm) thick. Cut out with small biscuit cutters and transfer to a lightly greased baking sheet. Brush the tops with lightly beaten egg, then dust with grated Parmesan or finely chopped hazelnuts. Bake just above the centre of the preheated oven until a pale golden (25–35 minutes). Lift off with a palette knife and cool on a wire rack. Serve cold as an 'appetizer' (preferably with an apéritif).

Makes 5 dozen shortbread

Chefs: Roger Grime and Melvin Jordan
Proprietors: Michael, Kenneth and Hanni Gill

ROTHAY MANOR

Ambleside, Cumbria

One imagines 'whet-appetits' being consumed by portly Pickwicks, and after a few days of Bronwen Nixon's cooking at Rothay Manor you would have no difficulty finding latter-day equivalents. After a day trekking over the fells or rowing across Lake Grasmere, the appetite only needs this sliver of cheese and anchovy to get it going. (More often, it is a case of keeping it on a tight leash until safely inside the dining-room.)

These small *bonne bouches* are a Georgian recipe, plundered by Mrs Nixon from her collection of antiquarian cook books. It is impossible to conceive of anything so simple acting as an 'open sesame' to the appetite but this, judging from the relish with which guests attack their dinner, is exactly what it does. It is one of many Georgian delicacies which Mrs Nixon's sleuthing has produced and which now grace the tables at Rothay Manor. She does, occasionally, devote a whole evening to cookery of this period and then Whet-appetits are joined by Almonde hedgehog soup, Herb pudding, Betrothal cake and countless others. The Pickwicks reappear for wine evenings held in November and December. Here dishes of a particular region in France are married with complementary wines from neighbouring villages.

Whet-appetits

---

4 anchovy fillets
a little milk
4 slices of bread
½ oz (15g) butter
2 oz (50g) grated Cheddar

1 egg, lightly beaten
oil *or* fat for frying

sprigs of parsley to garnish

Put the anchovy fillets on a saucer and cover with milk. Leave for 15–30 minutes, then drain and pat dry with kitchen paper.

Butter the bread, then remove the crusts. Cut each anchovy fillet in half and place two pieces on one half of each slice. Cover with grated cheese. Fold each slice over to cover the filling and pinch the edges together. Cut in half diagonally. Dip each triangle in beaten egg and fry in deep fat (or fry both sides in butter in a frying pan). Serve hot, garnished with a sprig of parsley.

Serves 4 as an 'appetizer'

Chef and proprietor: Bronwen Nixon

Soups

This Bouillabaisse a noble dish is –
  A sort of soup, or broth, or brew,
Or hotchpotch of all sorts of fishes,
  That Greenwich never could outdo:
Green herbs, red peppers, mussels, saffron,
  Soles, onions, garlic, roach, and dace:
All these you eat at TERRÉ's tavern
  In that one dish of Bouillabaisse.

from The Ballad of the Bouillabaisse,
W. M. Thackeray

There used to be a time when the same soups turned up with monotonous regularity on every restaurant menu. Worse still, they turned up in the same three colours: cream (usually leek and potato, with the emphasis on the latter), russet (tomato or carrot, possibly both) and mahogany (consommé or the ubiquitous 'Windsor-brown'). Country restaurants could at least be relied upon to provide a good vegetable soup being, as they were, surrounded by the stuff. But even they have fallen prey to modern advances and many are now producing soups with a disturbing technicolour glow.

For some reason, soups have never quite 'made it' as far as glamour and excitement go. They have never had the same magnetic appeal on a menu as prawn cocktail, pâté and melon. No one seems to expect much of them except that they should be hot (cold soups still get an icy reception in the country), cheap and filling. Who can blame restaurateurs then for trying to disguise them with exotic sounding names? *Potage bonne femme*, *Vichyssoise* and *Potage Crécy* all sound a good deal more inviting than their English counterparts (Vegetable, Leek and potato, and Carrot soup).

The following chapter provides unequivocal testimony to the efforts being made by certain country restaurateurs to restore the good name of homemade soup. Their creations are imaginative and flavoursome, comparable to the French in their shrewd use of seasonal ingredients and in the quality achieved. Susan Keen's Walnut soup at The Old Bakehouse, George Perry-Smith's now classic *Soupe de poisson* (Riverside), Joyce Molyneux's Banana curry soup (Carved Angel) and the Curried apple soup at Lamb's are all examples of how appetizing the soup course has become.

MARLFIELD HOUSE

Gorey, Co. Wexford, Eire

The factors which determine a restaurant's success, making it more popular than another of comparable standard, are often as recondite as an Einsteinian theory. It is a chemistry which continues to delight customers and baffle prospective restaurateurs.

The advantage of a charismatic owner cannot be overestimated and nowhere is it better demonstrated than at Marlfield House. It soon becomes obvious that, despite the beauty of an ivy-covered Regency dower house in thirty-five acres of woodland, the main asset is the owner, Mary Bowe. The Irish would (and do) describe her as a 'dote'; she has an irrepressible sense of fun, is immensely kind and has the most infectious laugh in County Wexford.

She can collect herbs from the garden, feed the roaming guinea fowl, arrange flowers in the front hall and chat to three or four guests in the time it takes to order lunch. Yet the atmosphere at Marlfield House is unhurried and so tranquil that you're likely to be lulled into a trance. If you stay to dinner, you will be offered a four-course *table d'hôte* with copious choice. Amongst the dishes on it will be a selection of homemade soups and one might be this delicious fennel soup.

Cream of Fennel Soup

1 medium onion
3 fennel bulbs
2 oz (50g) butter
1 oz (25g) flour
2 pints (1·1 litres) chicken stock
½ pint (275ml) milk

1 bay leaf
salt and pepper
2 egg yolks
¼ pint (150ml) single cream

croûtons to serve

Slice the onion and fennel thinly. Melt the butter in a heavy saucepan, add the vegetables and stir until well coated with butter. Cook over gentle heat until they have softened but on no account must they brown. Draw off the heat and stir in the flour. Cook for 3 minutes, then gradually blend in the stock and the milk. Add the bay leaf, cover and simmer for 20 minutes. Remove the bay leaf, then pass the soup through a fine mouli or wire sieve and return to a clean pan. Check the seasoning and adjust if necessary.

Mix the egg yolks and the cream together and slowly whisk in about half a cup of hot soup. Then tip it all back into the pan and whisk into the soup. Reheat gently (taking care not to let it boil) and serve piping hot with fried bread croûtons.

Serves 6–8

Chef and proprietor: Mary Bowe

WELL HOUSE

Poundisford, Somerset

If you are planning to visit Well House, it would be as well to take a good navigator with you. The route, through the leafy depths of Somerset, is beautiful but baffling. Anticipating confusion, a map is sent to all first-time diners. This looks remarkably easy to follow until you get within a five-mile radius of the restaurant; then it becomes about as clear as a guide to Jupiter.

The absence of relevant signposts is disconcerting but as you pass The Greyhound in Staple Fitzpaine for the third time, a mild panic sets in. (Without the natives, who are friendly and armed with shortcuts to the restaurant, one might be circling there still.) Having found the drive at last and by now indecently late, you arrive flushed and full of excuses. Will there be a fierce reprimand from the *patron* or worse still, no table? But a pleasant surprise awaits, for eight years of late-comers have mellowed the owners and you are given, instead, a prodigal's welcome.

Late or no, the roaring fire in the dining-room is a glorious sight after a long and frosty drive. It is only improved by the smell of Graham Cornish's homemade soup as it is brought post haste from the kitchen.

Cream of Onion Soup with Coriander

1½ lb (675g) onions
2 oz (50g) bacon fat
1 tablespoon flour
½ pint (275ml) strong chicken stock
½ pint (275ml) milk
zest of 2 lemons

3 teaspoons ground coriander
salt and pepper
3 dessertspoons single cream

crisp bacon and chopped chives to garnish

Peel and chop the onions. Melt the bacon fat in a large pan and toss the onions in it. Cover and sweat the onions until softened. Stir in the flour and cook for a minute or two. Gradually pour in the stock and milk, blending in well. Add the lemon zest, coriander and season to taste with salt and pepper. Cook over a gentle heat for 20 minutes. Liquidize the mixture, then pour through a sieve into the pan. Add the cream and adjust the seasoning if necessary. Keep warm, being careful not to let it boil. When ready to serve, garnish with a sprinkling of chopped bacon and chives.

Serves 4

Chef: Graham Cornish *Proprietor:* Ralph Vivian Neal

DUNDERRY LODGE

Dunderry, Co. Meath, Eire

There seems to be a widespread belief that the success of a recipe is directly proportional to the number of ingredients in it. Unless it looks frightfully complicated, no one trusts it to rise above the ordinary. A recipe with less than six ingredients is seen as nursery fodder, while one with over eight automatically qualifies as *haute cuisine*. Magazines are filled with glossy food photographs, partnered with interminably long recipes which show how 'remarkably easy' they all are. Anyone can do them, but not one who has arrived home late, forgotten the garlic and has guests arriving in half an hour.

Catherine Healey, needless to say, does *not* make this soup because she is pushed for time but because the combination is a good one. There is no need to add further dashes of anything; the flavour is perfect. When her guests at Dunderry Lodge ask for the recipe, they refuse to believe that the one she gives them is correct. They assume that this subtle masterpiece could only be created through hours of preparation and a list of ingredients as long as your soup ladle. Her attempts to serve a more exotic concoction are met with polite resistance and further requests for vegetable soup. While her creative urge fights back, her common sense concedes that with soups at least, the simplest is quite often the best.

Creamy Vegetable Soup

2 large onions
1 large carrot
2 sticks of celery
$\frac{1}{2}$ head of cauliflower
2 oz (50g) butter
2 pints (1·1 litres) good
   beef stock

salt and pepper

chopped parsley to
   garnish

Start by preparing the vegetables. Peel the onions and carrot and chop finely. Rinse the celery and dice. Cut the cauliflower into small florets. Melt the butter in a large saucepan and when foaming, add the chopped vegetables. Cook gently over a low heat, stirring occasionally. When they are soft, add the stock and season well with salt and pepper. Bring up to the boil, then reduce the heat and simmer for a few minutes. Leave to cool slightly, then blend in a liquidizer until smooth. Pass through a sieve into the saucepan and gradually reheat. Just before serving, garnish with a sprinkling of chopped parsley.

Serves 6

Chef: Catherine Healey
Proprietors: Catherine and Nicholas Healey

POOL COURT

Pool-in-Warfedale, West Yorkshire

Michael Gill is one of the few *patrons* in this book who actually knew from an early age that he wanted to run a restaurant and so went straight from school to catering college. Even more unusual was his determination not to work at the Connaught, the Gavroche or 'chez Bocuse' but to start his own restaurant immediately. The moment he graduated from Leeds Technical College he began looking for suitable premises. After a patient search, he eventually found a spacious Georgian house in Pool-in-Warfedale, West Yorkshire. It had obvious potential but the capital to realize it was not quite as evident.

Undaunted, Michael did the conversion as a series of part-works. He took one room at a time and when several (including the kitchen) were presentable, he opened the restaurant in 1971. Since then, the building and decorating have continued unabated and there is now one sitting-room, two bars and three dining-rooms. But unlike many establishments, this expansionist policy has not meant the end of good food and personal service. Michael Gill is still at the door to greet the guests and will be as busy as any member of staff during the evening, pouring drinks, taking orders or delivering coffee. His wife and brother are also involved and they all seem to have an indomitable enthusiasm for the job.

100

Creamed Celeriac Soup with Lemon Croûtes

½ lb (225g) onions
2 lb (900g) celeriac
¼ lb (100g) butter
¼ pint (150ml) dry sherry
salt and pepper
3 pints (1·75 litres)
 homemade chicken
 stock *or* made from
 stock cubes
juice of ½ lemon

a little double cream to
 garnish
a little finely chopped
 parsley

Lemon Croûtes
2 slices of white bread
1½ oz (40g) butter
juice of ½ lemon
salt

Peel the onions and chop roughly. Peel the celeriac, remove the flat end and chop into small pieces. Melt the butter in a heavy saucepan and toss the onion and celeriac well in it. Cook over moderate heat, stirring occasionally, until soft but not brown. Add the sherry, a good seasoning of salt and pepper and the stock. Bring up to the boil, then reduce the heat and simmer for about 30 minutes. Liquidize the soup, then pass through a strainer into a clean pan. Add the lemon juice, correct the seasoning and slowly reheat. Just before serving, add a swirl of double cream, a dusting of lemon croûtes and parsley.

To make the lemon croûtes, remove the crusts from the bread. Cut into ¼-inch (·50cm) dice, place on a baking tray and leave in a warm place (e.g. in a cool oven) to dry out. Melt the butter in a frying pan and when really hot, add the bread cubes. Sauté until golden brown, shaking the pan to give them an even colour. When nicely browned, add the lemon juice and a sprinkling of salt. Lift out of the pan and keep warm until needed.

Serves 8

Chefs: Roger Grime and Melvin Jordan
Proprietors: Michael, Kenneth and Hanni Gill

BALLYMALOE

Shanagarry, Co. Cork, Eire

The magnificent drive leading up to Ballymaloe is flanked with so many rows of cabbage, cauliflower and carrots that by the time you reach the front door, thoughts of French peasant soup, colcannon and cauliflower cheese are already well established.

The house itself, grey stone Irish 'baronial' with corners dating back to the fourteenth century, is set in four hundred acres of farmland. Owned by the Allens for over thirty years, it becomes obvious the minute you cross the threshold that a family atmosphere prevails.

If you take a wrong turning and find yourself at the back door (as many guests 'accidentally' do), you will then find Mrs Allen, in the kitchen supervising the cooking. When she first began serving meals to the public in 1964, all the food was prepared in what is now the alcove of the main dining-room. Nine years later, when the claustrophobia and the customers threatened to overwhelm her, a new kitchen was built at the back of the house. This has provided much-needed space for the rapidly expanding kitchen team (who now number eight) as well as for storage. It has since become one of the most popular rooms in the house and it is not unusual to find a guest (often aged under ten) perched on a kitchen stool or on the back stoop, with a piece of freshly baked bread or chocolate cake in hand. While this would send most chefs heading for the meat mallet, Mrs Allen remains unperturbed; six children of her own and sixteen years of running the restaurant have left her with a nature as steady as a Beeton blancmange.

French Peasant Soup

6 oz (175g) streaky rindless bacon
½ large onion
2 small potatoes
3 large tomatoes
clove of garlic, crushed

3 oz (75g) cabbage, finely shredded
½ teaspoon sugar
salt and pepper
1¼ pints (700ml) good chicken stock

Start by chopping the bacon into small dice. Then peel the onion and potatoes and chop into small pieces. Wash the tomatoes and chop roughly.

Put the bacon into a large heavy saucepan and cook over moderate heat until it begins to colour, stirring frequently. Add the chopped onion, potatoes and crushed garlic. Cover with a buttered piece of greaseproof paper and 'sweat' for 10 minutes, or until soft but not coloured. Remove the paper and add the cabbage, tomatoes, sugar and a good seasoning of salt and freshly ground black pepper. Mix in the stock, cover with a lid and cook until the cabbage is soft (15–20 minutes). Taste and adjust the seasoning if necessary. Serve at once or keep warm until needed. (The flavour actually improves if made the day before; thus, a good candidate for cooking in advance.)

Serves 4

Chef: Myrtle Allen *Proprietors:* Myrtle and Ivan Allen

PENLAN OLEU

Llanychaer Bridge, Dyfed, Wales

If the BBC ever decides to treat food-lovers to a series of *Face the Moussaka*, I have a recipe that will baffle even Bernard Levin.

It can only be found in the tiniest dining-room in the remotest farmhouse in the most distant part of Wales. It will be served to you by one of the MacKeown family, in their hilltop restaurant, Penlan Oleu. Identification of the ingredients will lead to such a heated discussion that the soup will, in all probability, be quite cold when you taste it. There will be those who swear they spot a touch of saffron, others an affinity with tomato and a few stalwarts who claim that it is definitely apple. Only the owner of Penlan Oleu and the soup's creator, Ann Carr, will be able to establish unequivocally what its origins are. A pity, perhaps, to spoil the fun by revealing the secret below – but the first sip should still be a pleasant surprise.

Kashmir Soup

½ lb (225g) good-quality dried apricots (darkest colour possible)
1 pint (575ml) cold tea
1 pint (575ml) thick chicken stock
good handful of chopped mint
pinch of garam masala *or* curry powder

salt and pepper
¼ pint (150ml) double cream
3 fl oz (75ml) medium dry sherry

fresh mint to garnish

Rinse the apricots, then soak overnight in cold tea. The next day, put the apricots and tea into a saucepan and simmer until tender. Transfer the mixture to a blender and purée until smooth. Pour back into a large saucepan and blend in the chicken stock, chopped mint, garam masala and a good seasoning of salt and pepper. Finally, stir in the cream and sherry. If the soup seems too thick, thin slightly with extra chicken stock. Reheat gently then garnish with chopped mint or float a whole mint leaf on each individual serving.

Serves 4–6

Chef: Ann Carr
Proprietors: Ann Carr and Martin MacKeown

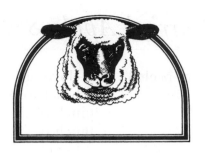

LAMB'S

Moreton-in-Marsh, Gloucestershire

It is, I think, more often the *idea* of fruit soups than their actual taste which puts people off them. One could imagine that black cherry soup, until you've tried it, might conjure up visions of half-melted ice-cream or a watery mousse. It sounds rich and cloying and more suited to the end, not the beginning, of the meal.

But fruit soups can be quite savoury and the version served at Lamb's is a convincing argument in their favour. Dished up, piping hot, in an earthenware bowl, it is a delicate blend of spicy and sweet flavours. Its rich, russet colour is set off by a swirl of cream and a confetti of finely diced green apple.

Curried Apple Soup

1 medium onion, peeled
stick of celery
1 carrot, peeled
1½ oz (40g) butter
2 level teaspoons mild
   curry powder
1 level teaspoon turmeric
1 level tablespoon flour
2 teaspoons tomato purée
2 pints (1·1 litres) chicken
   stock

2 cloves of garlic, crushed
2 bay leaves
pinch of thyme
pinch of oregano
2 large cooking apples
salt and pepper
a little redcurrant jelly
   (if needed)
chopped dessert apples
   and soured cream to
   garnish

Dice the onion, celery and carrot finely. Melt the butter in a large saucepan and add the vegetables. Sauté, stirring from time to time until the vegetables have softened but not browned. Stir in the curry powder, turmeric, flour and tomato purée. Blend well and cook over a low heat for several minutes. Gradually add the chicken stock, stirring continuously, then the crushed garlic, bay leaves, thyme and oregano. Cook gently for about 30 minutes.

Meanwhile core and slice the cooking apples (no need to peel them, simply wash and dry well). Add to the soup, remove the bay leaves, then liquidize the mixture until smooth. Pour through a sieve into a clean pan and bring slowly to the boil. Add salt and pepper to taste. If the soup seems slightly thin, thicken it with a small amount of cornflour slaked in water. If the flavour seems a little too sharp, a little redcurrant jelly or caramelized sugar will help to sweeten it. Lemon juice may be added if the soup lacks bite. Just before serving, garnish with chopped apples and soured cream.

Serves 6

Chef: Paul Barnard *Proprietor:* Ian MacKenzie

THE CARVED ANGEL

Dartmouth, Devon

'For my part, now, I consider supper as a turn-
pike through which one must pass, in order to
get to bed' – Oliver Edwards (1771–91)

This rebuff to gastronomy, which crowns the menu at The
Carved Angel, could never have been written by its
patrons. The only feeling is sympathy for the hapless
Edwards as one progresses through a meal of Cucumber
fritters with soured cream and dill, Venison with cherries
and *poivrade* sauce and Grapefruit sorbet.

Joyce Molyneux's menu is as inventive as it is well
executed and will provide hours of pleasure for any *bon
viveur*. You may choose, to start, from Hot, Cold or Fishy
Beginnings. Picking at random (though no one ever does)
from each section, there might be homemade *Fettucini alla
crema*, a Game terrine with spiced damsons or Fresh prawns
with *aioli*. 'Today's soup' (which may turn up under Hot,
Cold *or* Fishy Beginnings) provides further testimony of the
Molyneux flair. Besides the ever-popular *Soupe de poisson*,
the menu may feature a Fresh mussel soup, a creamy
lobster bisque or a hot pumpkin soup. They will all be
served in rough, earthenware bowls, accompanied by

three different types of homemade bread to mop up the final juices.

A good example of the originality to be found at The Carved Angel is this Banana curry soup – a rare treat for any tastebud.

Banana Curry Soup

¾ lb (350g) very ripe
   bananas, peeled
juice of ½ lemon
¼ lb (100g) onion, peeled
1 oz (25g) butter
1 teaspoon curry powder

1 teaspoon flour
1½ pints (850ml) chicken
   or lamb stock
salt and pepper
a little double cream

Purée the peeled bananas and lemon juice in a liquidizer until smooth. Chop the onion finely and sweat in the butter without colouring for 5 minutes with the curry powder. Add the flour, mixing it in well, then add the banana purée and the stock. Bring to the boil, stirring frequently, season to taste with salt and pepper and cook gently for 15 minutes. Finish with a little double cream and adjust the seasoning if necessary.

Serves 4

Chef: Joyce Molyneux
Proprietors: Joyce Molyneux and Tom Jaine

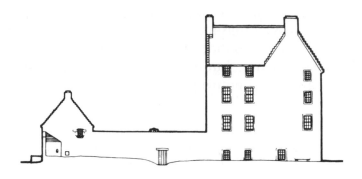

HOUSTOUN HOUSE

Uphall, West Lothian, Scotland

When Penny and Keith Knight bought the Royal Hotel in Comrie in 1961, they found the results of their first winter slightly disheartening. Customers were standing elbow to elbow in the bar but the dining-room was totally deserted (in four months, they served six dinners, to the same three people on two consecutive nights)!

For Keith this was particularly discouraging as it gave him no opportunity to flex his culinary muscles. Deciding that things couldn't possibly get worse, the Knights flung the *à la carte* out the window and settled instead for a four-course set dinner, based on unusual, and, for that part of Scotland, wildly adventurous dishes. The gamble paid off and they were soon besieged with diners.

Even though the Royal was doing well, it was still very quiet during the winter and the Knights decided, after five years, that they would like to be busy all year round. After a long search, extensive renovations and a marathon effort to get a restaurant licence, they opened at Houstoun House in 1969. Again, they instituted set lunches and dinners with no choice but, strangely, these were not received with the same enthusiasm as they had been at Comrie. For the first few months set meals were regarded rather suspiciously and even *The Good Food Guide* found this

110

policy 'dictatorial'. But Keith Knight continued in his inimitable way, building up a repertoire of interesting dishes. It takes a confident chef to put Curried parsnip soup on a set menu – but he has done it and, furthermore, now has guests clamouring for it.

Curried Parsnip Soup

1 large parsnip
clove of garlic
3 oz (75g) butter
$\frac{1}{4}$ lb (100g) chopped onion
1 tablespoon flour
1 rounded teaspoon mild curry powder
2 pints (1·1 litres) homemade beef stock *or* made from stock cubes

salt and pepper

$\frac{1}{4}$ pint (150ml) double cream, lightly whipped
croûtons
chopped parsley *or* chives

Peel the parsnip and the garlic, then chop both finely. Melt the butter in a heavy saucepan. Put in the parsnip, onion and garlic and stir until well coated in the butter. Cook gently for 10 minutes. Add the flour and the curry powder, blending in well, and cook for 1–2 minutes. Then blend in the stock. Simmer gently with the lid on until the vegetables are soft. Put into a liquidizer and blend until smooth. Pour through a sieve into a clean pan and season to taste with salt and pepper. Slowly reheat, then serve with dollops of lightly whipped cream, and a sprinkling of croûtons, chopped parsley or chives.

NB. The secret of this soup lies in the balance between the flavour of the parsnip and the curry.

Serves 4

Chef: Keith Knight *Proprietors:* Penny and Keith Knight

RIVERSIDE

Helford, Cornwall

George Perry-Smith has, besides a gentle and sensitive nature, a modesty which belies his talent and experience as a restaurateur. Unlike many chefs, he has no desire to talk about his cooking, preferring to discuss the latest *chef d'oeuvre* by Elizabeth David or the restaurants of his protégés. Getting him to acknowledge his own recipes is like pulling toffee. To him, they are simply interpretations of classic recipes; while to others, they are distinguished by their originality. His version of Mackerel brandade, *Bourride*, Salmon *en croûte* with ginger and currants and *St Emilion au chocolat* appear on more restaurant menus than you could possibly count.

With Heather Crosbie (also with him at 'The Hole') running the front of the Riverside, Perry-Smith is now left completely free to cook. Everything is made from scratch and his kitchen is always filled with the smell of fresh brioche, wholemeal bread or hot croissants. Ingredients for the now-famous *Soupe de poisson* come from 'Hawkins the Fish' in Helston. It arrives at the table in a rich garlic steam, with a ruby knob of *sauce rouille*.

Soupe de Poisson

½ lb (225g) onions, peeled
2 sticks of celery
4 inches (10cm) cucumber
½ small green or red
    pepper
3 cloves of garlic, peeled
olive oil
herbs (dill or fennel and
    thyme, parsley, basil)
spices (saffron or paprika
    or coriander/cumin/
    fenugreek, not a lot of
    any of these)
salt and pepper

14-oz (397g) tin
    tomatoes
¼ lb (100g) smoked
    haddock, chopped
2 pints (1·1 litres) very
    good fish stock (page
    115)
½ bottle dry white
    wine
lemon juice

aioli (page 260)
sauce rouille (page 260)
garlic croûtons

Chop the vegetables and garlic finely, then sweat in a little olive oil for 10 minutes (until soft but not coloured). Add the herbs, spices and a good seasoning of salt and pepper and fry a little longer, stirring well. Add the tomatoes, chopped smoked fish (or smoked fish trimmings wrapped in muslin and removed later would do), stock and wine. Simmer for 30 minutes, check the seasoning and, if necessary, add a little lemon juice.

Serve with *aioli*, either beaten into the soup when just off the boil or handed separately, *sauce rouille* (should definitely be served separately as some might find its flavour too strong) and garlic croûtons. (To make the croûtons: cut 2–3 slices of stale bread, crusts removed, into ½-inch (1cm) dice. Heat butter and oil in a large heavy frying pan and when hot, add 2 crushed garlic cloves. Stir over moderate heat for 1 minute, then add the bread dice and cook quickly until nicely browned on all sides.)

Serves 8

Chef: George Perry-Smith
Proprietors: Heather Crosbie and George Perry-Smith

THORNBURY CASTLE

Thornbury, Avon

Despite the fact that Kenneth Bell has been the *chef-patron* of Thornbury Castle for sixteen years, most people still associate him with his first restaurant, The Elizabeth, in Oxford. For many of them, as students, professors or simply tourists, it was a first introduction to really outstanding food and wine.

The menu was very long and featured specialities like Prawns with rice and *aioli* (5s), *Langoustine dieppoise* (18s 6d), Paella (12s 6d), Syllabub (3s 6d) and Cream Elizabeth (3s 6d). Vegetables were included in the price of the main dish and these also showed originality in their presentation. The restaurant's only drawback was that it had no licence. Only those who joined The Elizabeth Club forty-eight hours before dining could sample its wines, displayed temptingly round the restaurant as there was no proper cellar.

The reputation of The Elizabeth flourished during the early sixties but by 1965 Kenneth Bell was champing to try something new. Within a year he had bought and moved into a sixteenth-century castle in Thornbury, a few miles north of Bristol. The Elizabeth was sold to his head waiter, Antonio Lopez (who runs it still), and Bell settled down to running a 'first-class country restaurant' (which it has been ever since).

Crab Soup

1 medium-to-large cooked
   crab *or* a 1-lb (450g)
   packet frozen crab, half
   white, half brown meat
fish trimmings, onion
   skins, celery tops,
   parsley stalks,
   mushrooms stalks,
   chopped carrot and
   2 pints (1·1 litres) water
   for the stock
salt and pepper
1 medium onion

1 large carrot
2 sticks of celery
¼ lb (100g) butter
2 tablespoons tomato
   purée
1 teaspoon dry English
   mustard
1 wineglass Bual *or*
   Verdelho Madeira
¼ pint (150ml) double
   cream
a little brandy

Pick all the white and brown meat out of the cooked crab, or completely thaw the frozen crab.

Make a stock by putting the fish trimmings (get heads and bones from the fishmonger when you buy the crab) into a large saucepan with the water, onion skins, celery tops, parsley stalks, mushroom stalks and chopped carrot. Season well and simmmer for 30 minutes only, then strain.

Dice finely the onion, carrot and celery. Melt the butter in a large heavy saucepan and soften the chopped vegetables in it. Add the tomato purée and allow this to singe slightly. Pour in 1½ pints (850ml) of fish stock and simmer for 10 minutes. Add the mustard, Madeira and crab meat and simmer for a further 10 minutes. Season to taste with salt and pepper and blend in the cream. Serve very hot, adding a little brandy at the last minute. (If the soup is too thick, add more fish stock or cream. If the flavour isn't quite strong enough, add more Madeira or part of a chicken stock cube.)

Serves 6

Chef and proprietor: Kenneth Bell

SHARROW BAY

Ullswater, Cumbria

On a clear day, the view from Sharrow Bay would make
Lake Como look dull by comparison. With snow-capped
peaks in the distance and Ullswater, dotted with sailboats
and glistening in the sunlight, the scene seems more Italian
than English. The long terrace with a loggia at one end
reinforces this impression and you almost expect the waiter
to be humming '*o sole mio*' or delivering a chilled glass of
Frascati.

Inside, there is a feeling of elegance and comfort. Plump
sofas, priceless porcelain and gilt-edged paintings fill the
rooms. It seems incredible that when Francis Coulson
bought the house in the late 1940s, it was rather nondescript, with no outstanding features. He moved in with
nothing more than a suitcase, a large dog and a small
kettle, the idea of a hotel only a blurred vision in his head.
For the first few months he slept on the floor, working all
hours of the day and night to make the place habitable.

As soon as there were enough chairs to sit on, Francis
opened for business (1949). He started with teas, then
added lunches and dinners which, with rationing still in
effect, required ingenuity as well as stamina. A farmer
across the lake obligingly provided fresh eggs, butter and
cream, but only under cover of darkness. Francis tells

116

hilarious tales of picking up 'contraband' on lonely country roads: a lamb or piece of beef which would be left by pre-arranged signal in the boot of his car. His rich scones, cakes and biscuits seemed like manna in post-war Cumbria, and serving tea to a hundred people a day was not unusual. At the now ludicrous price of half a crown, it was a tea that everyone could afford, especially as each guest was given a bunch of flowers to take away.

Carrot Vichyssoise

2 potatoes
4–5 carrots
2 onions
2 leeks
ham bone *or* 2–3 rashers
    of bacon
2 bay leaves
2½ pints (1·4 litres) chicken
    stock

1 dessertspoon sugar
salt and pepper
½ pint (275ml) single
    cream

carrot cut in fine strips to
    garnish

Peel the potatoes, carrots and onions, then chop into small pieces. Trim and shred the leeks. Put all the vegetables into a large saucepan with the ham bone or chopped bacon, bay leaves and stock. Cover and simmer over a low heat until the vegetables are tender. Remove the bay leaves and ham bone and liquidize until smooth (or put through a sieve). Add the sugar, then season to taste with salt and freshly ground black pepper. Blend in the cream, then slowly reheat (taking care not to let it boil) or chill thoroughly. Just before serving (hot or cold), garnish with fine strips of carrot.

Serves 8

Chef: Francis Coulson
Proprietors: Francis Coulson and Brian Sack

117

SHIPDHAM PLACE

Shipdham, Norfolk

While enthusiasts fight for Real Ale and Real Cheese, Justin de Blank is waging his own war against Really Awful Bread. And he's winning, for we are all enjoying the spoils of his campaign.

Ten years ago, when supermarkets, bulk buying and 'special offers' were becoming fashionable, Justin de Blank opened his first food shop in London. Ignoring the current trend, it combined the nicest aspects of the old corner store: personal service and fresh produce, free from plastic corsetry. He filled it with pâtés, cheeses (English and obscure French ones), charcuterie, cooked foods, fruits, vegetables, herbs and a mountain of freshly baked bread. In France, it would have been commonplace; in London, it stood out as a rare and endangered species.

But while cheese was a hobby, bread to de Blank was a passion. Two, then three bakeries came under his umbrella. He searched the country for good millers and unusual flours, determined to produce old-fashioned bread with distinctive flavour and texture. Now white, wholemeal, granary, wheatmeal, poppyseed and cottage loaves, plus brioches and croissants, line his shop windows.

In the summer of 1979 he and his wife Melanie launched a new venture, a country house hotel in Shipdham, Norfolk. Run on a small scale, it has six bedrooms and a dining-room which holds thirty people. As well as Justin's irresistible wholemeal rolls, they serve beautifully cooked four-course lunches and dinners.

Shipdham Spinach Soup

1 large onion
1 oz (25g) butter
2 lb (900g) fresh
   spinach
1½ pints (850ml) good
   strong chicken stock
juice of 1 lemon

¼ oz (7g) crushed
   coriander *or* 1½ teaspoons
   ground (but it's not as
   good)
salt and pepper
¼ pint (150ml) single
   cream *or* creamy yogurt

Peel the onion and chop finely. Melt the butter in a large saucepan and add the onion. Cover with buttered paper and sweat until soft but not coloured. Wash the spinach, remove the stalks and drain well. Add to the pan and cook until it has reduced down. Put through a liquidizer with 1 pint (575ml) of the stock. Return to the pan and stir in the remaining stock, lemon juice and coriander. Season to taste with salt and pepper. Heat slowly until just below boiling point. Stir in the cream or yogurt (yogurt can curdle if it's the firm sort, in which case do not add it directly but stir some of the hot soup into it first, then pour it all back into the pot). Serve hot or cold with swirls of cream on top.

Serves 6–8

Chef: Melanie de Blank
Proprietors: Melanie and Justin de Blank

TULLYTHWAITE HOUSE

Underbarrow, Cumbria

Tullythwaite is an attractive stone farmhouse, almost hidden from its neighbours by gnarled hedges and high stone walls. It was built in 1636 as a tannery, and 'a jolly old tanner' (as described by the present owner) later added a sitting room which boasts an imposing Adam fireplace and alcove. The sideboard, specially built by Waring and Gillow to fit the alcove, is now a collector's item and a striking conversation piece. The room where the tanning was done is one of two small dining-rooms. Each is filled with gleaming brass and copper antiques, old Spode and polished oak tables. The tanning room also lays claim to the 'naughty corner', the table to which Fanny Craddock was banished when she booked at Tullythwaite under an assumed name, only to be recognized on arrival by the doughty Mrs Johnson.

Dinner is served promptly at 7 o'clock and guests drift in earlier to sip sherries in the sitting-room. They come armed with their own bottles as Tullythwaite has no licence. It is a set meal of five courses with choice only for starters and puddings. The food is outstanding home cooking, prepared and presented to a high standard.

Everything is made in the Tullythwaite kitchen, from the bread rolls to the biscuits served with cheese. Soups are made from their own homegrown vegetables, with Cauliflower, Leek and watercress and Carrot and orange being the favourites. Main courses are served with three or four different vegetables (again from the garden) and each table is given two sweets, left so that guests can help themselves to as much as they have room for.

Leek and Watercress Soup

3 large leeks
1 medium onion
¼ lb (100g) butter
clove of garlic, crushed
2 medium potatoes, peeled and diced
2 bunches of watercress, coarsely chopped

1¼ pints (700ml) good chicken stock
8 fl oz (225ml) milk
8 fl oz (225ml) single cream
salt and pepper

watercress to garnish

Clean the leeks well, then shred finely. Peel the onion and chop into small dice.

Melt the butter in a large saucepan. Add the leeks, onion and crushed garlic. Cover with buttered greaseproof paper and 'sweat' over moderate heat until the vegetables are soft. Remove the paper, then add the potatoes and the watercress. Cover with the chicken stock and simmer for 25 minutes. Put the soup through a sieve or liquidizer until smooth, then return to the pan. Add the milk and cream and a good seasoning of salt and pepper. Slowly reheat without boiling and when piping hot, serve garnished with small sprigs of watercress. (Or serve it chilled, with a dollop of cream on top.)

Serves 6

Chefs: Mary and Barbara Johnson
Proprietor: Mary Johnson

LA POTINIÈRE

Gullane, East Lothian, Scotland

If you happened to be strolling through the village of Gullane (that golfers' mecca about thirty miles east of Edinburgh), you might notice a small restaurant called La Potinière. Pinned inside a display case beside the front door, a neatly printed *carte du jour* reveals what lies inside.

Without too much effort one can see that it is written in French, but there is still further cause for amazement. On closer examination, all the dishes hint at a style of cooking totally foreign to the East Lothian coast. The thought of *Potage St Germain, Chachouka, Porc à la crème forestière* and *Citron surprise* will be enough to make you give up golf and book in here for a week. A plan which, alas, might be difficult to implement as all the tables at La Potinière are booked up several weeks in advance. The owners, David and Hilary Brown, have adopted unorthodox opening times (initiated by the previous *patronne*) and their hungry customers must be content with lunches Monday to Friday and Sunday, and dinner on Saturday. However, this doesn't mean that the Browns spend every evening with their feet up, reading Brillat-Savarin in the original or mentally ordering the next bin of Château Beychevelle. The restaurant is booked most evenings by private parties and as these are usually regular customers, it is more like cooking for friends. An atmosphere which suits the Browns very well.

Potage St Germain

2 medium onions
2 oz (50g) butter
heart of a lettuce
pinch of dried thyme
1 medium potato
water *or* stock

1¼ lb (575g) shelled peas
salt and freshly ground
    black pepper

cream, croûtons and
    thyme for garnish

Peel and finely dice or slice the onions. Cook gently in the butter until softened but not coloured. Shred the lettuce finely, then add to the pan with a pinch of dried thyme. Mix together and cook for several minutes more.

Peel and dice or slice the potato. Add to the onion mixture and cover with enough water or stock to cover the vegetables generously. Boil rapidly until the vegetables are cooked (about 40 minutes). Top up with more water or stock if necessary. Add the peas, stir well, then bring back to the boil. Continue to boil for about 5 minutes. (It is very important that the soup doesn't boil longer than this, otherwise it will lose its lovely green colour.)

Liquidize the soup, then put through a mouli or sieve to remove the skins of the peas. Season to taste with salt and pepper. Slowly reheat but try to serve it as soon as possible once reheated so that the colour is not lost. Garnish with a swirl of cream, a few croûtons and a sprinkling of thyme (fresh if possible).

Serves 6–8

Chef: Hilary Brown *Proprietors:* Hilary and David Brown

TULLICH LODGE

Ballater, Aberdeenshire, Scotland

If you dream of castles in the air, then try one instead in
Aberdeenshire. It is Tullich Lodge, a mid-Victorian castle,
described by one of the guides as 'sub-baronial'. (Built, I
suppose, for a slightly imperfect baron.) Compared to
nearby Balmoral, it is extremely small, with an atmosphere
more like a friendly country house. It was bought a decade
ago, a sad shadow of its former self, by Neil Bannister
and Hector Macdonald. After years of hard work, they
have now made it a paragon of Scottish castledom,
inside and out.

The dining-room, panelled in gleaming walnut, is
dominated by a magnificent sideboard, holding decanters
of wine and port, a plate of freshly baked bread and a
sizeable cheeseboard. In the morning, it displays eggs,
bacon, kippers and hot toast in impressive silver chafing
dishes. Polished wood floors stretch from dining-room to
entrance hall and here there stands a large Victorian glass
kiosk. It looks like a mahogany-trimmed bell jar and with
chair, table and telephone inside, is guaranteed to start or
stop the conversation.

Though delightfully old-fashioned, Tullich Lodge is in
no way faded or out-of-date. For those who anticipate

freezing floors, draughty corridors and lukewarm water, a pleasant surprise awaits. Modern conveniences (i.e. central heating and private bathrooms) have been discreetly installed, providing unexpected comfort in the spartan north.

All the vegetables and herbs used in the restaurant come from a large garden in the castle grounds. Those which fail to respond to the magic touch of Bannister and Macdonald are obtained from local farmers.

Beetroot Soup

1½ lb (675g) cooked beetroot

1½ pints (850ml) chicken stock

2 tablespoons tarragon vinegar

salt and white pepper

¼ pint (150ml) soured cream *or* yogurt, and 1 tablespoon chopped chives to garnish

Chop the beetroot finely. Liquidize it, small amounts at a time, with the stock. Add the vinegar and season to taste with salt and pepper. Serve chilled and garnished with a generous swirl of soured cream or yogurt and a sprinkling of chopped chives.

Serves 4

Chef: Neil Bannister
Proprietors: Neil Bannister and Hector Macdonald

MILLER HOWE

Windermere, Cumbria

There is a cooking style now which is distinctly 'John Tovey'. It is characterized by an innovative flair which, though totally unorthodox, produces spectacular results. It can be seen in its purest form at Miller Howe (where its permutations change daily) and with individual variations in countless restaurants throughout Britain and Ireland.

The great strength of John Tovey's cooking lies in his ability to create original dishes, sometimes from seemingly incompatible elements (for example, Calves' liver with gin and lime), and present them with panache. On paper they may look barely digestible, but on the plate they are sensational. He gets away with culinary murder and some of the more traditional chefs still regard him as a rather delinquent child. His creations may not always be to your taste but they are, unquestionably, inventive.

When John opened at Miller Howe in 1970, and later when articles on his cooking began to appear in *Caterer and Hotel-Keeper*, he was looked upon in the trade as a revolutionary. This was at a time when *nouvelle cuisine* was only a glimmer in Bocuse's eye and most country restaurant cooking was based on Elizabeth David, Constance Spry and Cordon Bleu. The articles may have raised eyebrows but they also triggered off a 'rethink' about cooking. Even if the chefs didn't swallow his recipes completely, at least they were curious enough to try them out.

His influence was particularly strong amongst young chefs, with techniques and repertoires still in an embryo stage, who were attracted by the freshness and novelty of his cooking. Despite its obvious theatricality, it has an unpretentiousness which is utterly engaging. John's favourite recipes from childhood, 'My Nan's tipsy trifle' and Lancashire hot pot (introduced in his recent cookery book, *Entertaining with John Tovey*, by the exclamation, 'Ooh, I do love a Lancashire Hot Pot!') are used as frequently as the newer dishes such as Savoury apple with tarragon cream, Cheese and herb pâté and Radish and red Windsor soup, the perfect soup for a summer's evening.

Radish and Red Windsor Soup

18 large radishes, cleaned, topped and tailed
four 5-fl oz (150ml) cartons natural yogurt
½ pint (275ml) single cream
¼ lb (100g) Red Windsor cheese, finely grated
clove of garlic, crushed with ½ teaspoon salt
1 tablespoon tarragon vinegar
2 hard-boiled eggs, finely diced
6 cocktail gherkins, finely chopped
chopped mint

Finely grate the radishes. Mix the yogurt and cream together, then blend in all the remaining ingredients, adding the radishes at the end. Check for seasoning, then cover and put in a cold place until well chilled.

Serves 6

Chef and proprietor: John Tovey

THE WIFE OF BATH

Wye, Kent

This is another progeny of The Hole in the Wall in Bath, its creator, Michael Waterfield, belonging to the group of young chefs who trained there with George Perry-Smith. Its location near Canterbury lends further credence to its Chaucerian connections and it has, since its opening in 1964, satisfied hungry pilgrims from all parts of the country.

Though geographically *en route* to France, The Wife of Bath appeared in an area that was gastronomically destitute. It must have come as a pleasant surprise to Kent visitors and residents to find a restaurant featuring thick, garlicky *bourride* or iced Cucumber and fennel soup as its *potage du jour*. And a further treat to sample Michael Waterfield's Sea bass *à la grecque*, Duck with spiced peaches and *Poulet à l'estragon*. The locals still describe the *Petits pots de café* and Blackberry sorbet with delight. In the early seventies, Mr Waterfield donned another cap and became *vigneron* as well as restaurateur. With the planting of his own vineyard, he was soon able to offer Wife of Bath diners a *dégustation* of his Marriage Hill wines.

In 1977, in order to have more time for lecturing and writing, Michael Waterfield handed over to his partner-chef Bob Johnson. Since then, Bob has been at the helm, doing all the cooking and assisted out front by another partner, Brian Boots. The style of the restaurant remains the same, with the emphasis still on French provincial cooking.

Though cold soups, as a rule, rate low in popularity, this one seems to be the exception. Its rich magenta colour is given striking bands of lime green with slices of ripe avocado pear.

Gazpacho

1 cucumber, peeled
2 small fresh chillis
2 green peppers
two 1¾-lb (793g) tins
  tomatoes
6¾-oz (190g) tin
  pimentos, well drained
2 medium onions

2 cloves of garlic
4 tablespoons olive oil
2 tablespoons white wine
  vinegar
large pinch of sugar
salt and pepper to taste

2 avocado pears, peeled
  and sliced

Chop the vegetables and garlic roughly, then blend, small amounts at a time, with the olive oil and vinegar in a liquidizer. Pour into a large bowl and if the mixture seems too thick, add a little water. Season with sugar, salt and pepper. Put in a cool place until well chilled.

When ready to serve, ladle into bowls, adding an ice cube and a few slices of avocado pear to each one.

Serves 8

Chef: Robert Johnson
Proprietors: Robert Johnson and Brian Boots

CHURCHE'S MANSION

Nantwich, Cheshire

If it hadn't been for the Myott family, Churche's Mansion could have suffered the same fate as London Bridge and might now be dispensing ice-cream and souvenirs in the Arizona desert. Put up for public auction in 1930, this magnificent Tudor house, built during the reign of Elizabeth I for a prosperous Cheshire merchant, was rescued from forced exile to America by a young doctor and his wife, Edgar and Irene Myott. Then followed several years of back-breaking work (done on their own and, through necessity, by candlelight) to make the house habitable and a further seventeen to restore it to its original condition. Their son Richard and his wife carried on the work and gradually built up an outstanding collection of period furniture so that the house today is very much as it was when the Churches originally lived there.

To celebrate the four hundredth birthday of the house in 1977, the Myotts hosted an Elizabethan banquet for eighty friends, dressed in period costume. The Avocado and walnut soup was only one of seven courses; others included Asparagus *mille-feuille* with quail pâté, Baked turbot with mousseline of chicken and Smoked fillet of beef with tongue and horseradish sauce.

Avocado and Walnut Soup

2 oz (50g) walnut kernels
½ pint (275ml) milk
2 ripe avocado pears
¾ pint (425ml) strong
 chicken stock
¼ pint (150ml) double
 cream
½ pint (275ml) plain
 yogurt
¼ pint (150ml) tomato
 juice

dash of Tabasco
salt and pepper
1 oz (25g) butter
1 teaspoon grated onion
1 oz (25g) flour

lightly whipped cream to
 garnish

Remove as much skin as possible from the walnuts and chop finely. Scald the milk and pour over the nuts. Leave to infuse for 30 minutes.

Peel the avocados, remove the stones and mash the flesh until smooth. Gradually whisk in the chicken stock, cream, yogurt, and tomato juice. Add a dash of Tabasco and season well with salt and freshly ground black pepper. Put to one side.

Melt the butter and soften the onion in it. Stir in the flour to make a roux and cook for a minute or two. Strain the milk then gradually blend it in, stirring until smooth. Then blend in the avocado mixture. Bring slowly to the boil and correct the seasoning. Turn into a bowl and chill thoroughly before serving. Garnish with the chopped walnuts and a dollop of cream.

Serves 6–8

Chefs: Mrs Myott and Ian Allen
Proprietors: Mr and Mrs Richard Myott

Main Courses

If you happen to be a potato, don't pretend to
be a turnip. Be yourself. Be your best self, of
course, and no one else. And whatever you have
to cook must be the same; let it be the best ...
Never attempt to hide or camouflage food: your
job is to see that it is dressed properly ... and
not masquerading as something it was never
expected to be.

Escoffier

Sobering words from the great Escoffier to his fledgling
chefs, curbing their flights of fancy and encouraging a
more down-to-earth approach. His words reflect the
philosophy of most country restaurants, whose attitude
to food has always been unaffected. They have not tried
to mimic their urban counterparts by offering out-of-
season delicacies or a lengthy *à la carte*. Instead, they
have concentrated on a smaller range of dishes, tailored
to seasonal produce, whose execution usually depends
on the skill of one person. The results are, inevitably,

more personal than they would be in a large hotel or city restaurant and allow more room for individual interpretation.

The thoroughly modern main course is a good deal simpler than its predecessors. It is now allowed to leave the kitchen without the classic wrapping of 'mother' or 'daughter' sauce and, on occasion, to go without one at all. The emphasis on top-quality ingredients has generated a respect for their intrinsic flavours. Every effort is made, by cooking methods and accompaniments, to enhance rather than obscure these. Fish particularly has benefited from this and a blanket of white sauce is no longer considered *de rigueur*. At The Horn of Plenty, fresh hake is baked in foil, then served with a buttery hollandaise. Neil Bannister (Tullich Lodge) takes fresh sea trout and serves it poached or baked with thin discs of sorrel butter. Dried-out salmon steaks are now as common as a brontosaurus; in their place, juicy fillets with *beurre blanc* or *sauce verte*. At The Old House in Wickham, Annie Skipwith keeps brill deliciously moist by cooking it *en chemise verte*, in a delicate casing of lettuce.

Chicken, often the most predictable item on the menu, has undergone major surgery. It's goodbye to Chicken Maryland, Chicken Kiev and Coronation chicken and hello *Poulet en croûte*, Chicken bouillabaisse and Chicken indienne. The vogue for *coq au vin* seems to have been superseded by *coq au cidre, poulet normand* and Chicken with Pernod and tarragon.

Though Saturday night has traditionally been steak night, other meats are beginning to crowd it out. Game, always a mainstay of country menus, is having a heyday. Pheasant is roasted, then served with a Port, orange and chestnut sauce at White's, while at The Bear in Nayland it appears under a thin layer of pastry as their tasty Pheasant pie. Venison, pigeon, partridge and wild duck are all sharing the limelight.

LONGUEVILLE HOUSE

Mallow, Co. Cork, Eire

There may always have been a strong matriarchal tradition in Ireland but today it seems to be flourishing more than ever in the catering trade.

Some of the most successful restaurants in the country are run by women who, after raising a family or still in the process of doing so, have opened their doors to the public. Relying on common sense, hard work and personal flair, they have produced a standard of cooking which would make many professional caterers blush. Myrtle Allen had only cooked for her six children before she started the restaurant at Ballymaloe and now chefs from all over Ireland come to train in her kitchen. Mary Bowe, the only one to have had a formal hotel training, has produced such a paragon of comfort and cuisine at Marlfield House that she is always fully booked.

Jane O'Callaghan, the youngest of the Irish *patronnes* in this book, is in the kitchen at Longueville House every night of the week, cooking dinners for thirty to fifty guests, while coping somehow with four small boys as well. Whenever she feels inspiration running short, she rushes down to Arbutus Lodge for dinner or across the channel to John Tovey's advanced cookery course at Miller Howe. Now that the vineyard at Longueville is planted, she hopes to accompany the *vigneron* (her husband Michael) on his frequent trips to France, with the prospect of more French-inspired dishes on the menu. At the moment, she takes the best local ingredients she can find (e.g. Blackwater salmon, Longueville lamb) and finds or invents a recipe to go with them. Her cooking has gradually evolved from 'good home cooking' to cooking done with confidence and unerring flair.

The lamb served at Longueville has usually been grazing on the front lawn until coralled by Michael O'Callaghan for the dinner table. He still does all the butchering, though after a recent sale of livestock this now means only lamb.

Shoulder of Longueville Lamb with Herb Stuffing

1 small shoulder *or* loin of lamb

Herb Stuffing
1 small onion
1 oz (25g) butter
5 tablespoons fresh white breadcrumbs
1 teaspoon each of chopped fresh parsley, mint and chives (halve quantity if using dried herbs)

3 tomatoes, skinned and deseeded
salt and pepper
1 small egg

oil *or* dripping
1½ pints (850ml) water
1½ tablespoons flour
1 tablespoon redcurrant jelly

Preheat the oven to gas mark 5, 375°F (190°C). Bone out the shoulder or loin of lamb or, better still, have your butcher do it, but do ask for the bones as these are essential for the stock.

Chop the onion finely and sauté in the butter until soft but not coloured. Transfer to a bowl and mix in the bread-

135

crumbs, herbs and tomatoes. Season well with salt and freshly ground black pepper. Beat the egg lightly and use to bind the mixture together.

Season the meat well with salt and pepper, then spread the stuffing over the inside surface. Roll up and tie securely (but not too tightly or it will burst). Heat some oil or dripping in a roasting tin and, when hot, put in the meat. Baste well, then put in the preheated oven and roast for about 1½ hours.

Meanwhile, brown the bones with some vegetable trimmings if you have any, then add 1½ pints (850ml) water and let it simmer away while the meat is cooking. When the meat is ready, transfer it on to a serving platter and keep warm. Tip off the fat from the pan, being careful to leave the sediment and meat juices. Stir in the flour and cook, stirring all the time, until golden. Strain the stock from the bones and blend in. Cook for several minutes, then strain and return to the pan. Reduce by boiling until syrupy. Season well and mix in the redcurrant jelly. Bring back to simmering point, then pour into a warmed jug and serve with the meat.

Serves 6–8

🍷 Claret – the best Médoc you can run to

Chef: Jane O'Callaghan
Proprietors: Jane and Michael O'Callaghan

MALLORY COURT

Tachbrook Mallory, Warwickshire

The world is full of good cooks but few of them could (or would want to) prepare three faultless courses for forty people every evening. Even fewer would be able to combine it with the role of *hôtelier*, supervising chambermaids, acting as night porter and preparing breakfast. Which makes the success achieved at Mallory Court all the more surprising – for Allan Holland, its proprietor, was originally the owner of a thriving menswear business. Cooking was only a hobby and, with no professional training, he decided with a colleague, Jeremy Mort, to run a country house hotel. Having found a manageable manor house just outside Leamington Spa, they spent six months converting it and then opened for business in 1976. Through their unstinting efforts, Mallory Court has gained, in a remarkably short time, a reputation for first-class comfort and *cuisine*.

The advantage of being a self-taught cook is that the only bad habits you acquire are your own. Nothing is automatic and recipes, as well as techniques, tend to be more innovative. This is immediately obvious from Allan Holland's menu, an amphibious blend of classical dishes and those of his own devising. Among the main courses, there might be a traditional Beef Wellington plus the more daring *Flétan en chemise verte* (halibut cooked in lettuce leaves and served with a chive sauce) or the *Selle d'agneau en feuilletage* (roast stuffed loin of lamb in puff pastry) given below. The gradual evolution of the menu, becoming bolder and more assured each year, holds a wealth of promise for the future.

Selle d'Agneau en Feuilletage

Stuffing
5½ oz (165g) butter
¼ lb (100g) mushrooms, finely chopped
¼ lb (100g) calves' liver, cut into ¼-inch (0·50cm) dice
3 shallots *or* spring onions, finely chopped
salt and freshly ground black pepper
½ lb (225g) fresh spinach, washed, dried and roughly chopped

1 boned loin of lamb, about 3 lb (1·5 kilos), trimmed of excess fat, leaving an ⅛-inch (0·25cm) layer on top

12–13 oz (350–375g) puff pastry, homemade if possible (page 386)
1 small egg, lightly beaten (for egg wash)

First prepare the stuffing. Melt 2 oz (50g) of the butter in a sauté pan and sauté the mushrooms over a moderately high heat until lightly coloured. Add the liver and shallots (or spring onions) and sauté the mixture for 1–2 minutes to brown the liver, but leave it pink inside. Season lightly with salt and pepper. Transfer the mixture to a bowl. In the same pan, melt a further 2 oz (50g) of butter and add the chopped spinach. Cook over a moderate heat for 8–10 minutes until the spinach has wilted and the moisture has evaporated. Season lightly and combine with the liver mixture. Taste and adjust the seasoning if necessary. Allow the stuffing to cool.

Open the loin of lamb, fat side down, and flatten it slightly between two sheets of cling film. Spread the stuffing over the inside of the lamb and roll up from the thick end. Tie with string at one-inch intervals and twice, lengthwise, to contain the stuffing. Melt the remaining 1½ oz (40g) of butter in a sauté pan and over a high heat brown the lamb well all over. Transfer to a wire rack and leave to cool. Remove the strings from the lamb.

Preheat the oven to gas mark 8, 475°F (240°C). Roll out the pastry into a rectangle about ⅛ inch (0·25cm) thick and large enough to enclose the lamb completely. Beat the egg lightly and use to moisten the edges of the pastry. Enclose the lamb completely, making sure that there are no gaps at the ends. Decorate the pastry with leaves cut from the trimmings, then brush the whole with the egg wash. Prick the top lightly to allow steam to escape. Place the lamb, seam side down in a shallow roasting tin and bake in the preheated oven for 25 minutes for medium rare meat. (If you prefer the meat medium, cover the pastry with a sheet of foil, and reduce the oven temperature to gas mark 7, 425°F (220°C) after 20 minutes and bake for a further 15 minutes.) Allow the lamb to stand on a rack for 10 minutes before carving into ½-inch (1cm) slices. Serve with *Gratin Dauphinois* (page 276).

Serves 8

▮ Could stand up to the weight of an Australian red such as Shiraz or perhaps a more accessible Rhône

Chef: Allan Holland
Proprietors: Allan Holland and Jeremy Mort

POPJOY'S

Bath, Avon

The scene of some revelry in its day, Beau Nash House in Bath is now the home of Popjoy's restaurant. Originally built in the mid-nineteenth century by Richard Nash, *soi-disant* 'King of Bath', it was there that he spent the latter years of his life. His mistress at the time, Juliana Popjoy, was a flamboyant character who enjoyed scandalizing Bath society. Such was her love for Nash that when he died she swore that she would never sleep in a bed again. From that day onwards, she lived a nomadic life, gathering herbs by day and sleeping in an empty tree trunk by night.

The informality of Popjoy's owners, Stephen and Penny Ross, is slightly at odds with the period setting. Thus the new bar, which is cosy and small, automatically breaks the ice. Being next door to the kitchen, it gives Stephen Ross a chance to circulate before dinner. It means that he can pop out occasionally to chat, discussing the *plats du jour* or comparing notes on wine. Upstairs, the formality of the dining-room is eased greatly by Penny's charm and the enthusiasm of the waitresses. As they are also 'part-timers' in the kitchen, helping out with some of the cooking, they treat the food with genuine respect.

Popjoy's Navarin d'Agneau

1 shoulder of lamb, about
4½ lb (2 kilos), boned
and tied

several tablespoons olive oil
2 large onions
¼ lb (100g) streaky
rindless bacon
3 cloves of garlic
rind and juice of 2 oranges
salt and pepper

1 bottle full-bodied red
wine
½ lb (225g) slicked carrots
sprig each of rosemary
and thyme, tied
together
½ lb (225g) haricot beans,
soaked overnight in cold
water
½ lb (225g) sliced
courgettes

Preheat the oven to gas mark 3, 325°F (170°C). Heat a few tablespoons of oil in a large casserole and when very hot add the lamb and brown quickly on all sides. Remove from the pan and put to one side. Peel and chop the onions, dice the bacon and crush or chop the garlic. Add all of these to the casserole and toss well in the oil. Cook, stirring occasionally, until they are soft and nicely browned. Add the orange rind and juice with a good seasoning of salt and black pepper. Put the lamb back into the pan and pour over the red wine. Add the carrots, the bundle of herbs and the haricot beans which have been well drained. Cover and cook in the preheated oven for 2 hours. Remove the lid, add the courgettes and cook uncovered for a further 30 minutes.

When ready to serve, strain the pan juices into a saucepan and skim off any excess fat. If necessary, reduce quickly for several minutes to thicken. Place the lamb on a spacious serving dish and pour over the sauce and the vegetables. Serve with baked potatoes or noodles.

Serves 6

▮ Red burgundy

Chef: Stephen Ross *Proprietors:* Penny and Stephen Ross

DUNDERRY LODGE

Dunderry, Co. Meath, Eire

Dunderry Lodge, like Well House in Somerset, is a place you need to go to with a good appetite and a good map. Located in Dunderry, about an hour's drive from Dublin, it is so well concealed that finding it usually involves a consultation with the locals.

It is the first restaurant that Catherine and Nicholas Healey (both in their early thirties) have owned and the effort they have put into it is clearly evident. Before this ambitious plunge, Catherine worked for several years as a private cook and then briefly at Jaws restaurant in Navan. Nicholas started off at the Grand Hotel in Leicester, followed by a gruelling but rewarding two years' work with Père Bise at his stunning three-star restaurant overlooking Lac Annecy, then a short spell in the wine trade.

Once the enormous job of making the farm buildings habitable had been completed, in 1977, the Healeys decided to attract custom by offering outstanding food at outstandingly low prices. This policy proved so popular that two years later they abandoned lunches and began serving dinner only. But the remarkable value remains.

Noisettes of Lamb
with Fresh Apricot Sauce

Fresh Apricot Sauce

½ lb (225g) fresh apricots
½ pint (275ml) dry white
  wine
3 oz (75g) sugar
4 tablespoons Marsala *or*
  sweet sherry
salt and pepper

8 large *or* 12 small
  noisettes of lamb
1½ oz (40g) butter

twists of orange and sprigs
  of parsley to garnish

Start by making the sauce. Halve the apricots and remove the stones. Put into a pan with the white wine and sugar (they may require less sugar if very ripe). Cover and cook over gentle heat until the fruit is soft (20–30 minutes). Leave to cool slightly, then put into a liquidizer or food processor and blend until smooth.

Melt the butter in a heavy frying pan and, when foaming, add the noisettes (do them in two lots if you have to, but don't crowd them). Cook until nicely browned on both sides (about 3–4 minutes each side) but still slightly pink inside. Remove from the pan and keep warm.

Add the apricot purée to the pan with the Marsala and a good sprinkling of salt and pepper. Keep over a moderate heat and stir constantly until the sauce is well reduced and shiny. Arrange the noisettes on a warm serving platter and pour the sauce over. Garnish with twists of orange and sprigs of parsley.

Serves 4

▮ Vouvray, preferably one with some age and richness

Chef: Catherine Healey
Proprietors: Catherine and Nicholas Healey

GRAVETYE MANOR

East Grinstead, West Sussex

There is a tendency amongst restaurateurs, once they have become established and successful, just to lie back and gaze at their Michelin stars. They seem reluctant to change in any way, for fear of upsetting the customers. Once the Stilton soup, *Boeuf en croûte* and Grand Marnier soufflé have become so famous that customers are driving from Exeter and Inverness to taste them, only a madman would take them off the menu. The latter graduates from hand-written sheet to printed glossy card, thus guaranteeing a further inflexibility as it now becomes expensive as well as unpopular to change it.

With this in mind, it comes as a particularly welcome surprise to find a prosperous restaurant like Gravetye Manor going, ostensibly, in a backwards direction. This is not to say that they have begun serving hamburgers instead of fillet steaks but that the style and menu have become 'liberated'. From a long printed menu, they have moved back to a hand-written one (now duplicated, thanks to Rank Xerox, in a matter of minutes). This not only gives a greater immediacy to the menu but reflects the frequent experimentation in the kitchen. It changes now, not when the glossy cards run out, but according to seasonal fluctuations and the number of new dishes being produced by the kitchen team.

144

The current menu will feature a selection of recent creations, with a rotating crop of old favourites. Michael Quinn, the *chef de cuisine*, feels strongly that he and his brigade are not there simply to indulge their culinary fantasies but to please the customers. Thus, there are always a few dishes (for instance, *Champignons farcis frits*) which are included because they are long-standing favourites and frequently requested.

Noisettes d'Agneau aux Trois Purées

1–2 tablespoons olive oil
5 oz (150g) unsalted
    butter
12 small noisettes of lamb,
    trimmed and seasoned
5 fl oz (150ml) dry
    vermouth
salt and pepper

Carrot Purée
1 lb (450g) carrots
pinch of salt
2 oz (50g) butter
½ oz (15g) castor sugar
black pepper

Sweet Potato Purée
1 lb (450g) sweet potato
pinch of salt
2 oz (50g) butter
black pepper

Parsnip Purée
1 lb (450g) parsnips
pinch of salt
2 oz (50g) butter
black pepper

finely chopped parsley to
    garnish

Start by making the purées. Peel and chop all the vegetables and place in three separate pans. Add a good pinch of salt to each one and just barely cover with water. Cook gently until tender (10–15 minutes), then drain well. Purée each one with the butter (and sugar if specified) in a liquidizer (or put through a mouli) and season well with salt and pepper. Keep warm until the noisettes are ready.

Heat a tablespoon of oil in a large heavy pan, then add 1 oz (25g) of butter. When really hot, add the noisettes and cook quickly on both sides until nicely browned but still pink inside (approximately 4 minutes each side), adding a little more oil if necessary. Lift out of the pan and keep warm. Pour off any excess fat, add the vermouth and swirl it round the pan. Then scrape the bottom of the pan to loosen the sediment and let the vermouth simmer for 1–2 minutes. Take off the heat and whisk in the remaining butter, small pieces at a time. Season to taste with salt and pepper. (This sauce must be served immediately.)

To serve: arrange three noisettes on each plate. With two tablespoons, mould a generous portion of each purée and place on the plates opposite the lamb. Spoon a little of the vermouth sauce over each noisette. Dust each purée with a little finely chopped parsley.

Serves 4

🍷 Hermitage at the beginning of the month, Crozes Hermitage at the end!

Chef: Michael Quinn *Proprietor:* Peter Herbert

MIDDLE FARM SHOP

Further south in Sussex is one of the largest farm shops in the country. At Middle Farm, you will find an extensive range of European and English (including the elusive Blue Vinny) cheeses, with freshly baked bread and rolls to go with them. Baskets are filled with fresh vegetables and fruit (pears and apples are a speciality) and the butter is shaped from old moulds. Farm eggs, cream, bacon, ham, joints of beef, lamb and pork are also available. Homemade jams, chutneys and local honey fill several shelves at the back.

WHITE'S

Lincoln, Lincolnshire

Big is not necessarily beautiful when referring to country restaurants and in fact the opposite seems to apply. This is vividly illustrated by White's restaurant in Lincoln, which opened in 1979.

It occupies the front room of an historic house, with proportions that can only be described as Lilliputian. The atmosphere is informal, yet it soon becomes evident that the *patron*, Colin White, is a chef of considerable talent. With his wife Gwen, he is running a restaurant which, in Michelin terms, is 'worthy of a detour'.

The emphasis is on French provincial cooking and, again, the influence of Elizabeth David can be seen. The now classic dishes of *Poulet à l'estragon*, *Estouffade* of pigeon and *Blanquette d'agneau* are prepared with skill and confidence by Colin White. In these, as in the dishes specifically his own, the presentation is faultless. His *Poulet en croûte*, a juicy breast of chicken filled with mushrooms and bacon, arrives at the table in a golden casing of puff pastry and its own pot of hot herb sauce. It is accompanied by four different vegetables, left on the table for second helpings.

When the chef gets hungry, the dish below is inevitably

147

what he heads for: succulent lambs' kidneys, laced liberally with mustard and accompanied by a crisp green salad.

Lambs' Kidneys with Mustard Sauce

2 lb (900g) lambs' kidneys, skinned, trimmed and halved
2 oz (50g) butter

Mustard Sauce

2 shallots, finely chopped
$\frac{1}{4}$ pint (150ml) medium *or* dry white wine

$1\frac{1}{2}$–2 tablespoons Dijon mustard
$1\frac{1}{2}$ oz (40g) butter, at room temperature
juice of $\frac{1}{2}$ lemon
salt and pepper
chopped parsley

Preheat the oven to gas mark 3, 325°F (170°C). Melt the butter in a heavy pan and fry the kidneys in it gently for about 5 minutes. Then put them into the oven and cook for a further 5 minutes.

Lift the kidneys out with a slotted spoon, transfer to a serving dish and keep warm. Cook the shallots in the pan juices until softened. Add the wine, scrape the bottom of the pan to loosen the sediment and reduce the liquid by three-quarters. Mix $1\frac{1}{2}$ tablespoons of the mustard with the softened butter, then add this and the lemon juice to the sauce *off the heat*. Whisk in well, then season to taste with salt and pepper. Whisk in more mustard if liked, then reheat the sauce gently. Add a good sprinkling of chopped parsley and pour over the kidneys. Serve at once.

Serves 4–6

🍷 Chianti Classico

Chef: Colin White *Proprietors:* Gwen and Colin White

148

SHIPDHAM PLACE

Shipdham, Norfolk

Shipdham Place is more country house than hotel and staying there is so relaxing that one soon forgets everything else (including, if not prompted, the bill).

Melanie and Justin de Blank must have psychic as well as culinary talents, for they have anticipated every need. The bedrooms, with crisp white duvets, marble-topped wash basins, wicker armchairs, nutmeg soaps, icy bottles of Perrier, wild flowers and fruit bowl, put each guest into a comfortable lap of luxury. As both de Blanks are very much in evidence, the feeling of being looked after by the hosts, rather than faceless proprietors, increases. The atmosphere of the house with its crackling fires, inviting sofas and candlelit dining-room is a perfect antidote to city life and considerable effort is needed to keep from dozing off beside the fire before or after dinner.

Justin runs the front of the house, welcoming guests and dispensing aperitifs and post-prandial drinks with a rare blend of speed and charm. Melanie supervises the kitchen and dining-room, usually emerging at the end of the meal for an after-dinner chat. Though never formally trained as a cook, she spent several years in the kitchen of Justin's London shop (page 151) before and after they were married. Now, despite two small children, she still does the bulk of the cooking for the restaurant herself.

At Shipdham Place, this dish might be prefaced by a spicy Tomato *en cocotte* or Shipdham spinach soup (page 119). A popular finale would be the Iced lemon mousse (page 319).

Boiled Beef and Herb Dumplings

Stock
2 carrots, peeled and
   sliced
2 onions, peeled and sliced
2 tomatoes, chopped
2 sticks of celery, chopped
several bay leaves
12 peppercorns
salt

Dumplings

$\frac{1}{2}$ lb (225g) self-raising
   flour
$\frac{1}{4}$ lb (100g) shredded suet
good pinch of thyme
good pinch of chopped
   parsley
pinch of ground bay leaf
salt and pepper to taste

3-lb (1·5 kilos) rump of
   beef

4 carrots, peeled and
   sliced
4 onions, peeled and
   quartered
1 lb (450g) parsnips,
   peeled and sliced
1 lb (450g) celery, cut
   into matchsticks

chopped parsley to
   garnish

Put all the stock vegetables into a large pan with the beef on top. Pour over $5\frac{1}{2}$ pints (3 litres) of water, cover and cook very gently for 3–4 hours.

Make the dumplings by blending all their ingredients together with as little water as possible. Roll into rounds the size of golf balls.

When the meat is tender, take out the stock vegetables and add the remaining vegetable ingredients and the dumplings. Cover with a lid and cook gently for 15–20 minutes.

Lift the beef on to a warm serving platter and surround with the vegetables and dumplings (and keep warm if the stock needs to be reduced). Taste the stock and if weak, reduce by rapid boiling. Then spoon a little over the meat and pour the remainder into a warmed jug. Dust the meat and vegetables lightly with chopped parsley, then serve.

Serves 8

🍷 Chianti, preferably Classico, should have enough zip to complement this substantial dish.

Chef: Melanie de Blank
Proprietors: Melanie and Justin de Blank

JUSTIN DE BLANK
PROVISIONS

If, after dining at Shipdham Place, you want another sliver of farmhouse St Nectaire or a regular supply of Justin's wholemeal rolls, they can both be found at his shop in Elizabeth Street, London. He also stocks an impressive range of English and French cheeses, charcuterie, cooked foods, greengroceries, wine, fresh herbs and bread from his bakery.

McCOY'S

Staddle Bridge, North Yorkshire

Eating at McCoy's is like shopping at the old Biba's in Kensington High Street on a Saturday afternoon. The customers are as riveting as the décor.

There is the same smoky glow of cocoa and chocolate brown, punctuated here and there by chromium glitter. The decorative style is eclectic, borrowing huge potted plants from the Palm Court era, Japanese parasols to shade the tables and music from the thirties.

Only the McCoy brothers could have pulled off this *coup d'éclat* for they are genuinely eccentric and blessed with irresistible charm. They all look the part and Eugene McCoy, who runs the front of the restaurant, will probably appear in flapping plimsolls, giant owl-like spectacles and an outsize apron. He or Alison (who claims to be the general dogsbody but is generally indispensable) will recite the *plats du soir* and talk you through the menu (this is essential as the latter is written in felt pen and after being hugged by a few gin and tonics will be practically indecipherable). It comes as such a surprise to find a restaurant of this standard (it won Egon Ronay's Restaurant of the Year award in 1978) so delightfully unorthodox that everyone relaxes immediately.

McCoy's Fillet of Beef

4-lb (2 kilos) fillet of
  beef
1½ oz (40g) butter
a little oil
¾ pint (425ml) espagnole
  sauce (page 381)
a little redcurrant jelly
handful of finely chopped
  mushrooms

fried cucumber strips to
  garnish

Marinade
1 bottle full-bodied red
  wine (burgundy if
  possible)
a few shallots, peeled and
  finely chopped
a few juniper berries
a little finely chopped
  parsley
2 bay leaves
2 cloves of garlic, peeled
  and chopped

Mix all the marinade ingredients together. Strip the fillet of all fat and sinews, then put it into a bowl and pour over the marinade. Cover and leave in the refrigerator to marinate for 48 hours, basting from time to time.

Strain the marinade into an equal amount of espagnole sauce. Transfer to a sauté pan and reduce by rapid boiling to a pouring thickness. Add the redcurrant jelly and mushrooms. Simmer for 10 minutes, then check the seasoning. Keep warm until needed.

Slice the fillet into rounds ½ inch (1cm) thick. Heat a little oil in a large frying pan and when really hot, add the butter. When melted, quickly sauté the meat, a few slices at a time (they will need about 2 minutes each side). Transfer to a warm serving platter or individual plates and coat with a little of the sauce (hand round the rest separately). Garnish with thin strips of cucumber which have been sautéed quickly in butter.

Serves 10–12

🍷 Rioja or a similarly hearty red

Chefs: Tom and Peter McCoy
Proprietors: Eugene, Tom and Peter McCoy

LA POTINIÈRE

Gullane, East Lothian, Scotland

There are not many people who go out to eat in a restaurant and then end up buying it. But this, apparently, is what Hilary and David Brown actually did.

Both extremely fond of good food and wine, they made regular pilgrimages from their home in Glasgow to a tiny restaurant just east of Edinburgh. Called La Potinière, it was run in true Provençal style by a Frenchwoman, Christiane Moodie. There was never any choice but the *table d'hôte* was magnificent. Hilary, at this time, was a teacher and David, an industrial design consultant. Their ideal was to find a job which would allow them to pursue their gastronomic interests. When they discovered, one evening at La Potinière, that it was up for sale, they jumped at it.

They have continued in much the same style as Mrs Moodie. The *table d'hôte*, a set meal of four beautifully prepared courses, is remarkable value. David's wine list is the stuff that dreams are made of: an extensive range of outstanding bottles at old-fashioned prices. It is well matched by the cooking which Hilary does single-handed and with a professional aplomb that would put more densely populated kitchens to shame.

154

Steak au Poivre Vert

6 rump *or* sirloin steaks, at room temperature
flour seasoned with salt, pepper and pinch of thyme
1–2 oz (25–50g) butter
¼ pint (150ml) good red wine
¼ pint (150ml) strong chicken stock
½ pint (275ml) double cream
3 firm tomatoes
1 teaspoon green peppercorns, well rinsed
salt

Toss the steaks in the seasoned flour. Heat 1 oz (25g) of butter in a large frying pan until very hot. Fry the steaks on both sides (3–4 minutes each side, depending on thickness), keeping them rather underdone as they will cook in the oven while the sauce is being made. Cook the steaks in two lots (adding more butter if necessary) rather than overload the pan. Transfer them to a plate and keep warm in a low oven until needed.

To the residue left in the pan, add the wine. Turn the heat up high and scrape the bottom of the pan to loosen all the sediment. Reduce the wine by boiling rapidly until only a small amount remains. Pour in the chicken stock and reduce by half. Stir in the cream and carry on reducing the sauce until it becomes thick and smooth, stirring frequently. Meanwhile, skin, chop and remove the seeds from the tomatoes.

Once the sauce has reached the right consistency, add the tomatoes, peppercorns and a little salt if necessary. Remove the steaks from the oven and pour any juice from them into the sauce. Arrange the steaks on a serving platter or individual plates and coat with the sauce.

Serves 6

▯ St Emilion or Pomerol or other Merlot-based wine

Chef: Hilary Brown *Proprietors:* Hilary and David Brown

MILLER HOWE

Windermere, Cumbria

Dinner at Miller Howe is blatantly theatrical but the performance is impressive. It has the same feeling of suspense and anticipation that accompanies an opening night. There are those who scoff at this stage management, saying that such artificial means shouldn't be necessary to draw attention to the food. They shouldn't be to *Good Food Guide* contributors but, as some people couldn't tell you a day later what they had eaten, perhaps Mr Tovey has, in desperation, been driven to these dramatic lengths. Use of the dimmer-switch guarantees that the guests' attention will be focused not on the magnificent view of Lake Windermere nor the Dior creation at the next table but on the dishes put in front on them. Staged it may be, boring it is not.

The evening ritual is carefully orchestrated by John Tovey with a sense of timing and dramatic effect that would be the envy of any theatrical director. By combining elements which generate their own excitement – the luxurious dining-room, the flourish which accompanies the service, and the imagination and effort put into each dish – he produces a dazzling result.

Calves' Liver
with Gin and Lime Sauce

1 lb (450g) calves' liver, cut into 4 steaks
seasoned flour
oil and butter for frying

Gin and Lime Sauce

½ oz (15g) butter
¼ lb (100g) finely chopped onion
2 level tablespoons apricot jam
1 level teaspoon tomato purée
½ level teaspoon Moutarde de Meaux
¾ pint (425ml) pig's trotter stock *or* good beef stock
grated rind and juice of 3 limes
2 teaspoons white wine vinegar
2 tablespoons gin
1 rounded tablespoon arrowroot mixed with some of the stock
dash of Worcestershire sauce

First make the sauce: melt the butter in a large heavy pan, then add the onion and cook until soft but not coloured. Gradually blend in all the other ingredients and then simmer for 35 minutes. Liquidize until smooth and keep warm.

Lightly coat the liver steaks with seasoned flour and simply cook in a mixture of hot oil and butter. BUT the success of this dish lies in how LITTLE you cook the liver and not how long. As soon as you see small bubbles of blood burst through, turn the liver over and do the other side for a similar length of time.

Pour a small amount of sauce over the liver steaks and hand round the rest separately.

Serves 4

🍷 A good Beaujolais 'cru' – Moulin-à-Vent

Chef and proprietor: John Tovey

NO. 3

Glastonbury, Somerset

Interest in the fourteenth-century Abbot's Kitchen in Glastonbury must be waning now that a more active one has emerged a few hundred yards down the road. But as a place of interest, it will undoubtedly appeal to gourmets rather than tourists. It is a 'temple of gastronomy', in the true French sense. Eating is taken seriously here.

An imposing Georgian residence, it has a crescent-shaped drive and massive front door with brass knocker. An entry hall, chequered with black and white tiles, stretches the length of the house and leads out into a garden at the back. But there is little time to admire the view for the efficient Mr Foden will whisk you into a small ante-room for a drink before dinner. Here, modern chairs and stern signs admonishing latecomers are uncomfortably reminiscent of a doctor's surgery. A smile from the host would do much to ease the tension but one has to rely instead on his admirable *kir*, a speciality of the house.

The two small dining-rooms, decorated with fire-engine red wallpaper, framed prints of starred restaurants in France and bosomy flower arrangements, create a rosy warmth. The dinner, served impeccably by Charles Foden and one other, is a series of perfect dishes. Midway, a devastatingly good sorbet of lemon and cognac is served to refresh the palate. This is followed by a main course that might be Chateaubriand with mushrooms and garlic butter, Severn salmon with hollandaise, or Escalope of veal with lemon, vermouth and fresh rosemary.

Escalopes of Veal with Lemon, Vermouth and Fresh Rosemary

2 good-sized escalopes of veal, each about 6 oz (175g)
1–2 tablespoons flour
salt and black pepper
2 oz (50g) butter
4 tablespoons good beef stock

4 tablespoons dry vermouth
1 spring onion
sprig of parsley
pinch of finely chopped fresh rosemary
½ small lemon, sliced very finely

Slice the escalopes into thin strips about ½ inch (1cm) wide. Season the flour well with salt and black pepper, then dust the veal lightly with it. Melt the butter in a heavy frying pan and, when foaming, add the veal strips. Sauté very quickly, then add the beef stock and vermouth and reduce until slightly thickened. Chop the spring onion and parsley and scatter over the meat with the rosemary. Add the lemon slices to the pan and cook for a further 2–3 minutes. Serve at once with a green vegetable and new potatoes.

Serves 2

🍷 A lightish Italian – Barbera or perhaps a Cabernet or Merlot from Friuli

Chef: George Atkinson
Proprietors: George Atkinson and Charles Foden

GRAVETYE MANOR

East Grinstead, West Sussex

It may sound romantic to have your own kitchen garden but in practice it's not always so blissful. Peter Herbert, the owner of Gravetye Manor, reckons that for the amount it costs him to keep up the garden, constantly expand it and keep the gardener in new boots, he could have vegetables flown in from Covent Garden.

With the numbers they serve at Gravetye (about forty for lunch, slightly more for dinner), it would be far more economical to buy vegetables wholesale. But, partly because the house is famous for its garden (started by the Victorian gardener, William Robinson, and now lovingly maintained by the Herberts) and partly because the vegetables have an undeniable freshness and flavour, the kitchen garden has become Gravetye's mad folly. It is an inestimable luxury to have *mange-touts, haricots verts* and tiny courgettes so near, with only minutes between the time that they are picked and cooked. Tarragon, chervil, dill, rosemary, thyme, basil, sage, mint, chives and parsley grow in profusion, making a fragrant herbaceous border. A well-trodden path takes them at the peak of freshness to the back door of the kitchen and straight into the hands of the chef, Michael Quinn. The impossibility of finding such quality or range of herbs elsewhere makes this part of the garden indispensable.

The *Côte de veau aux fines herbes* uses five herbs from the garden and its quintessential flavour depends largely on their quality and freshness.

Côte de Veau aux Fines Herbes

6 veal cutlets, each about 6 oz (175g), trimmed and seasoned

¼ lb (100g) unsalted butter

1 teaspoon each of finely chopped fresh basil, chives, tarragon, parsley and rosemary (only fresh herbs can be used)

¼ pint (150ml) dry vermouth

squeeze of lemon juice

salt and pepper

Put a large heavy frying pan over a moderate heat and when hot, add 1½ oz (40g) of the butter. As soon as it has melted, add the cutlets (do them in two lots rather than crowd the pan) and sauté them quickly. When almost cooked (they will need about 4 minutes each side), sprinkle on half the herbs.

When the cutlets are nicely browned and cooked through, lift out of the pan and keep warm. Drain off any excess fat, then pour in the vermouth. Scrape the bottom of the pan to loosen the sediment and simmer gently for 1–2 minutes. Add the lemon juice and the remaining herbs. Take the pan off the heat and whisk in the remaining butter, small pieces at a time. Season to taste with salt and pepper. (If the sauce is too sharp, add a small pinch of sugar.) Pour over the cutlets and serve at once.

Serves 6

🍷 A Côte d'Or white burgundy, or perhaps Mâcon Blanc

Chef: Michael Quinn *Proprietor:* Peter Herbert

THE CARVED ANGEL

Dartmouth, Devon

The Carved Angel, sitting a few feet from the water's edge, has a magnificent view of the Dart estuary. The high ceilings and expansive windows do full justice to the panorama outside, while giving the interior an almost dazzling brightness during the day.

The ground floor is one large room, with the restaurant in front and the kitchen, in full view, at the back. Polished wood surfaces, porcelain moulds, copper pans and vintage bottles produce a warm, gastronomic glow. It is fascinating to see how effortlessly the kitchen operates, a stone's throw from the diners, yet at the same time completely unobtrusive. Tom Jaine, the lanky manager and erstwhile history scholar, acts as go-between, pouring wine and ferrying orders from the kitchen. His enthusiasm for the cooking is apparently infectious as once the dishes are described, the choice becomes even more impossible. There is a passionate attention to detail: huge bowls of shiny olives and cheese morsels accompany the aperitif; homemade breads and crunchy croûtons come with the soup; various biscuits top the ice-creams and a plate of homemade fudge arrives with the coffee. Vegetables are not *à la carte* but 'according to shopping' and the menu, written in graceful script, changes daily.

Blanquette of Veal with Sorrel

1 lb (450g) lean veal, cut
  into ½-inch (1cm) dice
6 oz (175g) carrot, peeled
  and cut into batons
6 oz (175g) button onions,
  peeled
½ pint (275ml) veal *or*
  chicken stock
salt and pepper
bouquet garni
strip of lemon peel,
  without the pith
1 oz (25g) butter
1 oz (25g) flour
1½ oz (40g) sorrel
  (if unavailable, use
  fresh spinach)
1 egg yolk
2 fl oz (50ml) double
  cream
squeeze of lemon juice

Put the veal, carrots, onions, stock, seasoning, bouquet garni and lemon peel into a saucepan. Bring to the boil, cover and cook gently until just tender (about 40–60 minutes). Strain the liquid and put to one side. Tip the contents of the sieve (minus the bouquet garni and lemon peel) into a small bowl.

In another saucepan, melt the butter and stir in the flour. Cook for a minute or two to make a light roux. Gradually blend in the liquid, stirring continuously. Simmer for several minutes until you have a smooth, shiny sauce. Mix in the meat and vegetables. Wash and strip the sorrel leaves, then chop roughly. Blend the egg yolk with the cream. Add the sorrel and a squeeze of lemon juice to the sauce. Mix the yolk and cream together in a cup, add a little of the hot sauce, then tip all of it back into the saucepan. Reheat gently without boiling.

Serves 4

▮ Good white burgundy, Meursault perhaps

Chef: Joyce Molyneux
Proprietors: Joyce Molyneux and Tom Jaine

THORNBURY CASTLE

Thornbury, Avon

Perhaps it's since he's become a *vigneron* (with Thornbury wines now on the tables) or it may be the confidence of a sixteen-year tenure, but the *patron* of this sixteenth-century castle has definitely mellowed. While the emphasis, both at Thornbury and at The Elizabeth in Oxford, has always been on pleasing the customers, it seems now to be even more pronounced. Kenneth Bell admits that his own taste in food no longer prevails and that the menu is more attuned to the customers' preferences. He recognizes that a certain proportion of his clientele come to Thornbury as much for the ambiance as for the food. For them, it is a social occasion rather than a gastronomic event.

Thus, while experimentation continues in the kitchen unabated, the menu always caters for simple, as well as exotic tastes. One week it might include starters as diverse as Melon with port, Terrine of duck with pistachio nuts and Onion soup. On the list of main courses there might be a straightforward Roast loin of pork with two sauces or Dover sole with hollandaise sauce plus the more adventurous Haunch of venison with port and chestnut sauce, Stuffed breast of chicken with Pernod and cream or Paupiette of veal with apricot and rum stuffing.

164

Paupiette of Veal
with Apricot and Rum Stuffing

6 escalopes of veal, each
  about 6 oz (175g)
1 onion, peeled
1 medium carrot, peeled
large stick of celery
2 oz (50g) butter
1 teaspoon tomato purée
1 tablespoon flour
¼ lb (100g) mushrooms,
  sliced
1 bottle full-bodied red
  wine burgundy
  bordeaux *or* Rhône if
  possible)
1 chicken stock cube
scrap of garlic
pinch of fresh thyme *or*
  rosemary
salt and pepper

Apricot and Rum Stuffing

3 oz (75g) dried apricots
¼ pint (150ml) cider
2 eggs
5 oz (150g) fresh white
  breadcrumbs
1 oz (25g) slivered
  almonds
salt, pepper and Aromat
  (if available)
a little chopped parsley
a little finely chopped
  celery
2 tots of rum

Start by making the stuffing. In a small pan, simmer the apricots in the cider until the latter has dried up and the apricots are tender but not mushy. Chop the apricots. Beat the eggs in a mixing bowl, then mix in the breadcrumbs, chopped apricots, almonds, salt, pepper, Aromat, parsley, celery and rum. The stuffing should be moist but not sloppy.

Bat out the escalopes into even-sized pieces (not too thin or they will fall apart during cooking). On each one, put a portion of stuffing and make into a neat rectangular parcel. Tuck the ends in carefully and tie with fine string.

Preheat the oven to gas mark 4, 350°F (180°C). Dice the onion, carrot and celery neatly. Melt the butter in a flameproof and ovenproof casserole. When it is beginning to sizzle, put in the escalopes – not all at the same time –

and let them colour on all sides. Lift them out and put to one side. Add the vegetables to the casserole and allow them to colour slightly. Then add the tomato purée and the flour and cook for 1–2 minutes. Add the mushrooms, the wine, the stock cube, garlic and fresh thyme or rosemary. Cook for a few minutes to amalgamate the sauce, then check the seasoning. Place the *paupiettes* in the casserole, cover with a lid and cook for about 30 minutes in the preheated oven.

Take the *paupiettes* out and keep warm. Simmer the sauce to reduce it and adjust the seasoning if necessary. When you are happy with the sauce, remove the string from the *paupiettes* and put them back in the sauce to reheat. Serve with *Gratin Dauphinois* (page 276) and a green salad.

NB. One of the most difficult parts of this recipe is to cook the *paupiettes* without their falling apart. If your veal is of the best quality, well trimmed and batted out, this should not happen.

Serves 6

♟ A full-bodied red such as Dão from Portugal

Chef and proprietor: Kenneth Bell

LOAVES AND FISHES

Wootton Bassett, Wiltshire

Loaves and Fishes enjoys the unique distinction of being the only restaurant in this book run by two women. Two young women at that. Nikki Kedge and Angela Rawson managed their own catering business in Wiltshire for three years before deciding to cook *and* serve in the same place. Local rents and purchase prices were so exorbitant that in the end they commandeered a wing of Angela's family home in Wootton Bassett to use as a restaurant. Its size is also notable for, with a maximum of four tables and seating for twenty, it must be one of the smallest restaurants anywhere. A city caterer would find it mind-boggling, wondering how a restaurant this size could be financially feasible. But somehow the Rawson/Kedge team make it work, with a full house almost every night of the week.

They offer a fixed-price, three-course dinner with choice only for starter and pudding. Their range is not extensive but what they do serve is beautifully prepared and presented. Angela, who does all the cooking (while Nikki performs the triple role of waitress, *sommelier* and accountant), comes by her talent honestly, as her aunt was Iris Syrett, founder of the famous Tante Marie cookery school

167

in Woking. Her dishes are based on fresh seasonal ingredients: the vegetables are bought in the market in Marlborough, the game comes from Stuart Webb, the delightfully old-fashioned butcher in Malmesbury, and the fish is supplied by local anglers. Soups are a speciality and come with Angela's own wholemeal or poppyseed rolls. By far the most popular main courses are the roast pheasant with all the traditional accompaniments, the Brandied lamb (roasted with consommé and fresh rosemary, then topped with a brandy cream sauce) and this recipe for Pork with lemon and mushroom sauce.

Pork with Lemon and Mushroom Sauce

4-lb (2 kilos) loin of pork, boned and rolled

Lemon and Mushroom Sauce

6 oz (175g) butter
10 oz (275g) button mushrooms, thinly sliced
3 oz (75g) flour
scant 1½ pints (830ml) milk

2 teaspoons freshly chopped herbs (any combination of parsley, thyme, chives)
juice and finely grated rind of 2 lemons (a little more if liked)
1 dessertspoon castor sugar
salt and black pepper

finely chopped parsley to garnish

Roast the loin of pork at gas mark 6, 400°F (200°C) for about ¾ hour, then reduce the heat to gas mark 5, 375°F (190°C) and cook for a further 1¼ hours.

Put 3 oz (75g) of the butter into a saucepan and add the mushrooms. Put over a gentle heat and stir until they change colour. Remove from the heat and save to add to the sauce later. Put the remaining butter in another saucepan and, when melted, add the flour. Cook for 1–2

168

minutes, then add the milk, little by little, beating it in well (you may not need all the milk; at this stage you do not want it too runny). Add the herbs, lemon juice and rind, sugar, mushrooms and their juice. Season well with salt and pepper.

When the meat is ready, skim off any fat from the pan juices, then tip the latter into the sauce and blend in well. Slice the meat thinly and arrange on a serving platter or individual plates. Pour the sauce over and garnish with parsley.

Serves 8

🍷 A more substantial German such as Rheinpfalz Spätlese

Chef: Angela Rawson
Proprietors: Nikki Kedge and Angela Rawson

SPACKMAN'S

A detour off the M4, en route to Loaves and Fishes, will be rewarded by a visit to Spackman's. This old-fashioned grocery shop, in Hungerford's High Street, is filled with edible treasure. A large farm basket by the door is brimming with granary, French and cottage loaves. Local produce (butter, cream, jams, honey, sweet-cured hams, sausages etc.) are on sale as well as an outstanding range of foreign exotica. The cheese counter is exemplary, stocking varieties from all over England and Europe. The Spackmans (looking like benign doctors in their white coats) specialize in providing 'personal service'.

WHITE MOSS HOUSE

Rydal Water, Cumbria

I suspect that if Wordsworth were alive today he would have changed his domicile from Dove Cottage to White Moss House (which he actually owned but let to his son for a peppercorn rent). This would not be due to the house's superb situation overlooking Rydal Water, nor to its cheap water rate ($12\frac{1}{2}$p yearly for a private water supply), nor even to its graceful Georgian exterior. More likely, he would want to be closer to the attractive Mrs Butterworth, and her cooking.

Now acclaimed as one of the Lakeland's most outstanding cooks, Jean Butterworth provides a set five-course dinner which is the stuff that dreams are made of. There is no choice until the pudding but the courses until then are so inspired that you will be conscious only of being deliciously spoiled. She and her husband Arthur have been running the house as a 'restaurant with rooms' for ten years, after deciding to retire early to the Lake District. They started modestly with bed and breakfast, gradually adding dinner to their repertoire. Despite success and accolades from the guides, they have refused to expand and still serve only eighteen.

Loin of Pork
Stuffed with Prunes and Bacon

1· loin of pork, 3–4 lb
(1·5–2 kilos), skin
removed but kept,
kidney and belly flap
still intact

10 large prunes

water *or* cold tea
1 onion
1½ oz (40g) butter
2 rashers smoked bacon
¼ lb (100g) dried
breadcrumbs
salt and pepper

Soak the prunes overnight in water or cold tea, then remove the stones. Peel and chop the onion finely, then sauté in the butter until soft. Transfer the onion and pan juices to a large bowl. In the same pan, cook the bacon rashers (with rind removed) until crisp. Drain on kitchen paper, then chop into small pieces. Add to the onion with the breadcrumbs and mix well, adding a little more melted butter and salt and pepper if necessary.

Preheat the oven to gas mark 7, 425°F (220°C). Remove the kidney (if there is one) and cut into strips, discarding the core. Put a shallow layer of stuffing on the thin inside of the loin, cover with strips of kidney (if you have it), a layer of prunes, then the rest of the stuffing. Roll and secure with poultry pins or skewers down either side and lace together with string. Put a piece of foil over the lacing to keep the stuffing in place and put in a roasting tin, fat side up. Roast in the preheated oven for 2–2½ hours.

Meanwhile cut the skin into thin strips and cook in a pan in the oven (above the meat) for 15–20 minutes, pouring off any fat as it forms. Sprinkle with salt before the last 5 minutes of cooking. Use to garnish the meat.

Serve with a sage and onion sauce (page 377).

Serves 6

¶ The warmth of a red burgundy would be ideal

Chef: Jean Butterworth
Proprietors: Jean and Arthur Butterworth

LOWER BROOK HOUSE*

Blockley, Gloucestershire

Bob Greenstock represents the new breed of chef who, with or without a formal training, is unregimented in his approach to cooking. Gone is the obsession with classical French *cuisine* and in its place, a desire to develop an individual repertoire, based on new ideas and techniques. Running a country hotel and restaurant has made him particularly interested in the cooking done by Francis Coulson at Sharrow Bay and by John Tovey at Miller Howe. At the same time, he is attracted to the *nouvelle cuisine*, and the recipes of Bocuse, Guérard and the Troisgros hold a similar fascination.

His cooking is characterized by its inspired blend of ingredients, well illustrated by the following recipe. Though effortless to make, its taste is nothing short of sensational.

* As this book went to press, Lower Brook House changed hands.

Fillet of Pork
with Apple, Raisins and Calvados

3 pork fillets, each 1 lb
(450g)

¼ lb (100g) seedless raisins
4–6 tablespoons Calvados
or brandy
salt and freshly ground
black pepper

a little oil
1 oz (25g) butter
3 dessert apples
¾ pint (425ml) double
cream

Twenty-four hours beforehand, put the raisins into a bowl and add enough Calvados to cover them.

Trim all the fat off the pork, then cut the fillets diagonally into ¼-inch (0·50cm) slices. Bat out lightly with a meat mallet or rolling pin and season well.

Heat a little oil in a frying pan, then add the butter. When very hot, add the pork slices. Cook for 3–4 minutes on each side, then take out of the pan and keep warm. Quarter, core and slice the apples (no need to peel them). Add to the pan and cook quickly until golden, turning from time to time. Stir in the raisins and Calvados and set alight. Extinguish the flames by pouring the cream into the pan. Increase the heat and bring to the boil. Add the pork to the pan and mix in well. Check the seasoning and serve with crisp *haricots verts* or a green salad.

Serves 6

🍷|Really good cider or Corbières could 'cut' the richness nicely

Chef: Robert Greenstock
Proprietors: Robert and Gillian Greenstock

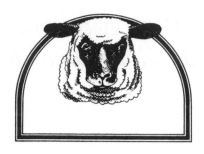

LAMB'S

Moreton-in-Marsh, Gloucestershire

Ian MacKenzie is one of those rare people who is able to combine artistic flair with the practical expertise needed to run a restaurant. With the benefit of cooking and management experience (he was at Hunter's Lodge in Broadway for eight years, then up the road at Dormy House until 1977 when he bought Lamb's), he has created a restaurant which is stunningly attractive and which actually works.

The building itself, a warm sandstone with gracefully arched windows, is tucked into one corner of the bustling market town of Moreton-in-Marsh. Originally a Georgian stable block, it was occupied by the Lamb family from the mid-nineteenth century and used as a shoemaker's business until 1975. Once the sale was completed, Ian Mackenzie did extensive structural work and redecoration and has now produced a clever juxtaposition of small rooms: a bar, sitting-room and five communicating dining-rooms. A courtyard in the centre has been glassed over to create a conservatory effect and now houses a proliferation of greenery and a large pine dresser filled with old crockery. All the dining-rooms (they vary from cloister-sized to cosy) are lit by table lamps or spotlights on the paintings overhead. The overall effect is soft and muted, with a quiet sophistication which belies its country origins.

174

Pork Allumettes
with Cider and Spices

1 lb (450g) pork fillet
large pinch of ground
　ginger
large pinch of mixed
　spice
pinch of cayenne
½ onion
1 green pepper
2 oz (50g) butter

2 tablespoons olive *or*
　vegetable oil
6 oz (175g) button
　mushrooms
5 fl oz (150ml) cider
5 fl oz (150ml) double
　cream
salt and pepper

Cut the pork fillet into slices ¼-inch (0·50cm) thick and then into thin strips. Dust lightly with ginger, mixed spice and cayenne. Peel the onion and slice thinly, then remove the white pith and seeds from the green pepper and cut into thin strips. Put the butter and oil into a large frying pan and gently sauté the onion and pepper until soft. Increase the heat, then add the pork and the mushrooms, cut into quarters. Cook for 5 minutes, then pour in the cider and continue cooking until it has reduced slightly. Lower the heat, blend in the cream and heat gently until the sauce thickens (5–10 minutes). Season to taste with salt and pepper and serve at once.

Serves 3

🍷 Cider or a Torres red from Penedes

Chef: Paul Barnard *Proprietor:* Ian MacKenzie

LE TALBOOTH

Dedham, Essex

At the tender age of twenty-four, Sam Chalmers, *chef de cuisine* at Le Talbooth, runs a kitchen which would defeat many chefs twice his age.

He has a way of making dinner for eighty look as easy as tea for two. His chefs know exactly what to do next and glide round the enormous kitchen like Olympic skaters. There seem to be surprisingly few fireworks and the team effort is obviously genuine.

This is undoubtedly due to Sam's calm temperament and his ability to inspire confidence and respect. He is further helped by the fact that all his chefs are young and share his enthusiasm for the new, lighter style of cooking. They are now constantly engaged in building up a repertoire which reflects this change in emphasis. Dishes are always being tested and perfected for future menus, and recent additions have been Fillet of pork flavoured with fresh sage and served with peaches, *Truite braisée 'Mon Ecluse'* (boned river trout filled with a julienne of fresh vegetables and glazed with a light cream sauce).

The recipe below was one of the first of Sam's recipes to appear on the menu after his arrival at Le Talbooth in 1976. The light *chemise* of spinach cocoons the chicken, keeping it moist and juicy and allowing the flavour of the filling to permeate up through the meat. Peel and

Suprême de Volaille aux Epinards

8 chicken breasts

4 shallots

½ lb (225g) mushrooms

2 oz (50g) butter

2 fl oz (50ml) dry white wine

salt and pepper

½ lb (225g) fresh spinach, washed and stalks removed

chop the shallots finely. Wipe the mushrooms and cut into small dice. Put 1½ oz (40g) of the butter in a small frying pan and when foaming, add the shallots. Sauté until they have softened, then add the mushrooms and continue cooking until they have darkened. Add the white wine and continue cooking for about 5 minutes. Season to taste with salt and pepper. Blanch the spinach in boiling, salted water for 2 minutes. Then refresh under running cold water and drain well. Put to one side.

Preheat the oven to gas mark 8, 450°F (230°C). Carefully bone the chicken breasts and tuck a large dollop of the mushroom stuffing in between the 'fillet' (or flap) and the main part of the breast. Wrap each one in several spinach leaves, then wrap again in a parcel of foil. Place in a buttered dish and bake for 15–20 minutes in the preheated oven. Take out, remove the foil and serve at once.

Serves 8

🍷 The spice of a Gewürztraminer from Alsace would suit this well

Chef: Sam Chalmers *Proprietor:* Gerald Milsom

177

THE PLOUGH INN

Fadmoor, North Yorkshire

One of the joys of travelling in France is discovering, in the middle of nowhere, a tiny restaurant with exquisite food. A pleasure which can still be elusive in this country but, for the intrepid gourmet, there are real treasures to be found.

The Plough Inn, buried deep in the North Yorkshire moors, is one of these. To the casual tourist and first-time diner, it looks remarkably unassuming: a white-washed pub, perched on the edge of a deserted village green. Inside, the locals are ranged along the bar or clustered round the coal fires, looking more interested in their pints of Cameron's Strongarm than in *haute cuisine*. But when the menu arrives, be prepared for a shock that will send you reeling from the bar stool. When all the pubs for miles around are serving Steak and kidney pudding and Shepherd's pie, how can this one be featuring *Soupe au pistou* and Salmon mousseline with sorrel sauce?

The answer lies in the kitchen with Kath Brown who, over the last eleven years, has steadily built up a stock of imaginative and well executed dishes. Assisted by her husband Don, she produces a menu and standard of cooking that, anywhere else in the county, would attract queues half a mile long. As it is, she is continually expanding and improving the repertoire, cooking for anyone game enough to try it.

Supremes of Chicken with Tarragon Cream Sauce

Tarragon Cream Sauce

2 fl oz (50ml) good quality
Bual Madeira
1 teaspoon chopped fresh
tarragon ($\frac{1}{2}$ teaspoon if
using dried herb)
$\frac{1}{4}$ pint (150ml) double
cream
salt and white pepper

4 chicken breasts, skinned
and boned
1$\frac{1}{2}$ oz (40g) butter
seasoned flour

Heat the butter until foaming, but not coloured, in a large frying pan that can hold the chicken breasts without crowding. Toss the breasts lightly in seasoned flour, then seal them quickly in the hot butter. Reduce the heat and fry them for about 5 minutes on each side until firm to the touch (overcooking will harden them). Lift out on to a plate and keep warm.

Turn up the heat, add the Madeira and tarragon (crumbling it with your fingers if using dried to release the flavour) and when the Madeira is bubbling, pour in the cream. Continue cooking until it thickens, scraping round the sides and bottom of the pan to loosen the sediment from the chicken. If the frying pan is wide, the cream will bubble and thicken almost immediately. Season lightly with salt and white pepper, then pour over the chicken breasts and serve at once.

Serves 4

🍷 Needs something powerful – California Chardonnay would suit well

Chef: Kath Brown
Proprietors: Kath and Don Brown

179

POPJOY'S

Bath, Avon

It's quite possible that if you asked anyone who had eaten at Popjoy's and at Thornbury Castle what they had enjoyed most, the answer might be the same: Chicken with Pernod and tarragon.

This simple dish has long been a cornerstone of Kenneth Bell's repertoire and its appearance on a menu twenty miles away is explained by the fact that Stephen Ross, *chef-patron* of Popjoy's, has spent many a happy cooking hour in the kitchen at Thornbury. After graduating in economics from Bristol University, Stephen decided to indulge his long-held hobby of cooking. He went first to work with Kenneth Bell at Thornbury Castle, then to The Cottage in the Wood for another year.

Impatient by now (1972) to branch out on his own, he began to look seriously for restaurant sites in Bristol. About ten months later, he discovered that Beau Nash House in Bath was up for sale. It had been used as a restaurant but despite its grandiloquent origins was in appalling condition. It took six months to build a proper kitchen and completely redecorate the house.

The Rosses finally opened in 1973, hoping that there would be enough customers to sustain yet another restaurant in Bath. (The Hole in the Wall was by now firmly established as 'the' restaurant but, ironically, this was the same year that George Perry-Smith sold it and moved to Helford.)

Stuffed Breast of Chicken with Pernod and Tarragon

Stuffing
4½ oz (125g) butter
2 medium onions, peeled and finely chopped
¼ lb (100g) mushrooms
rind and juice of 2 lemons
1 teaspoon chopped fresh tarragon (½ teaspoon if using dried herb)
1 teaspoon fresh thyme (½ teaspoon if using dried herb)
salt and pepper
1 egg

5 oz (150g) fresh white breadcrumbs
1 teaspoon chopped fresh parsley

8 boned chicken breasts
2 oz (50g) butter
7 tablespoons Pernod
¼ pint (150ml) double cream
handful of chopped fresh tarragon (2 teaspoons if using dried herb)
salt and pepper

Start by making the stuffing. Melt the butter in a pan and toss the onions in it. Cook over a moderate heat, stirring from time to time, until the onions are soft but not coloured. Dice the mushrooms and add to the pan with the lemon rind, juice and seasonings. Continue cooking until the mixture begins to look dry (about 15 minutes). Take off the heat and leave to cool. Then beat in the egg, breadcrumbs and parsley. Cover and chill until ready to use.

Preheat the oven to gas mark 5, 375°F (190°C). Make a slit along the length of each chicken breast (not right through) to make a pocket. Fill with a good dollop of stuffing, then close the pocket neatly to keep the stuffing in. When ready to cook, dot each chicken breast gener-

181

ously with butter and wrap in foil. Cook in the preheated oven until no pink juices run out when pierced with a skewer (approximately 25–30 minutes).

To serve: unwrap the chicken and place on a heated ovenproof dish (or individual dishes), retaining all the butter and juices. Pour the butter and juices into a saucepan and stir in the Pernod, cream and tarragon. Season to taste with salt and pepper. Put over a moderate heat and reduce by boiling until the sauce has a smooth silky texture (about 5–10 minutes). Coat the chicken with the sauce and serve with rice and a green salad.

Serves 8

🍷 A lightish claret (anything too special could be ruined by the Pernod)

Chef: Stephen Ross *Proprietors:* Penny and Stephen Ross

CHEWTON CHEESE DAIRY

The Cheddar served at Bowlish House comes from the prize-winning Chewton Cheese Dairy, at nearby Chewton Mendip, an area which has, for centuries, been famous for its Cheddar. Here, the cheese is made in the traditional method, entirely from the milk of their own herd. They sell whole cheeses (20-lb), the popular 5-lb 'truckles' or pieces by the pound. The shop is also stocked with homemade gingerbread, biscuits, wholemeal loaves, jams and local honey. The cheese can be ordered and sent by post.

BOWLISH HOUSE

Shepton Mallet, Somerset

Catering seems a far cry from fork-lift trucks and Formula 3 cars but Brian Jordan has coped with all three successfully. He started off as a racing cyclist in the U.K., Ireland and France, moved on to motor racing on the international circuit and then became managing director of an American subsidiary which dealt with mechanical handling, based in the Oman.

As frequent visitors to The Toastmaster's Inn and friends of the owners (Judith and Gregory Ward), Brian and his wife Pat had long been attracted to the idea of running their own country restaurant. On their return from the Middle East in 1977, they began to look seriously for a house suitable for restaurant conversion. By happy coincidence, the house they found and liked most was owned by someone they knew already (Nicholas von Preussen who, with Gillian Abbott, had been running Bowlish House as a restaurant for several years). Contracts were quickly exchanged and the Jordans were ready to open for business in February 1978.

Major restoration work had recently been done on the house (built in the 1770s, with a magnificent Palladian frontage), so it only needed minor structural work and redecoration. Having agreed that the restaurant was their top priority, they converted ten pokey bedrooms into five good-sized ones. These are now available at a modest price to anyone dining in the restaurant.

Poulet en Croûte

3-lb (1·5 kilos) chicken
8 fl oz (225ml) medium
  sherry
¼ lb (100g) lean veal *or*
  pork
½ onion, peeled and
  chopped
salt and black pepper
dash of Worcestershire
  sauce
dash of angostura bitters
  (optional)
pinch of chopped oregano
pinch of chopped tarragon
¼ pint (150ml) double
  cream

¼ lb (100g) cooked ham
1 oz (25g) chopped mixed
  nuts *or* pistachios

¾ lb (350g) puff pastry
  (for homemade, see
  page 386)
1 egg, beaten

Sauce
¼ lb (100g) button
  mushrooms
1½ oz (40g) butter

Roast the chicken in a moderately hot oven – gas mark 5, 375°F (190°C) – basting frequently, for about 1¼ hours (have it slightly moist rather than overdone). Leave to cool.

Remove the skin, then slice the breast meat from the chicken and arrange in a flat dish; cover with half the sherry and allow to marinate for at least 1 hour. Remove all the rest of the flesh from the chicken and mince together with the veal or pork and the onion. Season this mixture with salt, pepper, Worcestershire sauce and angostura bitters (if liked) and blend in the herbs and half the cream. Slice the ham into thin strips and mix with the nuts. Roll out the pastry and lay the slices of breast meat down the middle, cover with the farce and then with the ham and nuts. Paint the edges of the pastry with beaten egg, then fold over to make a parcel. Prick the top lightly with a fork to let the steam escape and decorate with any remaining pastry trimmings. Chill until needed. When ready to bake, preheat the oven to gas mark 7, 425°F (220°C). Brush the pastry completely with beaten egg and transfer to a greased and floured baking sheet. Bake in the oven for 15–20 minutes or until golden brown.

To make the sauce, slice the mushrooms and sauté in the butter. Add the remaining sherry and the strained marinade and continue cooking until it has reduced by half (5–10 minutes). Stir in the remaining cream and season to taste. Keep over a low heat until needed.

When nicely browned, take the pastry 'parcel' out of the oven and cut into slices. Transfer to a serving platter. Pour the sauce into a warmed jug and hand round separately.

Serves 8

▯ Claret or one of its close relatives such as Bergerac

Chef: Martin Schwaller *Proprietors:* Pat and Brian Jordan

WELL HOUSE

Poundisford, Somerset

Well House has undoubtedly one of the most romantic settings of any country restaurant. Once you've mastered the tortuous approach (a nightmare for navigators), you are welcomed by a guard of honour – a double row of spreading limes. Then traditional procedure is reversed and you enter this stately house through the back door. A short walk across the cobbled courtyard (past the eponymous well) takes you by the open door of the kitchen where the chef, Graham Cornish, and his team are in full view. The sights and smells of this detour are so tantalizing that an aperitif is barely necessary.

On entering the main house, you will be greeted by Graham's wife Maggie who guides you through to the garden (weather permitting) or to one of two sitting-rooms to order dinner. The dining-room itself was the original Tudor kitchen, an all-purpose room used for cooking, eating and family gatherings. Its vaulted ceiling is dizzyingly high and rows of mullioned windows face each other across the room. Porcelain moulds, precious china and other artefacts from former days are ranged along their sills. The fireplace runs the whole width of the room, and during the winter there is always a fire burning and in the summer months it is filled with flowers from the garden.

186

Chicken with Green Pepper and Cardamoms

3-lb (1·5 kilos) chicken
 or 4–8 chicken pieces,
 depending on size
salt and pepper
2 oz (50g) butter
1 large green pepper
8 whole cardamoms
5 fl oz (150ml) sweet
 white wine or sweet
 vermouth

1 teaspoon meat glaze or
 well-reduced beef stock
 or Marmite
½ pint (275ml) double
 cream

watercress to garnish

Joint the chicken into 8 pieces and season well with salt and pepper. Melt the butter in a large frying pan and fry the seasoned joints (legs first) until cooked and nicely browned (they'll need 20–25 minutes). Transfer to a serving dish and keep warm.

Slice the green pepper and remove the stalk, white pith and seeds. Put into the frying pan with the chicken juices and the seeds of the cardamoms. Pour in the wine, scrape the bottom of the pan well to loosen the sediment and cook over moderate heat until well-reduced (about 10 minutes). Add the meat glaze and the cream. Reduce by boiling for a further 5 minutes or until it thickens. Season to taste with salt and pepper.

Pour any juices from the chicken in the serving dish into the sauce. Blend well, then pour the sauce over the chicken and garnish with watercress.

Serves 4

🍷 The pungency of an Austrian white would complement this spiciness

Chef: Graham Cornish *Proprietor:* Ralph Vivian Neal

THE WIFE OF BATH

Wye, Kent

Bob Johnson, the *chef-patron* of The Wife of Bath, provides a classic example of how easy it is to fall into a *métier* by accident. In the late sixties, he started part-time work as a waiter at The Wife of Bath to supplement his regular job as a dental technician. By 1972, his obvious flair and interest in cooking was enough for Michael Waterfield (the *chef-patron* at that time) to persuade him to give up his job and cook full-time at the restaurant. For the next three years, he did an intensive apprenticeship, cooking his way through The Wife of Bath repertoire. When Mr Waterfield left in 1977 to pursue other interests, Bob took over completely.

The menu, a *table d'hôte* with half a dozen starters and main courses, changes daily. It is a bi-partisan blend of French provincial and traditional English dishes. The Wife of Bath specialities (e.g. *Beignets de fromage, Escalopes de dinde 'aux trois épices', Filets de sole vert-pré*) feature regularly as well as the more recent Johnson innovations: Turbot with prawns and brandy sauce, and a spicy Lamb marocaine served with avocado sauce. With a total of three in the kitchen (sometimes only two), the pace can become marginally too hectic when serving forty lunches, and sometimes as many as seventy dinners.

188

Escalopes de Dinde aux Trois Epices

1 oz (25g) butter
4 spring onions, finely chopped
1 oz (25g) flour
¼ pint (150ml) dry white wine
½ pint (275ml) water
½ oz (15g) cumin seeds, ½ oz (15g) cardomom seeds, 1 oz (25g) coriander seeds, all powdered to a fine dust

clove of garlic, crushed
salt and pepper
a little butter
4 large turkey escalopes, sliced thinly, *or* 8 slices fresh turkey breast
seasoned flour
¼ pint (150ml) double cream

Melt the butter in a frying pan and add the spring onions. Cook until softened, then stir in the flour. Continue cooking for a minute or two, then add the wine, water, spices, garlic and a good seasoning of salt and pepper. Cook for 10–15 minutes until well blended and slightly thickened.

Melt a little butter in another pan and cook the turkey breasts (which have been lightly tossed in seasoned flour), a few at a time. As soon as they are nicely browned on one side (this takes 5–10 minutes), lift out of the pan. When they have all been browned on one side, return them to the pan (uncooked side down) and pour over the onion, spice and wine mixture. Continue cooking for about 5 minutes, then add the cream. Simmer gently for a further 5 minutes until the sauce browns and thickens. Serve at once with a green vegetable or salad.

Serves 4

🍷 Needs a fairly full red – from California or Eastern Europe, for instance

Chef: Robert Johnson
Proprietors: Robert Johnson and Brian Boots

THE TOASTMASTER'S INN

Burham, Kent

The Toastmaster's Inn distinguishes itself in many ways, not the least of which is its unassuming appearance. From the outside, it looks the sort of place where you might get a good pint of Young's and a fistful of crisp packets. Inside, there is the totally unexpected pleasure of seeing a battered lunch card, propped against a soda siphon, which lists cassoulet, jugged hare and game pie! It is enough to make you abandon the journey to Dover and simply eat here for a week.

A week would be just enough time to work your way through the menu, which includes half a dozen starters and main courses. With a bit of careful planning, you could arrive in time to get the best of both weeks, as the menu changes on Saturday. It is a labour of love by chef Tim Daglish and prepared with his *commis*, Paul Duval. There is a strong bias towards classical French dishes, yet the lightness of the sauces shows a definite liaison with *nouvelle cuisine*. The evolution of the menu, particularly in the last few years, has brought it much closer to the new style of country restaurant cooking in France. In a kitchen the size of a broom cupboard, Daglish and Duval produce dishes that would be completely at home in any first-rate French *auberge*. Scallops served in a choux pastry case with a green herb sauce, a rich *Bouillabaisse de poulet* or Dark field mushrooms *en chapelure* with homemade *sauce tartare* would be only three of the starters offered on one particular day.

Duck is a Daglish speciality and as well as the recipe given below, he does a crispy wild duck, served with a sage-flavoured sauce of port and cherries.

Duck Breasts
with Green Peppercorns and Livers

4 duck breasts cut from
   two 6-lb (2·75 kilos) fresh
   ducks (retain the legs
   for future use)
several tablespoons of
   clarified butter
a little oil
4 duck livers, trimmed, *or*
   use chicken livers

fresh watercress to garnish

Green Peppercorn Sauce
3 tablespoons brandy *or*
   Armagnac
3 teaspoons green
   peppercorns
7 fl oz (200ml) rich gravy
   or espagnole sauce (page
   381)
3 fl oz (75ml) double
   cream
salt and black pepper

Season the duck breasts on both sides, then prick their skins all over with a needle. Melt a little of the clarified butter with a small amount of oil in a heavy frying pan and when really hot, sear the breasts, skin side first, on both sides. Then turn over to the skin side again and cook for a further 4–5 minutes over a low heat (keeping the heat low is important, otherwise the breast will shrink). The flesh must be a rosy pink when sliced so be careful not to overcook. Lift out with a slotted spoon and place in a cool oven to keep warm, skin side up.

191

Strain the excess fat from the pan, leaving about a table-spoon of fat and all the sediment. Increase the heat and drop in the livers. Cook on each side for 2–3 minutes (they must be underdone). Warm the brandy, pour into the pan and flame. Lift out the livers with a slotted spoon and keep warm. Add the peppercorns and gravy to the pan. Scrape the bottom of the pan well to lift all the rich sediment. Whisk until smooth, then whisk in the cream. Heat gently until it thickens, then season to taste with salt and black pepper.

To serve: make two horizontal incisions in each duck breast. Cut each liver in two and place these in the incisions. Coat with the sauce and garnish with fresh watercress. Serve with new potatoes tossed in garlic butter and a green salad.

Serves 4

▮ The savoury dryness of a Barolo

Chefs: Tim Daglish and Paul Duval
Proprietors: Judith and Gregory Ward

FINDON MANOR

Findon, West Sussex

Running a restaurant may be riddled with headaches but running a 'restaurant with rooms' can mean a permanent migraine. There are barely enough hours in the day to get a decent, let alone imaginative, meal on the tables as it is. By the time you've been to the market, chivvied a few suppliers, spent half an hour on the phone trying to replace chipped crockery, paid a few bills and billed a few customers, it's almost time to serve lunch.

When you add rooms, first you have to spring out of bed an hour earlier to deliver morning tea. Then you feel morally obliged to provide fresh croissants, as well as a hearty British breakfast. As most guests come equipped with hollow legs, there will be a cry, at what seems like thirty seconds later, for a pot of coffee and a few biscuits (homemade, of course). At the Savoy, where you have waiters and customers in equal quantities, this presents no problem. But in the country, it means that the *patron* is in a state of perpetual motion.

Mary and Adrian Bannister thought they knew what busy meant when they owned and ran their own restaurant ('Bannisters') in Brighton. But now that they are at Findon Manor, which has five bedrooms in addition to the restaurant, they wonder what they did with their time.

Even though their business is tiny compared with many, the standard of comfort and *cuisine* which they offer takes energy and effort to maintain. They have lessened the workload slightly by only serving residents on Sunday evenings (who must be content with a modest supper of roast pheasant or cold lobster!) and lunches in the bar: terrines, hot pies and soups, with everything, including the French bread, made in the Findon Manor kitchen.

Le Caneton au Citron Vert

2 fresh limes
2–3 tablespoons brandy
1 pint (575ml) good duck
   stock *or* strong chicken
   stock
1 oz (25g) butter
Meaux mustard
fresh white breadcrumbs
salt and pepper

1 wild duck (if
   unavailable, use
   ordinary duck)

Preheat the oven to gas mark 7, 425°F (220°C). Remove the outer peel of the limes, using a vegetable peeler, taking care not to include any of the bitter white pith. Cut into very fine julienne strips and blanch quickly in boiling water. Refresh under running cold water, then leave to drain. Squeeze the juice of 1 lime. Cut the pith off the remaining lime and remove the segments.

Season the duck well then put it in a roasting tin and into the preheated oven for about 12 minutes, or until the breasts are cooked but slightly underdone. Lift the duck out of the tin. Remove the breasts, place on a serving dish and keep warm. Remove the legs and put under a hot grill for a few minutes. Then coat with a little Meaux mustard and fresh breadcrumbs. Continue grilling until crisp on all sides. Place on the serving dish and keep warm.

Deglaze the roasting tin with a little brandy, scraping the bottom of the pan well to loosen the sediment. Pour in the stock and reduce by half, boiling rapidly. Add the fresh lime juice. Take the pan off the heat and whisk in the butter, cut into small pieces, a little at a time. Season to taste with salt and pepper. Pour the sauce through a strainer into a warmed jug, add the julienne of lime peel and a little more brandy if you like. Make small incisions in the duck breasts and insert the lime segments. Serve the duck at once, handing round the sauce separately.

NB. The success of this dish depends on using a first-rate stock, well-reduced and with a good glaze. Even more important is the balance between the acidity of the lime and the 'gameyness' of the duck – neither flavour should be overwhelming. The breasts must be kept *underdone*.

Serves 3

♟ Claret or other Cabernet from a ripe year

Chef: Adrian Bannister
Proprietors: Mary and Adrian Bannister

KINCH'S

Chesterton, Oxfordshire

A dilapidated old barn in Oxfordshire, after a good deal of plaster surgery, got a new lease of life when Mr and Mrs Greatorex opened it as a restaurant in 1972. It is now one large room, cleverly decorated to leave its origins undisguised. You step first into a snug bar (a converted cowshed) no bigger than a pocket handkerchief, where the customers rub shoulders while ordering. When the crush threatens to upset the aperitif, guests are ushered upstairs to the loft overlooking the dining-room. Here, one is easily distracted by the watercolours painted by Frances Marsh (Mrs Greatorex) which provide a striking contrast to the *cappuccino* walls. From this eyrie, you also get a discreet view of the diners below, tucking into fresh Salmon mousse, Poussin with garlic and herbs or Blackcurrant sorbet (page 358). Occasionally there are special evenings when the wines from Kinch's impressive list are paired up with dishes of a particular region in France. There are music nights as well, with a string quartet playing in the loft or in the restaurant, tables pushed to one side, followed by a set dinner of four or five courses.

Duck is almost always on the menu at Kinch's, partly because of a good local supplier but largely because of

Christopher Greatorex's skill in cooking it. It is sometimes baked with apple and ginger, other times served with a black cherry sauce or 'as roasted by the *vignerons*'.

Duck as Roasted by the Wine Growers

4½-lb (2 kilos) duck
salt and pepper

2 lb (900g) white grapes
(should be quite tart)

sprigs of parsley to garnish

Preheat the oven to gas mark 6, 400°F (200°C). Season the duck well, inside and out, then prick the skin with a fork. Place in a roasting tin.

Halve and pip 12 grapes and put to one side. Place the remaining grapes in and around the duck. Roast for 1 hour in the preheated oven, then pour off the fat. Remove the grapes and juice and push through a sieve. Return the duck to the oven for a further 15–20 minutes. Pour the juices from the tin into a saucepan and skim off any fat. Add the grape purée, the 12 remaining grapes and a good seasoning of salt and pepper. (If the grapes are very tart, you might need to add a pinch of sugar.) Heat gently for 5–10 minutes. Carve the duck and arrange on a serving platter. Cover with the grape sauce and garnish with sprigs of parsley.

Serves 3

🍷 Côtes de Buzet or Madiran would be suitably ethnic

Chef: Christopher Greatorex
Proprietors: Frances and Christopher Greatorex

197

THE HORN OF PLENTY

Gulworthy, Devon

If you're lucky, you might just catch a glimpse of Sonia Stevenson in the restaurant – still in her Wellington boots. Though her husband looks more like a marmalade-loving Paddington Bear, she is the one who wears the boots. They are standard issue in the kitchen, as she shuttles back and forth from the garden. Homegrown herbs, vegetables and fruit, supplemented by seasonal game, fish and local meat form the cornerstone of her cooking.

The menu is characterized by a bizarre eclecticism, drawing ideas and recipes from all parts of the world. It might include Duck with Peruvian savoury rice (a recipe which is over five hundred years old) as well as the unusual *Fruits de mer en croustade Clément* and a traditional Cornish parsley pie. Game is often on the menu: perhaps a Roast pheasant with the old Devon country accompaniments – henge, hog's and black pudding slices, fried apple, bread sauce and a wine gravy.

Despite the fact that Mrs Stevenson has never taken a cookery course, she is able to produce dishes of staggering complexity. It is a skill that silences the severest critics. She is equally capable of cooking a Ham *en croûte* with truffles for ten people and, simultaneously, a delicate hot Crab mousse for two. Whatever the dish, it is done to perfection and with an ingenuity which is now synonymous with her cooking.

Venison Pie

2 lb (900g) cubed venison

1½ lb (675g) pickled pork *or* unsmoked streaky bacon in one piece

1 tablespoon tomato purée

1½ pints (850ml) red wine

zest and juice of 2 oranges

½–1 pint (275–575ml) good game *or* beef stock

salt and pepper

beurre manié to thicken

good pinch of marjoram

½ lb (225g) shortcrust pastry

egg wash

medium-sized, deep pie dish

Preheat the oven to gas mark 5, 375°F (190°C). Remove the bone and rind from the pork. Cut into medium chunks. Put into a large pan and fry gently until the fat runs. Add the venison and fry until the juice runs and coats the meat with a rich brown juice (this is very important). Add the tomato purée, the wine and orange zest. Mix well, scraping the bottom of the pan to loosen all the sediment. Add the orange juice, enough stock to cover the meat and a good seasoning of salt and pepper (allowing for reduction and the saltiness of the pork). Simmer until tender (about 45 minutes), then strain all the juice into another pan. Mix together equal amounts of butter and flour (*beurre manié*) and add, small pieces at a time, to thicken the gravy. Add the marjoram and simmer for a further 5–10 minutes.

Put the meat into the pie dish and cover with the gravy. Roll out the pastry and use to cover the filling completely. Cut a small hole or slits on top to allow the steam to escape. Glaze the surface with a little lightly beaten egg. Bake in the preheated oven for 30–40 minutes or until golden brown. Take out and serve at once.

Serves 4–6

🍷 Hermitage or Châteauneuf-du-Pape

Chef: Sonia Stevenson
Proprietors: Sonia and Patrick Stevenson

TULLICH LODGE

Ballater, Aberdeenshire, Scotland

Tullich Lodge is a miniature castle, built in the nineteenth century and converted to the twentieth with a minimum of fuss. On the surface, it remains unchanged. Fires glow in every room, the panelling is in pristine condition and the fine china and silver are in frequent use. Guests gravitate to the bar before dinner and this is served at no exact time, but when the gong sounds.

While Neil Bannister cooks, his partner Hector Macdonald slides easily between his roles as bartender and waiter. The dinner will be simple, showing skilful handling of the finest local ingredients. It may, for instance, be Stilton soup, Roast rib of beef and fresh vegetables, followed by Apple and orange crisp. For those who long for cheese a Scottish Dunlop, Islay and Stilton sit waiting on the sideboard. They are served with crisp 'butter puffs' from the local baker in Ballater or with his equally distinctive wholemeal 'Balmoral' loaf. The atmosphere, generated by the setting and attentive service, still hints at Victorian grandeur.

During the autumn and winter, Tullich Lodge is a popular rendezvous for shooting parties. You may, at this time, feel a little out of place if you walk in with a suitcase rather than a brace of pheasants.

Pheasant, Normandy Style

1 young cock pheasant *or* hen

a little olive *or* vegetable oil

2 oz (50g) streaky, rindless bacon, finely chopped

2 oz (50g) onion, finely chopped

clove of garlic, finely chopped

4 small cooking apples

salt and black pepper

¼ pint (150ml) medium cider

¼ pint (150ml) double cream

pinch of sugar (if needed)

watercress to garnish

Preheat the oven to gas mark 4, 350°F (180°C). Heat a little oil in a frying pan and add the bacon. Cook until the fat runs, then add the onion and garlic. Continue cooking until they are soft and lightly browned (about 5–10 minutes). Lift out of the pan and put to one side. Peel, core and slice the apples. Add to the same pan and brown slightly. Then lift out and put with the onions and bacon. Brown the pheasant in the remaining fat, then transfer to a casserole and surround with the apples, bacon and onion. Season well with salt, and freshly ground black pepper. Mix the cider and cream together, then pour over the pheasant. Cover and bake for 30–45 minutes.

Take the pheasant out of the casserole and place on a serving platter. Skim the sauce of fat, then liquidize until smooth. Season to taste, adding a pinch of sugar if necessary. Pour over the pheasant and garnish with watercress.

Serves 2–3

▮ Lash out on a good red burgundy from Côte-de-Nuits

Chef: Neil Bannister
Proprietors: Neil Bannister and Hector Macdonald

MARLFIELD HOUSE

Gorey, Co. Wexford, Eire

Mary Bowe, the owner of Marlfield House, has always had a problem with dining-rooms. When she worked at the Waldorf in London, the dining-room was too big; the customers felt as if they were eating in the Albert Hall. Then she moved back to her native Ireland and, several years later, started running the Esker Lodge in Curracloe, where the dining-room was far too small. Her cooking was so popular that guests were begging to eat on the landing, in the back hall or on the front doorstep.

In 1977 she bought and opened Marlfield House and, anticipating seating difficulties, she provided *two* dining-rooms. However ideal this might have been on paper, it didn't work in practice. For some inexplicable reason, all the customers (especially the 'regulars') wanted to eat in the front dining-room. No one, despite Mary's persuasive powers, wanted to eat in the back one which seemed to have everything going for it: wood panelling, exquisite décor, crackling fire and candlelit tables. It may be a strange Irish quirk (though Americans, Japanese and Germans seem to display it as well) but the reason they all like the front room is, apparently, the priceless silver collection on the mahogany sideboard!

202

After seeing the wild pigeons flitting across the lawn earlier in the day, it brings a small lump to the throat to see them on the menu that evening. However, as soon as one's back is turned on the garden, interest in this Mary Bowe *specialité* is soon revived.

Pigeon Breasts with Juniper Berry Sauce

4 pigeons
2 oz (50g) butter
4 slices brown bread,
    lightly buttered
4 rashers streaky rindless
    bacon

watercress to garnish

Juniper Berry Sauce

1 small onion, peeled
stick of celery
2 oz (50g) butter
1 oz (25g) flour
$\frac{1}{2}$ pint (275ml) red wine
1 dessertspoon redcurrant
    jelly
15 juniper berries, crushed
1 chicken stock cube
6 peppercorns
$\frac{1}{4}$ pint (150ml) port

Preheat the oven to gas mark 7, 425°F (220°C). Using poultry shears, cut the breasts off each pigeon and skin them. Rub them with some butter, set them on the lightly buttered slices of bread and cover each one with a bacon rasher, cut in half. Roast them in the preheated oven until they are cooked but still slightly pink (about 15–25 minutes).

Chop the onion and celery finely. Melt the butter in a saucepan, then add the vegetables. Cover and 'sweat' them until they are soft but not coloured. Stir in the flour and cook gently for 2–3 minutes until golden brown. Blend in the wine, redcurrant jelly, juniper berries, stock cube and peppercorns. Bring up to the boil and then simmer very slowly for 20 minutes. Add the port and cook for a further 5 minutes. Strain the sauce and pour into a warmed jug.

Lift the pigeons out on to a serving platter, coat with a little of the sauce and garnish with fresh watercress. Hand round the remaining sauce separately.

NB. The sauce can be made ahead of time but you may find in that case that it needs to be thinned slightly with a little more port. If the pigeons are being kept warm for any length of time, you may prefer to roast them on croûtes of toast rather than bread which becomes rather soggy if left too long.

Serves 4

🍷 Cahors or other robust red from south-west France

Chef and proprietor: Mary Bowe

MILSOM'S

With fishmongers becoming as scarce as red herrings, the opening of 'Milsom's' in Ipswich is a welcome sight. Its namesake and owner, Gerald Milsom, is the proprietor of Le Talbooth and of The Pier at Harwich (with a menu and style reminiscent of the quayside fish restaurants on the east and west coasts of America). East Anglian residents and visitors are now treated to an outstanding selection of fresh fish, poultry and game, bought with the benefit of Milsom's twenty-five years' experience in the restaurant trade. A smokehouse at the rear of the shop has recently been brought to life and all their fish is now smoked on the premises.

FISHES'

Burnham Market, Norfolk

When Gillian Cape moved from London to Norfolk six
years ago, it was to start an oyster farm and fish-smoking
business. When this failed to occupy her full-time, she and
her husband bought an old ironmongers' in Burnham
Market and opened it as a fish shop and restaurant. From
a modest start, it mushroomed quickly and soon overtook
the fish business. (This has since been abandoned and
though Mrs Cape still smokes her own fish and ham, it is
now mainly for the restaurant.)

As you walk into Fishes', you will be guided into a
sitting-room (which doubles as a dining-room during the
busy summer months) or the main restaurant. Both rooms
are distinctly 'homely' and you are likely to find as diver-
sion Leggo, Meccano or Donald Duck. There is a choice
of two menus: one a daily *table d'hôte*, the other a monthly
changing *à la carte*. As all the fish is caught locally, it is
wonderfully fresh but does, as a result, depend on availability. Though both menus are predominantly fish, there
are always one or two dishes for those who dislike it: a thick
vegetable *potage*, a potted Stilton pâté or sweet-cured ham
with fresh fruit.

Inside the front door, a long counter houses Mrs Cape's
smoked fish (salmon, trout, mackerel, cod's roe), cured

ham and various pâtés. These are sold to passing trade as well as to diners. Both shop and restaurant are open all year round, despite the fact that their business is distinctly seasonal (packed during the summer, then tailing off from October to March).

As the ingredients are so fresh, they seldom need anything other than careful cooking. Mrs Cape serves Norfolk trout poached or grilled, with bananas or, as below, with lemon sauce.

Norfolk Trout with Lemon Sauce

4 fresh trout, each about
    12 oz (350g), gutted
    and cleaned
dry white wine
lemon juice
salt and pepper
sprig of tarragon
2 bay leaves
2 sticks of celery, finely
    chopped

lemon slices, chopped
    parsley and a few
    toasted almonds to
    garnish

Lemon Sauce

2 oz (50g) butter
1½ oz (40g) chopped leek
¾ oz (20g) flour
3 fl oz (75ml) PLJ (pure
    lemon juice)
3 fl oz (75ml) orange juice
1 generous tablespoon dry
    white wine
good pinch of tarragon
    (dried will do)
1 small lemon, peeled and
    chopped into segments
salt and pepper
¼ pint (150ml) single
    cream
a little castor sugar if
    necessary
a few green grapes, halved
    and pipped

The trout should be poached in a covered pan (preferably a fish kettle) for about 8 minutes in a mixture of water, white wine, lemon juice, salt and pepper, tarragon, bay leaves and finely chopped celery. Do not overcook or the trout will fall to pieces.

To make the sauce, melt the butter in a large pan. Add the leek and cook until softened. Stir in the flour and cook for a minute or two. Remove from the heat, then add the PLJ and orange juice, stirring until well blended. Return to the heat, pour in the wine and add the tarragon, lemon segments and a little shredded lemon peel. Bring to the boil, stirring continuously, and simmer for 2 minutes. Season to taste with salt and pepper. Blend in the cream, then taste again. If too sharp, add a little castor sugar. If too thick, whisk in a little of the liquor that the trout has been poached in. Finally, add the halved and pipped green grapes. Pour over the trout and decorate with lemon slices, chopped parsley and a few toasted almonds.

Serve with a salad containing fresh fruit and nuts, perhaps chicory and/or celery.

Serves 4

♆ White burgundy, perhaps from the Côte Chalonnaise

Chef and proprietor: Gillian Cape

RIVERSIDE

Helford, Cornwall

The sale of The Hole in the Wall in 1974 caused much knashing of teeth and tearing of hair in Bath. There was a general outcry from residents and out-of-town gourmets, who failed to understand how George Perry-Smith could leave them for a tiny, backwoods spot on the Helford River.

It may also have been a shock to Perry-Smith, to find himself in the slow-motion world of Cornwall after the bustle of Bath. When he opened the Riverside in September 1974, it was quite a different restaurant from the one he had opened twenty-two years earlier. This was a 'restaurant with rooms', serving breakfasts to a maximum of six residents and dinners, five nights a week, to an average of thirty people. The menu was, and still is, a fraction the size of the one at 'The Hole' and offers a *prix fixe* meal with limited choice. The 'always' and 'sometimes' dishes allow for an unexpected delivery of lobster or a sudden shortage of salmon or lamb. The cold table, a cornerstone of 'The Hole', was tried at first but the diminutive size of the Riverside made it impractical.

The inventiveness and skill of Perry-Smith are just as evident here and his cooking would make any epicure swoon. It features Turbot plucky (done Greek-style with fennel), Goose *à la poitevine*, *Carré de porc provençale* and rich

Oxtail with grapes. (To ease the difficulty of deciding which of these to have, large bowls of glistening black olives and cheese tidbits arrive with the menu.) Vegetables are treated with imaginative respect and a creamy *Gratin dauphinois* might be paired with Courgettes and tomatoes with basil or Aubergine spiced with cumin.

Salmon Baked in Pastry with Currants and Ginger

2½ lb (1 kilo) fresh salmon
salt and pepper
¼ lb (100g) butter
3–4 globes of stem ginger, chopped
1 oz (25g) currants
rich shortcrust pastry, made with 1 lb (450g) flour, 10 oz (275g) butter
egg yolk
sauce messine (page 380) to serve

Preheat the oven to gas mark 8, 450°F (230°C). Skin and bone the salmon (or ask your fishmonger to do this), then season the resultant two thick fillets all over with salt and pepper. Cream the butter and mix in the chopped ginger and currants. Sandwich half this mixture in an even layer between the two fillets, then spread the remainder over the top. Wrap it neatly (i.e. not a great wodge of pastry at the ends but a neat parcel) in pastry, brush with egg yolk and make several small holes in the top for the steam to escape. Bake in the preheated oven for 30–35 minutes.

Serve with a *sauce messine* and a cucumber salad.

Serves 8

⟦♙⟧ Alsace Riesling has enough character of its own not to be cowed

Chef: George Perry-Smith
Proprietors: Heather Crosbie and George Perry-Smith

DUNDERRY LODGE

Dunderry, Co. Meath, Eire

When Catherine and Nicholas Healey bought Dunderry
Lodge, the part which is now the restaurant was greatly
in need of a builder. It was a draughty old barn with a
ramshackle shed on one side. Neither had much going for
it except a family of rats nibbling their way through the
skirting boards.

In a remarkably short time, the Healeys effected a trans-
formation, restoring beams and putting in new wood
floors, painting the walls in soft colours and filling the
dining-room with a large oak dresser and mahogany tables
of differing sizes. It is now difficult to distinguish its origins,
and in the evening, lit only by candles and firelight, the
warm glow is almost hypnotic.

One of the cowsheds has been converted to a cosy sitting-
room with a large fireplace and comfortable sofas to sink
into while you order dinner. Nicholas Healey will be on
hand to provide an aperitif and guide you through the
menus (one *table d'hôte*, the other *à la carte*). His presence
in the restaurant, as well as out front, guarantees the
smooth running of both. Though relaxed and informal,
there is no unnecessary wait between courses and the
waitresses are very proficient. It is a nice touch, reminiscent of France, to be shown the finished dish before it
is served.

Salmon en Papillote with Courgettes

4 salmon steaks, each
   1 inch (2·5cm) thick

2 courgettes
salt
$\frac{1}{2}$ oz (15g) butter, melted
2 tablespoons dry
   Dubonnet (if
   unavailable, use dry
   vermouth)

$\frac{1}{4}$ pint (150ml) double
   cream
pepper

chopped parsley to
   garnish

Slice the courgettes very thinly and sprinkle with salt. Leave for 30 minutes, then rinse clean and pat dry with kitchen paper.

Preheat the oven to gas mark 4, 350°F (180°C). Tear off a large piece of tin foil and use to line a roasting tin. Brush it lightly with melted butter. Arrange the salmon steaks on the foil, then put the courgettes on top. Mix the Dubonnet and cream together with a good seasoning of salt and pepper. Pour over the salmon and bring the sides of the foil up and fold over to make a large parcel. Put into the preheated oven and bake for 30 minutes.

Before serving, remove the skin and central bone from the salmon (this is easily done with the point of a sharp knife). Place the salmon on a serving dish, pour the sauce over and dust lightly with chopped parsley.

Serves 4

🍷 A white Rhône – Château Grillet or Condrieu would be really special

Chef: Catherine Healey
Proprietors: Catherine and Nicholas Healey

JOCKEY HALL

Curragh, Co. Kildare, Eire

Paul McCluskey could easily be the Irishwoman's answer to Michel Guérard. He has the same good looks, natural charm and infectious enthusiasm for food and wine. Though a shining example himself of *cuisine minceur*, a few of his customers look a bit *gourmand* for comfort (spoiled, no doubt, by the generous portions of his excellent cooking). The inspiration for Paul's cooking comes from France and while he admires Guérard and Bocuse, his heart is really with the Troisgros (Jean and Pierre, who run the celebrated *Les Frères Troisgros* restaurant in Roanne). For they, more than any of the other three-star chefs in France, have managed to produce 'serious eating' without taking the fun out of it. Their philosophy that nothing should interfere with the customer's enjoyment of the food is one that he shares. When the guest becomes so daunted by the restaurant's reputation that he hardly dares comment on the food, then the chef may as well be cooking for robots.

Though the *cuisine* at Jockey Hall is outstanding, the atmosphere is not intimidating. This is largely due to Monica McCluskey who runs the front of the house and acts as liaison between the customers and her husband in

212

the kitchen. One senses that here, unlike many restaurants of similar standard, the chef is conscious of cooking for individuals and not just table numbers.

This recipe, one of the favourites on the Jockey Hall menu, shows glimmerings of *nouvelle cuisine* and is an attractive prospect for both the eye and the palate.

Sole with Chives

4 sole, each about ¾ lb (350g)
salt and freshly ground black pepper
½ lb (225g) butter
dry white breadcrumbs
½ pint (275ml) fish stock (page 115)
2 tablespoons dry white wine

3 tablespoons Noilly Prat
½ pint (275ml) double cream
1½ rounded teaspoons tomato concentrate
several drops lemon juice
nut of butter
2 tablespoons chopped fresh chives

Preheat the oven to gas mark 5, 375°F (190°C). Take the dark skin off the fish and scale the white skin. Cut off the head diagonally. Season lightly with salt and pepper. Lightly grease a gratin dish with a knob of butter. (Use individual dishes or one large enough to hold two or more sole side by side. Not too large a dish or the liquid will boil away, but not too small or the soles will come into contact and damage each other.)

Melt the butter in a deep plate and dip the sole in it, then dredge the white-skin side only in breadcrumbs. Place in the buttered gratin dish, crumbed side up. Add the fish stock, white wine and Noilly Prat, taking care not to moisten the crumbs. Pour what remains of the melted butter over the breadcrumbs and put the sole into the preheated oven for about 15–20 minutes. (The sole is cooked when the flesh at the top is tender to the touch and is starting to come away from the bone.)

Transfer the sole to another dish. Carefully remove all the little bones and fins from around the edges and keep the fish warm. Reduce the cooking liquid until only about $6\frac{1}{2}$ oz (190ml) remain. Add the cream and tomato concentrate and reduce again until it begins to thicken, whisking all the time. Add a few drops of lemon juice and check the seasoning. When the sauce has nicely thickened (this takes 5–10 minutes), add one small nut of butter to give it a nice gloss. Place the soles under a hot grill to brown the crumbs lightly. While this is being done, sprinkle the chopped chives into the sauce and spread the sauce evenly over four hot plates. Carefully lay the soles on top of the sauce and serve at once.

Serves 4

☻ White burgundy, or Chardonnay from anywhere else

Chef: Paul McCluskey
Proprietors: Monica and Paul McCluskey

SHARROW BAY

Ullswater, Cumbria

'Life is too short for *cuisine minceur*' – *Paul Bocuse*

One hopes, after a meal or two at Sharrow Bay, that Bocuse is right. The menu is not only long, it is virtually irresistible. With twenty starters to choose from, there will be not one but at least three or four that appeal. Thus, before you even begin, the appetite has swung into a racing gallop. Of these, there might be several homemade soups (Carrot vichyssoise [page 117] or Pear and watercress), one of the now famous mousselines (salmon, duck or chicken), Morecambe shrimp bouchée, *Beignets de fromage* or Duck terrine with Cumberland sauce. The fish course offers no choice but will be cooked to perfection. It is often partnered with a *suissesse*, a feather-weight soufflé which is almost airborne.

A fresh fruit sorbet provides the pause between fish and main course. The latter is, thankfully, limited to five dishes (excluding various omelettes and cold meats for those who have indulged on previous days), otherwise one would need an hour to make the choice. If you ordered roast local farmhouse chicken, its generous form would be accompanied by a bed of vegetables with chervil, fruit and herb stuffing, bread sauce bouchée, curried rice, sausage and bacon. And then, to fill the odd centimetre of extra space, there are portions of carrots, swedes, dressed cabbage and three types of potato.

If you are still in an upright position, you can then choose one of eleven puddings. These would be a great deal easier to resist if they weren't displayed so temptingly at the dining-room door. Though you may feel full to brimming, Brian Sack will somehow persuade you to try 'just a mouthful' of Chocolate brandy cake, Sticky toffee pudding (page 283), Lemon syllabub or French apple tart (page 324).

Sole en Croûte

8 small sole fillets
2 oz (50g) butter
salt and pepper
$\frac{1}{2}$ pint (275ml) dry white wine
1 small onion, peeled
$\frac{1}{4}$ lb (100g) mushrooms

a little finely chopped parsley
1 egg, beaten

1 lb (450g) puff pastry (for homemade, see page 386)

shallow baking tin, well buttered

Preheat the oven to gas mark 3, 325°F (170°C). Arrange the fish fillets in the baking tin, then dot them with butter – about 1 oz (25g). Season well with salt and pepper and pour over the white wine. Cook slowly in the preheated oven for about 15 minutes until tender. Take out and leave to cool, reserving all the pan juices for the sauce.

While the fish is cooking, chop the onion finely. Cut the mushrooms into small dice. Melt the remaining butter in a frying pan and sweat the onion until soft but not coloured. Add the mushrooms and continue cooking until they have darkened in colour. Season with salt and pepper. Remove from the pan, add the chopped parsley and a little of the beaten egg to bind it together.

Increase the oven temperature to gas mark 5, 375°F (190°C). Place a small amount of the onion stuffing down the centre of each fish fillet. Roll out the pastry thinly and cut into pieces large enough to wrap each fillet completely. Moisten the edges with a little of the remaining beaten egg and pinch the edges to seal. Glaze each fish 'parcel' with beaten egg, then prick the tops lightly to allow the steam to escape. Place on a slightly dampened baking tray and bake in the preheated oven for 20–25 minutes or until golden brown. Take out and serve with a tomato or mornay sauce or the one given below.

Serves 8

White Wine Sauce

½ pint (275ml) dry white
wine
1 oz (25g) butter
1 oz (25g) flour
fish juices from the pan

salt and white pepper
a little cream
finely chopped parsley

Reduce the wine by rapid boiling to ¼ pint (150ml). Melt the butter in a small saucepan and add the flour. Cook for a minute or two, then gradually blend in the fish juices and wine (adding some milk if necessary to get the right consistency). Slowly bring up to the boil, stirring continuously, then simmer for 2 minutes. Season to taste with salt and pepper and add a small amount of cream if you like and a sprinkling of finely chopped parsley. Keep warm until needed.

🍷 |A dry (Trocken) wine from Germany

Chef: Francis Coulson
Proprietors: Francis Coulson and Brian Sack

217

CHURCHE'S MANSION

Nantwich, Cheshire

The menu at Churche's Mansion is outstanding for its variety and value. It must have been tempting, as the restaurant expanded and grew increasingly successful over a period of twenty years, to succumb to pure commercialism.

But the Myott family, owners of this Tudor mansion for half a century, have refused to do this, sacrificing neither quality nor originality. Everything that comes out of the kitchen is homemade, from the granary rolls made fresh each morning to the pastry, pâtés, mayonnaise, cakes, ice-creams and oatmeal biscuits. Despite the large numbers catered for (40–50 at lunch, 60–80 for dinner, with occasional coffees and teas in between) and the fact that one is eating in an 'historic house', guests are more conscious of being at the receiving end of personal hospitality.

Considering that there are usually only three people in the kitchen at one time, the volume and consistency of the cooking is impressive. The very reasonably priced luncheon menu provides six starters and twice as many main courses; the dinner menu is equally prodigious.

The Sole and prawn pudding was served for the first time at Churche's Mansion at a dinner to celebrate the house's four hundredth birthday in 1977.

Sole and Prawn Pudding

4 Dover sole
3 egg whites
¼ pint (150ml) double
  cream

pinch of ground nutmeg
salt and white pepper
½ lb (225g) prawns

Preheat the oven to gas mark 4, 350°F (180°C). Skin and fillet the Dover sole (or ask the fishmonger to do this). Put the fillets (there should be 16), one or two at a time, between sheets of greaseproof paper and pound flat. Grease four cereal bowls with butter and line each with two fillets, skinned side inwards. Mince four fillets and put them into the liquidizer with the egg whites (or blend the whole fillets with the egg whites in a food processor). Whiz just long enough to break down the whites, then add the cream, nutmeg and a good seasoning of salt and pepper. Blend again until smooth. Turn into a bowl and fold in the prawns. Divide the mixture evenly between the four bowls. Place one fillet over the top of each bowl (you have to cut them in half to make them fit). Cover with buttered greaseproof paper, then foil.

Bake in a bain-marie in the preheated oven for 15–20 minutes. When set, remove the papers, turn the baby puddings on to a plate and coat with a white wine sauce (page 375) flavoured with fresh herbs, or with a hollandaise sauce (page 378).

Serves 4

🍷 ¹Moselle

Chefs: Mrs Richard Myott and Ian Allan
Proprietors: Mr and Mrs Richard Myott

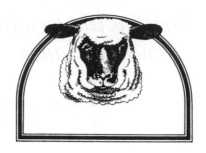

LAMB'S

Moreton-in-Marsh, Gloucestershire

It becomes obvious the moment you walk in the door at Lamb's that there is a definite emphasis on pleasing the eye as well as the palate.

Contrast in colour and texture is used to intensify both the food and the décor. Salmony pink tablecloths warm the steeliness of grey stone walls, modern chrome chairs in one room highlight those of rich mahogany in another. Stone flags alternate with thick carpet, and distinctly lit watercolours stand out against muted shades elsewhere.

The same care is taken with the presentation of the food. Arranged with an artist's eye, it arrives at the table attractively clad but not overdressed. The chef, Paul Barnard, feels strongly that the essence of the original ingredients should not be overwhelmed, and garnishes are used only if they enhance a dish. The dusky Duck and veal terrine is studded with light green pistachio nuts, a ribbon of magenta sauce across one corner. A Roast guinea fowl with crisp brown skin is accompanied by fresh oranges and toasted almonds. The creaminess of fresh brill is accentuated by a scattering of diced avocado and a sliver of lemon.

220

Fresh Brill with Lemon and Avocado Sauce

4 fillets of brill
¼ pint (150ml) dry
  vermouth
½ onion, peeled
1 ripe avocado

1 teaspoon lemon juice
8 fl oz (225ml) double
  cream
salt and pepper

shallow ovenproof (and flameproof) dish, lightly buttered

Preheat the oven to gas mark 4, 350°F (180°C). Wash the brill fillets and pat dry with absorbent kitchen paper. Spread out in the ovenproof dish and pour over the vermouth. Finely chop the onion, then scatter over the fish. Put into the preheated oven for 10–15 minutes or until cooked. Transfer to a serving dish and keep warm.

Peel the avocado and chop into small dice. Add to the vermouth in the ovenproof dish and stir in the lemon juice and cream. Simmer gently over a low heat until the mixture thickens and forms a sauce of coating consistency (5–10 minutes). Season to taste with salt and pepper, then pour over the brill. Serve at once.

Serves 4

▌ Sancerre, Pouilly Fumé or other Sauvignon

Chef: Paul Barnard *Proprietor:* Ian MacKenzie

THE OLD BAKEHOUSE

Colyton, Devon

The Old Bakehouse, a camellia-pink seventeenth-century building, stands in the centre of a sleepy Devon village. It is reminiscent of those small towns in provincial France, cocooned from the flow of traffic and tourists.

It was bought in 1972 by Susan and Stephen Keen, both gastronomes who enjoyed the prospect of running a 'restaurant with rooms'. A courageous move as neither had catering experience of any kind (she had been a model and part-time cook; he was a dealer in rare books). Frequent trips to France had generated an interest in its regional cooking and Susan began converting a vast collection of recipes to restaurant use. Stephen, an ardent wine-lover, filled the cellar with an interesting collection of bottles, some to suit the country style of cooking, others to delight the inquisitive and *gourmand*. The natural outcome has been a series of regional dinners, in which wines and dishes of a particular area are served together on specific evenings three or four times a year.

The fish on The Old Bakehouse menu certainly needs no recommendation; it is a *specialité de la maison*. Fresh red mullet, Dover sole, monkfish, sea bream, salmon, bass, brill, mussels, pike, herring, scallops and trout all feature regularly.

222

Daurade à la Bretonne

1 sea bream, about 2 lb (900g)
1 shallot, peeled
1 oz (25g) butter
6 oz (175g) mushrooms
¼ pint (150ml) white wine
1 tablespoon chopped parsley
6 sprigs of rosemary
salt and pepper
2 oz (50g) fresh white breadcrumbs
1 egg, beaten
3 lemons

Preheat the oven to gas mark 4, 350°F (180°C). Scale, gut and fillet the bream, keeping the fish in one piece with the head on (or ask your fishmonger to do this for you).

Finely chop the shallot and soften in the butter. Dice the mushrooms finely and add to the pan. Continue cooking for about 5 minutes, then add the wine, parsley, 1 sprig of rosemary and the seasonings. Simmer for a further 15 minutes. Take off the heat and leave to cool. Then blend in the breadcrumbs and enough beaten egg to bind the mixture together. Use to stuff the fish, then place it in a shallow baking dish with 3 sprigs of rosemary and enough water to cover the bottom of the dish. Cover the fish with buttered greaseproof paper and place in the preheated oven for approximately 30 minutes. Take out, transfer to a serving platter, decorate the fish with the remaining rosemary and surround with lemon wedges.

Serves 4–6

🍷 Muscadet, or Chablis on high days

Chef: Susan Keen
Proprietors: Susan and Stephen Keen

Lunch and Supper Dishes

'Carême, you will be the death of me; you send in such appetizing fare that I cannot help over-eating.'

'Sire, my duty is to tempt your appetite; yours is to control it.'

The Prince Regent and Carême in conversation

Country restaurateurs have always tried to offer, if not an extensive choice, then a varied one. Despite their remoteness, they have had to cater for the idiosyncrasies of taste as well as appetite. The latter, which differs so radically from one part of the country to another, is the most difficult to gauge. Appetites in Yorkshire are still robust while those in Sussex are distinctly 'slim-line': on the whole, they seem to have become a size or two smaller. This has led to the demise of gargantuan portions and six-course Lucullan feasts. Inflation (of the pound and the waistline) has been another factor and restaurateurs simply can't afford to pile the plates high with food if half of it ends up in the dustbin. Though *gourmets* still abound, the day of the insatiable *gourmand* is over.

Attuned to the foibles of their customers, chefs now compose their menus with a lighter hand. Some suggest (as at Gravetye Manor, White's and Lamb's) that any of the starters may be eaten as a main course. Many offer to cook plainer dishes for customers who, for one reason or another, desire only simple food. At Sharrow Bay, it is not unusual to see guests content to eat only one or two of the four courses provided (and though Brian Sack will be happier if you have more, there is no pressure to do so). At Longueville House, Jane O'Callaghan always puts one 'homely' dish on the menu every evening for guests staying one or two weeks. After several days of eating restaurant food, all they want is something uncomplicated like Grilled salmon, Irish stew or Roast lamb.

This chapter provides a collection of dishes which seem ideally suited to lunch or supper. Some, though technically starters, would make a satisfying meal in themselves. Others represent the *cuisine de ménage* aspect of country restaurant menus.

WHITE'S

Lincoln, Lincolnshire

Colin White, the *chef-patron* of White's in Lincoln, has an outstanding pedigree in country restaurant cooking. Not only has he worked in the kitchen at Sharrow Bay and The Hole in the Wall but also at The Pantry in Newport and The Old House in Wickham. His restaurant is convincing proof of the influence both Sharrow and The Hole have had in developing a new cooking style and in encouraging young chefs to branch out on their own.

At Sharrow Bay, where Colin worked early in his career, the efficiency of the kitchen and the professionalism of its master chef, Francis Coulson, was dazzling. Nothing left the kitchen unless it was perfect and the impeccably high standard was never allowed to slip. Colin reckons that this training, particularly the attention to detail, has stood him in good stead ever since. At The Hole in the Wall, no one worked harder than George Perry-Smith himself. There was never any one chef at the stove all the time; instead, everyone rotated round the kitchen. Even the waitresses did some of the cooking (doing preparation for the cold table or making the sweets) while the chefs occasionally doubled as waiters. As a result, the rapport between kitchen and restaurant was exemplary.

226

Though these restaurants may have had a formative influence, Colin White's style is now definitely his own. His menu is an interesting anthology of dishes, combining classic and country recipes.

Barbecued Spare Ribs

Marinade
1 tablespoon runny honey
1 tablespoon soy sauce
1½ tablespoons wine
vinegar
1 tablespoon tomato purée
2½ tablespoons tomato
ketchup
¼ pint (150ml) pork stock
(if unavailable use
chicken stock)
good pinch of salt

1 lb (450g) pork 'American cut' spare ribs (prepared weight)
1–2 tablespoons olive *or* vegetable oil

Mix all the marinade ingredients together and pour over the spare ribs, which have been put into a large bowl. Leave to marinate for several hours (or overnight), basting from time to time.

When ready to cook, preheat the oven to gas mark 4, 350°F (180°C). Transfer the ribs and marinade to a large saucepan. Warm gently until the sauce becomes runny, then carefully lift out the ribs. Wipe them dry with kitchen paper. Heat a tablespoon of oil in a shallow pan and fry the ribs in it, adding more oil if necessary. When nicely browned, transfer them to an ovenproof dish and finish in the preheated oven for 15–20 minutes until cooked through. Reduce the marinade in the saucepan by boiling rapidly until thick and well-flavoured (the sauce shouldn't be too copious).

Pour the sauce over the ribs and serve with finger bowls

or, if you want to go the whole hog (no pun intended), hot damp towels.

Serves 2 as a supper dish, 4 as a starter

🍷 Valpolicella or tea

White's Moussaka

1 large aubergine, about
   ¾ lb (350g)
salt
olive oil
1 medium onion, peeled
   and finely chopped
1 lb (450g) coarsely
   minced *or* chopped raw
   lamb *or* beef
1 dessertspoon tomato
   purée
2–3 cloves of garlic, crushed
plenty of fresh herbs
   (chopped parsley,
   marjoram *or* oregano,
   thyme, bay, basil)

pinch of ground allspice
black pepper
beef *or* lamb stock to
   moisten

Cheese Sauce

2 oz (50g) butter
1½ oz (40g) flour
1 pint (575ml) milk,
   warmed
2–3 oz (50–75g) tasty or
   mature Cheddar
salt and pepper

Rinse and wipe the aubergine, then remove the stalk end. Cut in half, then into thin horizontal slices. Spread out on a plate, salt well and leave for 1 hour. Rinse and pat dry with kitchen paper. Heat several tablespoons of oil in a large sauté pan. Fry the aubergine slices (not all at once) quickly on both sides, adding more oil when needed. Lift out and drain on kitchen paper.

Heat a little more oil in the same pan and add the onion and meat. Cook until the onion has softened, then stir in the tomato purée, garlic, fresh herbs, pinch of allspice and a good seasoning of salt and freshly ground black pepper. Add enough stock to moisten the mixture, then check again for seasoning.

To make the cheese sauce, melt the butter in a small saucepan. Stir in the flour and cook for a minute or two. Gradually blend in the warmed milk and simmer gently, stirring all the time, until slightly thickened. Grate the cheese and mix into the sauce. Heat gently until it has completely melted (making sure that it doesn't boil), then season to taste with salt and pepper.

Preheat the oven to gas mark 6, 400°F (200°C). Build up layers of aubergine, meat and cheese sauce in an oven-proof dish, ending with one of cheese sauce. Bake in the preheated oven until brown and bubbling (about 45 minutes). (If the top gets too brown, cover loosely with foil.) Take out and serve with a crisp green salad.

Serves 4

▼ Greek red such as Demestica, or one of Italy's more southern reds – Corvo, perhaps

Chef: Colin White *Proprietors:* Gwen and Colin White

JANE HOWARD

If you continue up the hill from White's, you will reach the Cathedral and, a few yards from it, a shop crammed with goodies. It is run with enthusiasm and efficiency by Jane Howard who, with her staff, is responsible for making a good proportion of the shop's contents. Jars of their own jams, chutneys and lemon curd line the shelves, with a special counter for homemade pâtés, taramasalata, quiches, curries, casseroles, salads, strudels, pies and cakes. Locally cured York and Bradenham hams (cooked at the shop), Parma ham, smoked salmon and Boston pork sausages are also available. One whole side of the shop is devoted to cheese, where over fifty varieties are featured (including eight different Bries, unusual Continental cheeses and various vegetarian ones).

ROTHAY MANOR

Ambleside, Cumbria

Lancashire and Cumbria have obvious links, both historical and geographical, but the most edible one is the succulent lamb 'hot pot'. Sometimes known as 'tatie pot', it has had many fans over the centuries, including John Peel, who claimed it was his favourite dish. In Cumbria, it is traditionally made with potatoes, black pudding, onions and local Herdwick lamb. It needs long, slow cooking so that the juices of the meat seep down through the vegetables and the potatoes on top become crisp and brown. To offset the richness, a large bowl of pickled red cabbage is usually served with it.

Rothay Manor is an obvious place to try Cumbrian hot pot as its owner and chef, Bronwen Nixon, is an expert on regional specialities. When she compiles the menu each morning, she chooses at least one Cumbrian dish or one gleaned from her vast collection of Georgian cookery books. As well as the popular favourites like Cumberland ham and Potted char, she might serve Grapes in wine jelly as a starter or Casseroled partridge as a main course. Alongside the four entrées on the menu, there will be several complementary wines from the manor's list. These are chosen by Bronwen's son Stephen. He is responsible for all the wine-buying at Rothay Manor, while his brother Nigel runs the restaurant.

Cumbrian Hot Pot

12 lamb chops *or* equivalent neck of mutton (allow 1½ chops per person)
1 pint (575ml) good meat stock
1 onion, thinly sliced
salt and pepper

2 medium onions, peeled
1 lb (450g) carrots, peeled
½ lb (225g) Cumberland sausage *or* pork sausage

2 teaspoons mixed herbs (if using fresh, include mint and sage)
salt and pepper
¾ lb (350g) black pudding (about 8 slices) if available
2 lb (900g) potatoes
chopped parsley

Preheat the oven to gas mark 4, 350°F (180°C). Trim the chops of excess fat and place in a shallow roasting tin. Cover with the stock and sliced onion. Season well with salt and freshly ground black pepper. Bake until the lamb is tender and falls easily off the bone (about 1 hour).

Increase the oven temperature to gas mark 5, 375°F (190°C). Carefully remove the bones and most of the fat. Put the meat into the bottom of a large casserole. Reserve the stock. Slice the onions and carrots thinly and cut the sausage into ½-inch (0.50cm) pieces. Arrange all of these on top of the meat and add a dusting of herbs and seasoning of salt and pepper. Put a layer of black pudding slices on top. Peel and slice the potatoes, reserving the end 'caps' for the top layer. Place the potato slices over the black pudding, putting the rounded 'caps' on last. Press down firmly. Fill up the casserole with the rich fatty stock from the chops and season well with salt and pepper. Bake until the potatoes are nicely browned (approximately 1–1½ hours). Take out, sprinkle with chopped parsley and serve with Mrs Nixon's pickled red cabbage (page 389).

Serves 8

🍷 A *vin du pays* or any other south of France red

Chef and proprietor: Bronwen Nixon

TULLYTHWAITE HOUSE

Underbarrow, Cumbria

The theory that people only go out to eat fancy or exotic food has been irrefutably disproved by the success achieved in the Lake District by Mrs Johnson. For three decades, she has been famous for the unpretentious cooking served from her farmhouse restaurant. She started first by serving teas in her old house, Hodge Hill, a few miles from where she is now. The queue of customers flocking to try her home-made breads, scones, jams, biscuits and cakes were ample proof of her expertise. She served over a hundred people a week and baked everything herself.

When Mrs Johnson moved to Tullythwaite House in 1964, she opened a few bedrooms and began taking over-night guests. With the help of her daughter-in-law, she served lunches and dinners, as well as teas. Again, everything was homemade with the emphasis on providing superlative home cooking. Four years ago, when the work load became too much, the two Mrs Johnsons decided to do only dinners and Sunday lunch. But the old favourites – Stilton soup, Jugged hare, Chicken pie and Pineapple meringue pudding (page 285) – remain pillars of the menu.

Though now a sprightly eighty-three, Mrs Johnson is still in the kitchen every day ('no one will ever do my vege-

232

tables') and makes the rounds after dinner to chat to the guests. The majority of the cooking is now done by her daughter-in-law and to assist them both is 'a little person' who comes daily to help with the starters and the washing-up. The two waitresses, who work alternate evenings, are as devoted to Tullythwaite as the Johnsons and have been there almost as long. They are both 'Mums' and Mrs Johnson despairs of ever getting youngsters with the same enthusiasm; she finds them all a bit too 'slaphazard'.

Jugged Hare

1 hare, skinned and cleaned
3 oz (75g) butter
salt
1 medium onion
8 cloves
1 glass claret *or* port wine
1 tablespoon lemon juice
6 peppercorns
bouquet garni (sprig of
   parsley, thyme, bay leaf)
1½ pints (850ml) stock
   (preferably game,
   otherwise chicken)
1 oz (25g) flour
salt and pepper

Forcemeat
2 oz (50g) rindless back
   bacon
¼ lb (100g) suet
3 teaspoons finely chopped
   parsley
rind of ½ lemon
1 teaspoon dried sweet
   herbs (basil, thyme etc.)
6 oz (175g) breadcrumbs
salt and pepper
2 eggs
2 oz (50g) butter

Preheat the oven to gas mark 4, 350°F (180°C). Cut the hare into small joints. Remove any membrane and wipe the joints well (any blood left on them will make the sauce curdle). Heat 2 oz (50g) of the butter in a frying pan and fry the joints, a few at a time, until well browned. Put them into a casserole with a little salt, the onion stuck with the cloves, half the wine, the lemon juice, peppercorns, herbs and the stock. Cover tightly and cook in the preheated

233

oven for about 3 hours. About 30 minutes before serving, knead the remaining butter with the flour and stir into the hot liquid in the casserole. Add the remaining wine and season to taste with salt and pepper. Bring up to the boil on top of the stove, boil for a minute or two, then replace the lid and return the casserole to the oven for the remaining cooking time.

Meanwhile, make the forcemeat balls: mince the bacon, suet, parsley, lemon rind and sweet herbs together. Mix in the breadcrumbs and a good seasoning of salt and pepper. Lightly beat the eggs and use to bind the mixture together. Shape into balls and fry in the butter in a deep frying pan for about 8 minutes, or until nicely browned.

When ready to serve, pile the hare joints on a hot dish. Strain the gravy and pour over. Arrange the forcemeat balls around the edge. Serve with redcurrant jelly.

Serves 6–8

♟ Red from Rioja

Chefs: Mary Johnson and Barbara Johnson
Proprietor: Mary Johnson

234

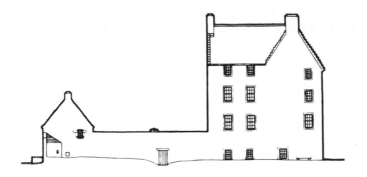

HOUSTOUN HOUSE

Uphall, West Lothian, Scotland

Though Keith Knight is in the kitchen every day and supervises the service of dinner, he is now principally involved with teaching his two young chefs, David McKendry and David Hamilton. He believes in teaching by example but knows from his own experience that the only way to learn is by actually having to do it yourself.

Keith trained as an architect, yet decided almost from the moment he graduated that he wanted to run a hotel more than anything else. To make a start in this direction, he went to work for Willie Heptinstall at Fortingall. Heptinstall had travelled extensively and worked in Parisian, Viennese and Hungarian restaurants. Consequently, his cooking style was cosmopolitan and his menus blended dishes of various nationalities.

The menu at Houstoun House shows the same interest in international cooking and is run along similar lines to Fortingall: set dinners and lunches with limited choice. The diversity of its sources can be seen in recipes like *Potage du Père Tranquille, Insalata de cavolfiore calda* (page 271), Virgin Island pie (page 330) and this *Brochette d'agneau marocaine*.

235

Brochette d'Agneau Marocaine

1 lb (450g) lamb gigot or
  chops, cut into 1-inch
  (2·5cm) cubes
4 rashers smoked rindless
  bacon
3–4 slices of pineapple
16 dates, stoned

Marinade
2 tablespoons oil
$\frac{1}{4}$ teaspoon ground cumin
pinch of ground cardamom
$\frac{1}{4}$ teaspoon ground
  cinnamon
$\frac{1}{4}$ teaspoon salt
$\frac{1}{2}$ clove of garlic, crushed
1 tablespoon lemon juice

Rice
a little oil
$\frac{1}{4}$ onion, peeled and finely
  chopped
1 breakfast cup long-grain
  rice
2 breakfast cups beef *or*
  lamb stock
salt and pepper

4 8-inch (20cm) skewers

Lime Sauce
$\frac{1}{4}$ onion, peeled and
  chopped
1 oz (25g) butter
four 8-inch (20cm) skewers
$\frac{1}{4}$ pint (150ml) double
  cream
juice of 2 limes (if
  unavailable, use 1
  lemon)
1 tablespoon desiccated
  coconut
salt and pepper
a little curry powder to taste

orange segments and
  watercress to garnish

Cut each bacon rasher into four and quarter the pineapple
slices. Thread each skewer with alternate pieces of lamb,
bacon, pineapple and date.

Mix the marinade ingredients in a bowl and pour over
the *brochettes*. Leave for 2–3 hours, turning the skewers at
regular intervals.

When ready to cook the rice, choose a saucepan with a tight-fitting lid. Add a little oil and fry the onion in it until softened. Add the rice and continue frying, turning the rice frequently, until it becomes opaque. Pour in the stock and add a good seasoning of salt and pepper. Bring up to the boil, then fit the lid on tightly and leave to simmer for precisely 17 minutes. By this time the liquid will have been absorbed and the rice will be ready to serve. Keep warm until needed.

To make the sauce: fry the onion in the butter until softened, then stir in the flour and cook for a minute or two. Blend in the cream and the lime or lemon juice. Bring up to the boil, stirring continuously, and simmer for 2 minutes. Stir in the coconut and season to taste with salt, pepper and curry powder. If necessary, thin with milk until the consistency of pouring cream.

Grill the brochettes, turning at intervals. (They will need about 7 minutes. The lamb should still be pink inside.) Serve on a bed of the hot rice, garnished with orange segments and watercress. Hand round the sauce separately.

Serves 4

▯ Any fairly basic red that takes your fancy

Chef: Keith Knight *Proprietors:* Penny and Keith Knight

BALLYMALOE

Shanagarry, Co. Cork, Eire

After living at Ballymaloe for sixteen years, the Allens were faced with such steep running costs that it became a choice between selling either some of the land or the house. Mrs Allen forestalled the decision with typical ingenuity. She put an advertisement in the local paper offering readers the opportunity to 'Dine in an Irish Country House'. The response was so enthusiatic that all members of the family were conscripted as waitresses, wine waiters, assistant cooks and bottle washers.

To start with, Mrs Allen offered a set menu of traditional dishes, based on produce from the farm. As her confidence and repertoire grew, she began serving lunches and adding choice to the menu. When the customers could no longer be squeezed into the main dining-room, another one was opened beside it and eventually bedrooms were made available to guests who seemed reluctant to leave.

Now, fifteen years on, the house has been completely converted to accommodate residential guests, though its essential character remains unchanged. The stable block has been transformed and so has the dower house at the end of the drive. At the height of the summer, there is always a full house, with about fifty guests in all.

238

Ballymaloe Pepper Beef Stew

6 rump *or* braising steaks, each about 5 oz (150g)

4 level teaspoons black peppercorns
4 teaspoons oil
1½ oz (40g) butter

2 medium onions, sliced
2 glasses dry white wine
¾ pint (425ml) good beef stock
2 cloves of garlic, crushed
salt

Preheat the oven to gas mark 4, 350°F (180°C). Crush the peppercorns and press them into the meat. Heat the oil in a large heavy casserole. When really hot, add the steaks (a few at a time) and sear for 2 minutes on each side. Lift out and put to one side. Wipe out the pot. Heat 1 oz (25g) of butter in the casserole and sauté the onions gently in it until soft and lightly coloured. Put the meat back in (with more crushed peppercorns if too many have been lost) with the wine, stock and garlic. Add salt to taste. Cover with a lid and cook gently in the preheated oven until the meat is tender (about 1½ hours).

When the meat is ready, lift it out on to a serving dish and keep warm. Reduce the sauce in the casserole by boiling quickly, then enrich with the remaining butter and check the seasoning again. When it reaches the right consistency (as thick or as thin as you like it), pour over the meat and serve at once with sauté potatoes and green salad.

Serves 6

♟ Claret, not necessarily anthing more special than AC bordeaux

Chef: Myrtle Allen *Proprietors:* Myrtle and Ivan Allen

PLUMBER MANOR

Sturminster Newton, Dorset

As *chef-patron* of Plumber Manor, Brian Prideaux-Brune must somehow satisfy the culinary demands of fifty people (sometimes more) five nights a week, in a county where there is virtually no other restaurant of this standard. Consequently, his menu must make a sporting effort to cater for all tastes, taking into consideration various-sized purses. The end result is a double-sided menu, with *à la carte* dishes on one page, a fixed price *table d'hôte* with a good deal of choice on the other. It is vaguely reminiscent of The Grange (King Street, Covent Garden) where Brian worked for two and a half years before leaving in 1973 to cook full-time at Plumber Manor. His kitchen apprenticeship was done under the eagle eye of Geoffrey Sharp, the man responsible for making The Grange as well known for its food as for its stylish David Hicks décor.

Main courses at Plumber Manor tend to be based on top-quality ingredients, cooked in a classic style. Beef Wellington, Chateaubriand, Escalope of veal with mushrooms and cream and Salmon hollandaise are now cornerstones of the menu. They are supplemented with Prideaux-Brune innovations: the Roast loin of pork with avocado, the *Carré d'agneau* with chestnut purée and burgundy sauce and the popular Chicken indienne.

240

Chicken Indienne

8 good-sized chicken
  breasts, boned
4 small bananas, finely
  sliced
24 white grapes, halved
  and pitted
4 tablespoons crushed
  hazelnuts
2 oz (50g) butter
12 fl oz (350ml) basic
  curry sauce (page 376)
8 fl oz (225ml) double
  cream

Preheat the oven to gas mark 5, 375°F (190°C). Remove the fillet (the underside 'flap') from the chicken breasts, then pound (not too vigorously) each breast until flat. Then flatten each fillet.

Stuff each breast with half a banana, 6 grape halves and $\frac{1}{2}$ tablespoon of crushed hazelnuts. Place the fillet on top and fold the ends over to make a rectangular parcel. Place the breasts, rounded side up, close together in a shallow roasting tin, in which 2 oz (50g) of butter has been melted. Bake in the preheated oven for 20–25 minutes, basting frequently, until cooked through and golden brown.

Make up the curry sauce (or use a prepared sauce) and whisk in the cream. Transfer the chicken to a shallow flameproof dish and pour over the sauce. Put over gentle heat until bubbling and slightly thickened. Remove from the heat and serve.

Serves 8

🍷 A medium dry white such as Vouray, or other Chenin Blanc

Chef: Brian Prideaux-Brune
Proprietors: Alison, Richard and Brian Prideaux-Brune

THE OLD HOUSE

Wickham, Hampshire

In the South of France, one feels compelled, either by the waiters or by the garlicky smell coming from the kitchen, to start at least one meal with the famed *bouillabaisse*. This rich concoction, more stew than soup, is made with several kinds of local fish, Provençal herbs, fennel, saffron, vegetables, garlic and wine. It is served with a thick knob of *rouille*, a smooth paste made from peppers, garlic and oil. It is undoubtedly true that because of the outstanding flavour and quality of these native ingredients, the soup never reaches the same perfection anywhere else in the world. In countries not blessed with the same profusion of fish and herbs, it is understandable that chefs should tailor the recipe to their own ingredients. At The Old House, Annie Skipwith uses chicken instead of fish as her *bouilla* base, with results that would come as a pleasant surprise to any Provençal fisherman.

The only drawback to a good *bouillabaisse* is that when served as a starter, it leaves very little room for main course or pudding. As a main course (which it is at The Old House) it can be consumed with gusto, with no fears of ruining the appetite.

Chicken Bouillabaisse

1 chicken about 2½–3 lb
(1–1·5 kilos), with its
liver
⅛ teaspoon ground saffron
2 tablespoons Pernod
8 tablespoons olive oil
salt and freshly ground
black pepper
2 medium onions, peeled
and sliced
4 cloves of garlic, crushed
6 tomatoes
1 small head of fennel
(white part only)

6 sprigs of parsley
4 medium potatoes, peeled
and chopped
4–6 slices French bread

Sauce Rouille

clove of garlic, peeled
4 small hot red peppers,
stalk end removed
2 fl oz (50ml) olive oil
1 tablespoon butter

Cut the chicken into 8 pieces and remove the skin. Put into a large flat dish or bowl. Mix the saffron, Pernod and 3 tablespoons of oil together and pour over. Season well with salt and pepper, then leave the chicken to marinate in this mixture for 30 minutes (turning the chicken from time to time).

Heat 3 tablespoons of oil in a large casserole and add the onions and garlic. Toss in the oil, then cook until barely golden. Skin the tomatoes, cut into quarters, remove the seeds and chop. Add to the pan and cook for 5 minutes, stirring frequently. Chop the fennel and parsley and stir in with the chicken pieces and their marinade. Add enough boiling water to cover the chicken. Season with salt, cover the casserole and bring to the boil. Reduce the heat and cook over low heat for 10 minutes. Add the potatoes and simmer covered for 20 minutes longer or until the chicken and potatoes are cooked. Remove the chicken and vegetables, keep warm. Reduce the liquid by boiling rapidly until slightly thickened.

Line a soup tureen with the sliced bread and sprinkle

the remaining oil over it. Pour the chicken, vegetables and sauce over the bread and keep hot.

To make the *sauce rouille*: put the garlic, hot peppers and olive oil into a liquidizer (or use a mortar and pestle). Blend until smooth . Sauté the chicken liver quickly in a little butter, then mash it well and add it to the garlic purée. Add 2 slices of potato from the *bouillabaisse* and blend or mash until the mixture is smooth again. Stir in 6 tablespoons of the *bouillabaisse* sauce and blend again. Serve the *sauce rouille* separately in a bowl.

Serves 4–6

☙ The dry rosés of Provence would go admirably

Chef: Colin Wood
Proprietors: Annie and Richard Skipwith

YE OLDE PORK SHOPPE

In the heart of Dorset is the town of Blandford Forum and Ye Olde Pork Shoppe. It lays an honest claim to the name as a pork shop has occupied this site since 1681. The present owners, Mr and Mrs Ford and their son Roger, moved from Derbyshire nine years ago, bringing the best pork pie traditions with them. All the pies sold in the shop are made by Roger in the kitchen at the back. Varieties include steak and kidney, chicken and ham, mushroom and bacon, cheese and onion, as well as the traditional pork pie. He makes four different types of sausage: pork, chipolata, English herb, pork and tomato, plus sausage rolls and pastries. Also displayed on the marble counter in the front of the shop are their own cured hams and bacon, black puddings, faggots, cold roast pork and brawn.

THE LLWYNDERW HOTEL

Abergwesyn, Powys, Wales

If you were to choose an idyllic setting for a country hotel, it could easily be the spot now occupied by The Llwynderw Hotel. A thousand miles above sea level, it sits on a hilltop in the heart of Powys lakeland, with views of nothing but sheep, palomino horses and rolling hills.

The setting, though Utopian, is not without its minor drawbacks. One forgets about suppliers who at the merest hint of precipitation abandon all promise of delivery, and about guests who, unused to Welsh signposts, arrive an hour late for dinner. Nor is it without pitfalls for the owner who, due to this very remoteness, is doubling as fire-officer, tax-gatherer, tea-lady, chief bottle-washer and innumerable other characters parts. On the occasions when he also becomes the chef, it is to find, inevitably, that the only ingredient crucial to the dinner's success is lying in a shop ten miles away.

But the natural attributes of Llwynderw outweigh all else and Michael Yates is anxious to preserve its tranquil character. His brochure makes it plain that this is a place for reading, bird-watching, walking, conversation and civilized eating. It is not for late-night sessions at the bar

245

(which there isn't), lounging in front of the television (which there is, but 'only for coronations') or impromptu meals (dinner is at 8 o'clock and must be booked in advance). It is run along the lines of an Edwardian hotel, where the proprietor's idiosyncrasies would stamp it as 'owner-run'. The guests whose feathers are ruffled by Mr Yates's 'hair-tax' (a supplement for those who bring dogs) are no doubt pacified by his cooking which produces purrs of contentment all round. Dinner is a four-course set meal, with no choice until the pudding stage (though there is occasionally an either/or choice of main course). The cooking leans towards Elizabeth David, Mrs Beeton and Escoffier (though not necessarily in that order) and is always of a high standard.

Prawns in Rice with a Nice Sauce

½ lb (225g) prawns
salt and black pepper
1 oz (25g) butter
1 teaspoon olive oil
3 oz (75ml) cooking
   brandy
¼ pint (150ml) double
   cream
few drops of lemon juice

pinch of grated nutmeg
½ lb (225g) long-grain rice
2–3 strips red pepper
a few black olives (in oil
   not brine)
2 oz (50g) Gruyère *or*
   Emmenthaler cheese

4 shallow ovenproof dishes *or* 1 small gratin dish, well buttered

Dry the prawns very well, then put into a bowl and sprinkle well with salt and pepper (toss to make sure it is evenly distributed). Melt the butter with the oil in a small frying pan and sauté the prawns in it for about 2 minutes (be careful not to overcook). Heat the cooking brandy and pour into the pan. Ignite the brandy and shake the pan vigorously (have a good blaze as this is what gives the delicious taste). Remove the prawns with a slotted spoon. Increase the heat and add the cream. Let it bubble until it thickens, scraping the bottom of the pan firmly but gently with a wooden spatula. Add a few drops of lemon juice and a pinch of nutmeg. Cover and keep warm.

Cook the rice according to the instructions on the packet (undercooking it slightly). Drain and put to one side. Blanch the strips of red pepper and dry. Halve the olives, remove the stones and chop them, with the pepper, finely. Put several spoonfuls of hot rice into each dish and top with a few prawns and chopped olive and pepper. Cover with the sauce and top with a small amount of grated Gruyère. Put under the grill until lightly browned (if cheese is very dry, dot with butter first). Serve at once, with a crisp green salad.

Serves 4

🍷 An Alsace wine

Chef and proprietor: Michael Yates

POPJOY'S

Bath, Avon

Stephen Ross, *chef-patron* of Popjoy's, is blessed with a team of suppliers who really care about food and take pride in producing top-quality ingredients. A local farmer delivers fresh herbs and vegetables to the back door every morning and a butcher up the road provides all the meat, even seemingly unobtainable cuts like noisettes of veal. 'The fish man' comes up from Cornwall every Thursday, bringing with him glistening sea bass, fresh lobster, crab and scallops. All the other fish comes from the market in Bath and consequently is simply billed on the menu as 'fresh fish according to the market'. The results of the shopping are described by Penny Ross (there are usually at least two, often three fish dishes offered every day) as you contemplate a menu already full of tempting prospects. Terrine of sole and salmon with *sauce verte* is a favourite, as is the Wye salmon poached in Muscadet, Brill with scallops and saffron and the *Oeuf Benedictine*.

Stephen Ross's version of the last differs slightly from the original Provençal dish. He makes a brandade of the smoked mackerel (instead of the traditional salt cod), garlic and olive oil, with poached egg and hollandaise sauce on top. It is rich and filling and would be suitable as a starter (followed by a light main course) or as a luncheon dish.

Popjoy's Oeuf Benedictine

½ lb (225g) smoked
  mackerel
rind and juice of 2 lemons
¼ pint (150ml) good olive
  oil
clove of garlic, crushed

salt and pepper
6 eggs
vinegar
6 tablespoons of
  hollandaise sauce
  (page 378)

6 ramekin dishes

Flake the mackerel well, being careful to remove all the skin and bones. Put it into a liquidizer or food processor with the lemon rind and juice, oil and garlic. Blend until you have a smooth purée. Season carefully as the fish tends to be salty.

Distribute the brandade equally in the bottom of the ramekins or cocotte dishes. Warm carefully in the oven, covering with foil if necessary. When your guests are ready to eat, poach the eggs in boiling water (you'll need two saucepans), to which a small amount of salt and vinegar have been added, for 2 minutes. Lift out with a slotted spoon and place an egg in each dish. Spoon over the hollandaise sauce and serve immediately with brown bread and butter.

Serves 6

🍷 Muscadet or any other basic dry white

Chef: Stephen Ross *Proprietors:* Penny and Stephen Ross

LE TALBOOTH

Dedham, Essex

Le Talbooth has an enviable roost: perched on the banks of the River Stour with a private view of the Vale of Dedham. With its timber frame and overhanging willows, it looks like the archetypal Constable painting and, not surprisingly, the house *was* painted by him (the picture now hangs in the National Gallery of Scotland). Built in the early sixteenth century, it didn't become a toll booth until about 1789.

When the present owner, Gerald Milsom, bought the house in 1952 it had become a tea shop, in sad repair. Undismayed by his first week's takings of 2*s* 6*d*, he soldiered on with light meals and teas for nine years, until the restoration work had been completed and he felt confident to re-open as a fully fledged restaurant. Since then, more changes have gradually been effected (in keeping with the style of the house) and the restaurant now consists of a riverside dining-room and bar, a new dining-room (suitably camouflaged) and two upstairs rooms which can be used for private parties and lunches.

An infusion of new blood arrived in 1976 in the shape of Sam Chalmers, a young head chef who trained at the Malmaison restaurant in Glasgow and at Gleneagles. The menu now bears his personal stamp and the cooking has won him stars in both the Michelin and Egon Ronay guides.

Soufflé Talbooth

Filling
1 oz (25g) butter
¼ lb (100g) button
   mushrooms, finely diced
¼ lb (100g) smoked
   haddock
¼ pint (150ml) single cream
salt and pepper
pinch of cayenne pepper

1½ oz (40g) butter
1 oz (25g) flour
8 fl oz (225ml) milk
1 oz (25g) Parmesan cheese
4 egg yolks
5 egg whites

4 large ramekin dishes, 4 inches (10cm) in diameter

Start by making the filling. Melt the butter in a medium saucepan and add the mushrooms. Cook until the mushrooms have softened and darkened in colour. Flake the haddock, taking care to remove all bones. Add to the pan with the cream and blend well. Season to taste with salt and pepper and add a pinch of cayenne pepper. Simmer gently over a low heat for about 10 minutes. Divide among the ramekins then put to one side.

Preheat the oven to gas mark 7, 425°F (220°C). In another saucepan, melt a further 1½ oz (40g) butter. Stir in the flour, then cook for a minute or two. Blend in the milk and cook over a moderate heat, stirring frequently, until the mixture thickens. Simmer for about 5 minutes, then add the cheese. Blend well, then leave to cool slightly. Slowly beat in the yolks, one at a time. Whisk the egg whites until very stiff and fold in lightly. Pile on top of the partially filled ramekins. Put straight into the preheated oven and bake for 12–15 minutes or until golden brown. Take out and serve at once.

Serves 4

🍷 An Italian white such as Orvieto or Frascati

Chef: Sam Chalmers *Proprietor:* Gerald Milsom

THE BEAR

Nayland, Suffolk

When asked who had taught him how to cook, Alexandre Dumas replied with characteristic solemnity, 'the greatest master of all – *La Necessité*'. Many country restaurateurs have shared the same tutor, with the choice of cooking well or being faced with an empty restaurant. It matters little whether they have had formal training; the proof is undeniably in the pudding. If it doesn't measure up, then the customers eat elsewhere.

Gerry Ford, one half of the husband and wife team who run The Bear restaurant in Nayland, trained first in agriculture, gaining a degree in animal husbandry and estate management. With no capital to buy his own farm and disliking the prospect of working for someone else, he and his wife Jane racked their brains for a job which would occupy them both. Being undisguised food-lovers and spare-time cooks, a restaurant seemed a good idea.

With a boldness which now, they admit, seems close to madness, they found a site in Colchester and after minimal decoration opened it in 1972 as 'Bistro Nine'. They decided wisely to concentrate on food which they personally liked and knew they could cook well. Modest dishes like Chicken and mushroom pie, Moussaka, Carbonnade of beef, Chocolate mousse and Apricot crumble soon became sellouts. Everything was homemade and the restaurant acquired a reputation for 'excellent food at reasonable prices'. Astonished by their success, the Fords decided to look for a larger place outside Colchester which would also accommodate their growing family.

In 1976, they opened The Bear in Nayland, a village with artistic, rather than gastronomic associations. Though originally intended to be a 'restaurant with rooms', the cooking and conversion of the house have proved so time-consuming that the bedrooms remain on the drawing board.

Pheasant Pie

1 pheasant, well hung
1½ pints (850ml) white stock *or* chicken *or* game stock
2 medium onions, peeled and chopped
2 sticks of celery, chopped
6 juniper berries
pinch of savory
pinch of thyme
¼ pint (150ml) medium dry white wine

2 oz (50g) garlic butter (page 73)
½ lb (225g) mushrooms, finely sliced
1 dessertspoon flour
1 tablespoon chopped fresh parsley
salt and pepper

½ lb (225g) shortcrust pastry (page 254)
egg wash

medium, deep pie dish

Soak the pheasant in salted water for a few hours or overnight. This removes the blood and improves the colour and flavour. Discard the salty water. In a covered pan, simmer the pheasant in the stock and add one chopped onion, one stick of chopped celery, four juniper berries, a pinch of savory, pinch of thyme and the wine.

When the pheasant is cooked (approximately 1 hour), remove from the pan and take the meat off the bones. Cut up into smallish pieces, removing any shot, gristle and tendons. Strain the stock and reduce to 1 pint (575ml) by quick boiling. Soften the second onion and piece of celery in the garlic butter over moderate heat. Add the mushrooms. Stir in the flour and add the hot stock, skimmed of fat. (This stock must be delicious as it is the basis of the pie.) Simmer for about 10 minutes and then add the diced pheasant, a little chopped parsley, the remaining juniper berries and a good seasoning of salt and pepper. Put this mixture into a pie dish and cover with shortcrust pastry. Cut a hole in the top to allow the steam to escape. Decorate with pastry leaves and glaze with egg wash. Keep the pie in the refrigerator until needed, then bake for 30–40 minutes in a moderate oven – gas mark 4, 350°F (180°C). (The liquid in the pie will certainly reduce and thicken during the final cooking, so make sure that there is plenty of juice and that it is not too thick.)

Serves 4

♟ A none-too-dry red such as Côtes-du-Rhône

French Leek Flan

Filling
1½ lb (675g) leeks
clove of garlic
2 tablespoons olive oil
1 oz (25g) butter
2 eggs
4 fl oz (100ml) double cream
2 oz (50g) Gruyère, grated
salt and pepper
pinch of powdered mace

½ lb (225g) plain flour
pinch of salt
6 oz (175g) butter, slightly
　softened
1 egg yolk
1 tablespoon cold water

9-inch (23cm) flan case, lightly buttered

254

Sieve the flour and salt into a basin and rub in the butter. Mix the egg yolk with the water and add to the flour. Combine ingredients with a fork and turn out on to a lightly floured surface. Knead the mixture gently until smooth, then roll into a ball. Wrap in cling film and leave to rest in a cold place for at least 1 hour.

When ready to bake the flan case, preheat the oven to gas mark 5, 375°F (190°C). Bring the pastry to room temperature, then roll out thinly and use to line the buttered tin. Prick the base lightly with a fork and line firmly with silver foil. Fill with dried beans and bake in the preheated oven until amost cooked (15–20 minutes). Remove the beans and foil and cool slightly before filling with the leek mixture.

Reduce the oven temperature to gas mark 4, 350°F (180°C). Roughly chop the cleaned leeks and the garlic. Put the olive oil and butter into a large pan, add the leeks and garlic and cover with a lid. Cook slowly until they have softened. In the meantime, whisk the eggs, cream and two-thirds of the Gruyère together. Liquidize the leeks with the egg mixture. Taste and season well with salt, pepper and mace. Pour into the prepared flan case and top with the remaining cheese. Bake in the preheated oven for 15–20 minutes or until firm and golden in colour.

Serves 8

🍷 A fairly spicy white such as Yugoslav Riesling or Baden wine

Chefs and proprietors: Jane and Gerry Ford

THE HUNGRY MONK

Jevington, West Sussex

This recipe may be one reason why there are no longer any hungry monks in West Sussex. The old habits are gone and the new are being created by Ian Dowding and Kent Austin. Both in their twenties, they seem wedded to the 'Monk' (Ian has been there since it opened, ten years ago) and between them, they have devised literally hundreds of recipes for the restaurant. Many of these are original; others are variations on a traditional theme. Very few stay the same and most evolve gradually or accidentally (as often happens when reliant on country supplies).

Like figures in an Austrian clock, one goes off as the other comes on (they each work three and a half days a week, overlapping at Sunday lunch). Their kitchen is the size of a large shoebox and it's a wonder they haven't been driven to *cuisine minceur* as a result. In this Lilliputian space, Ian or Kent produce, on average, fifty-five dinners a night. They share an inventive streak which appears to be irrepressible. Like two professors, they seem engaged in a never-ending series of culinary experiments. Their recipes are imaginative and straight-forward, though some require a bottle of wine in one hand, a jug of cream in the other. Collections of their recipes have been published (at the request of contented diners) in three slim volumes illustrated by 'Brother Grahame' who provides a well-fed-monk's eye of the food.

256

Sue and Nigel Mackenzie, who founded and still run The Hungry Monk, are frequent visitors to America. This is one of the recipes that came back in their baggage and has since been adapted to West Sussex specifications.

Hungry Monk Chicken Pie

3-lb (1·5 kilos) chicken
1 onion, peeled and sliced
1 carrot
1 bay leaf
1 bouquet garni
salt and pepper

2 sweet red pimentos
2 oz (50g) butter
½ lb (225g) mushrooms, sliced

2 oz (50g) flour
¼ lb (100g) cooked peas
4 hard-boiled eggs, peeled and chopped

12–13 oz (350–375g) puff pastry (for homemade, see page 386)
1 egg, lightly beaten
4 fl oz (100ml) milk

large, deep pie dish

Put the chicken in a large saucepan with the onion, carrot, bay leaf, bouquet garni, a good seasoning of salt and pepper and just enough water to cover it. Bring up to simmering point, cover with a lid and poach gently for 1 hour. Lift the chicken out and put to one side to cool. Reserve the stock.

Cut the pimentos into short, thin strips. Melt the butter in a large saucepan, then add the pimentos and fry for a moment or two. Add the mushrooms and continue cooking until they have softened and darkened in colour. Stir in the flour and cook for 2–3 minutes. Strain the chicken stock and gradually blend in 1 pint (575ml) of it. When it has all been incorporated, bring up to the boil and allow to bubble for a few seconds. Remove from the heat and add the peas and hard-boiled eggs. Season to taste with salt and freshly ground black pepper. Put to one side while you remove the meat from the chicken and chop into medium chunks. Carefully blend the chicken into the sauce and check the seasoning again. Transfer the mixture to a deep pie dish.

Roll out the puff pastry to fit the pie dish. Place over the filling, trim the edges with a sharp knife and cut a small hole in the centre for the steam to escape. Use the pastry trimmings to decorate the top. Mix the egg and milk together and use to brush the entire pastry surface. Chill until needed, then bake in a preheated oven – gas mark 7, 425°F (220°C) – for 30 minutes or until the pastry is golden brown.

Serves 6

Ⓨ Hock would be ideal

Chefs: Ian Dowding and Kent Austin
Proprietors: Susan and Nigel Mackenzie

THE VILLAGE STORE

Close to The Hungry Monk is a shop which would answer a thousand cooks' prayers. The Village Store in Alfriston is an old-fashioned grocers with turn-of-the-century mahogany fittings, brass scales, antique biscuit cabinet and hanging chalk boards for special offers. The cold counter features cooked meats, home-cooked ham on the bone, homemade sausage rolls, pasties and flans (any size, any filling to order) and a good range of English and French cheeses. Local vegetables, fruit, dairy products, honey and bread, plus home-grown herbs, are also sold. The sweets are equally old-fashioned with stocks of liquorice laces, sherbet fountains and homemade fudge. They even have a shelf of cookery books for customers to consult when recipe ingredients are forgotten.

THE CARVED ANGEL

Dartmouth, Devon

There is more connecting The Carved Angel in Dartmouth and The Riverside in Helford than the Devon-Cornwall coastline. The former's chef, Joyce Molyneux, spent many years cooking at The Hole in the Wall, the restaurant made famous by George Perry-Smith before he moved, six years ago, to the Riverside. They are now partners in each other's enterprises and Tom Jaine, manager of The Carved Angel and a Perry-Smith relation, provides a familial tie as well. While the restaurants couldn't be more different in appearance (one a cosy Cornish cottage, the other streamlined, with Scandinavian décor), their cooking is on a similar wavelength.

Elizabeth David, particularly through her *French Provincial Cooking* and *French Country Cooking*, has been a mentor to both Joyce Molyneux and Perry-Smith. Her interest in simple country cooking, unaffected by *haute cuisine* and the '*pompeuses bagatelles de la cuisine masquée*', is one they share. Freshness and top quality ingredients are the only gods they worship; after that the variety of dishes which can be created from country produce is infinite. It is essentially *cuisine bourgeoise*, with hare, rabbit, goose, duck, oxtail, tongue and all types of fish featuring regularly. The style is distinctly Provençal, with its specialities forming the back-

259

bone of the menu. The thick, garlicky *aioli* turns up in the *Tarte à la bourride* or an unusual *Bourride* of chicken (a garlic sauté, finished with *aioli*) or a simple dish of Brill, *aioli* and vegetables. Habitués plump for the *Soupe de poisson*, made not from the traditional *rascasse* but at least two different types of local fish, topped with a peppery knob of *rouille* and garlic croûtons. Further traces of Provence are found in *La queue de boeuf des vignerons* – an oxtail cooked slowly with white grapes, producing a sauce of rich colour and flavour.

The Carved Angel's *Tarte à la bourride* (thick chunks of fish, lightly coated in an *aioli* sauce and piled gracefully into a crisp pastry case) is served in a dish made by Colin Kellam, an outstanding potter who lives in nearby Totnes.

Tarte à la Bourride

Aioli

clove of garlic
salt
1 egg yolk
juice of ¼ lemon
¼ pint (150ml) olive oil

Sauce Rouille

1 tinned pimento
1 fresh chili, seeded
2 teaspoons olive oil
salt and pepper

4 shortcrust pastry cases,
   each about 4 inches
   (10cm) in diameter,
   baked blind

Filling

1½ oz (40g) chopped onion
2 tablespoons olive oil
3 oz (75g) tomato, skinned
   and sliced
1 fl oz (25ml) white wine
pinch of saffron
1 tablespoon chopped
   parsley
squeeze of lemon juice
salt and pepper
½ lb (225g) fillet of brill *or*
   turbot

chopped parsley and
   lemon wedges to garnish

Start by making the *aioli*. Pound the clove of garlic with a pinch of salt in a mortar. Add the yolk and the lemon juice. Using a small whisk, gradually add the oil as in making mayonnaise.

Make the *sauce rouille* by mixing all its ingredients in an electric blender until smooth. It should taste very hot, so another chili may be required if they are mild.

For the tart filling, sweat the onion in olive oil for about 3 minutes until soft but not coloured. Add the tomato, wine, saffron, parsley, lemon juice and seasoning to make a tasty mixture. Put the tart cases in a moderate oven to warm. Cut the fish into about twelve pieces and lay them in a dish. Pour over the onion sauce. Cover and cook on top of the stove for 5 minutes, or in the moderate oven – gas mark 4, 350°F (180°C) – for 12 minutes, until just tender. Drain off the liquid into a small saucepan and reduce by boiling to half its original volume. Add the *aioli* and whisk it over a gentle heat until it thickens. (It must not boil.) Check the seasoning and adjust if necessary. Put the fish into this sauce, turning gently, then divide the whole between the heated tart cases. Top with a teaspoon of *sauce rouille* and a sprinkling of chopped parsley. Serve with a wedge of lemon.

Serves 4

🍷 A crisp, dry, fairly neutral white such as Soave or Sylvaner

Chef: Joyce Molyneux
Proprietors: Joyce Molyneux and Tom Jaine

LA POTINIÈRE

Gullane, East Lothian, Scotland

La Potinière, for those whose French stops at *Encore une bouteille* and *C'est la vie*, roughly translated means 'the gossip shop': a place, like any French café, where you can go to eat, drink and chat for hours on end. The Scottish version, well camouflaged in the seaside town of Gullane, defines this more precisely, limiting the food, wine and chatter to Saturday evening and lunchtime during the week. It may be regarded as eccentric by the locals but it doesn't stop them beating a path to its door, along with food-lovers from afar. It could, with ease, be transplanted to any village in France and only the *patron*'s Scottish accent would betray its origins. The standard of both food and wine would satisfy the most exacting Gallic *gourmand* and the serving of cheese before the pudding would win his heart completely.

Quiche au Stilton

2½ oz (65g) margarine, at
    room temperature
2½ oz (65g) butter, at room
    temperature
½ lb (225g) plain flour
1 level tablespoon icing
    sugar
1 large egg (size 2)

Filling
1 large onion, peeled
3 oz (75g) back bacon
½ oz (15g) butter
6 oz (175g) Stilton
2 large eggs
1 egg yolk
½ pint (275ml) double
    cream
salt and pepper

9-inch (23cm) flan tin with removable base

Start by making the pastry. Place the fats in a bowl. Cream together using an electric whisk. Sift the flour and icing sugar into the bowl and add the egg. Beat at medium speed until *just* mixed together (it should form large lumps rather than being over-mixed). Knead very gently on a lightly floured work surface, then chill slightly.

Preheat the oven to gas mark 5, 375°F (190°C). Roll out the pastry and line the tin in your usual way. Prick the base lightly, then chill again for at least 30 minutes. Bake blind in the preheated oven. To avoid a soggy base, bake the pastry case completely (about 20–25 minutes), rather than leaving it slightly undercooked. Put to one side. Turn up the oven to gas mark 6, 400°F (200°C).

Finely chop the onion and bacon. Cook both in the butter until the onion has softened. Allow to cool. Using a very sharp knife, finely slice the Stilton. (This will be much easier if you put the cheese in the freezer for 30 minutes beforehand.) The finer the slices, the lighter the quiche. Beat together the eggs, yolk and cream with a good sprinkling of salt and pepper.

Place the onion and bacon in an even layer in the cooked pastry case (still in the tin) and cover with the Stilton. Ladle the cream mixture gently over the cheese. Carefully place the quiche in the preheated oven. Bake for 10 minutes, then turn the setting down to gas mark 4, 350°F (180°C) and bake for a further 20 minutes until puffy, golden and set.

Serves 8

🍷 Minervois, Roussillon, Corbières or thereabouts

Chef: Hilary Brown *Proprietors:* Hilary and David Brown

VIN SULLIVAN AND SON

This is a shop that has to be seen to be believed. Started by Vin Sullivan in 1960, it is now run by his wife and son, John. Their vigour and enthusiasm seem inexhaustible and no request is too much trouble. The shop is stocked with fifty different types of vegetable, coming from as far afield as Italy, Cyprus, East Africa and Carolina. In addition to native fruits, there is a huge selection of exotic ones, including passion fruit, paw-paws, kiwis, persimmons, pomegranates, fresh dates and figs. Fish and game are a speciality and the range provided is mind-boggling. Poussin, goslings, Norfolk duckling, guinea fowl, mallard, partridge, smoked quail and smoked turkey are just a sampling of what is available. Every imaginable wet fish is on offer, plus copious smoked and shellfish. The displays are dazzling, the quality top-class.

Vegetables

It is in the matter of vegetables and fruit that a country's eating habits evolve most rapidly.

Elizabeth David

There seems to be a well-established myth, no doubt perpetrated by small boys and fruit-growers, that no one really likes vegetables. They are regarded as the least interesting half of 'meat and two veg' and have therefore to play a delicate balancing act. Restaurateurs, in all but the most sophisticated establishments, have pandered to our prejudices and provided a most circumspect selection.

It is only recently that spinach has been seen in public, with carrots, cabbage and parsnips all making a comeback. Courgettes, *mange-touts*, salsify and aubergines are now not rarities but popular favourites on any country restaurant menu. This is, on the whole, the result of dedicated efforts by chefs and restaurateurs to woo their customers to more exotic fruits of the earth. With skill and imagination they have produced vegetable dishes which are as attractive as they are delicious and no longer the bland 'window dressing' for the main course.

Nouvelle cuisine has had enormous influence in making chefs and customers think again of the plate as a palette. Colours, and their combination with various flavours and textures, have gained a new importance. It is now the chef, like the artist, who determines the composite picture. Instead of offering vegetables *à la carte*, he will serve the freshest available that day, choosing them carefully to complement the main dishes. While this may restrict the choice, it guarantees that 'a selection of fresh vegetables' will mean exactly that. It is by far the most sensible policy for a country restaurant, dependent on irregular supplies, who might otherwise have to rely on frozen food.

Cooking methods have evolved at the same time, making it possible to highlight individual textures and to prevent a uniform consistency of mashed potato. The crunch of vegetables is now kept intact (and so, consequently, are the vitamins and colour) and cooking them no longer means their death by drowning. Cabbage, the most maligned of all vegetables, now turns up in a variety of guises: stir-fried with garlic and juniper berries, sautéed in butter and finished with a dollop of soured cream, or baked in the oven with apples, onions and cider.

Chefs still have to contend with a large section of the dining public who feel that vegetables shouldn't be 'messed about'. Anything more unusual than cauliflower cheese is greeted with the utmost suspicion (this is not why, incidentally, most country restaurants have dim lighting). To encourage a more adventurous spirit, country *patrons* have cleverly included their selection of vegetables in the price of the meal. If steaming hot dishes of *mange-touts*, roast parsnips and creamed spinach arrive at the table, they will be consumed with pleasure and alacrity. However, if those same vegetables had to be *ordered*, few would leave the kitchen.

The wealth of this glorious vegetable 'revival' is amply demonstrated in the pages which follow.

266

KINCH'S
Purée of Jerusalem Artichokes

2 lb (900g) Jerusalem
   artichokes
1 lb (450g) potatoes

¼ lb (100g) butter
sea salt and pepper

chopped parsley to garnish

Peel the artichokes (or scrub well) and potatoes, then chop
roughly. Put into separate pans with a good sprinkling of
sea salt and a small amount of water. Cover and cook
quickly until tender. Drain very well, then purée both
vegetables together with the butter. Season to taste with
salt and pepper. Garnish with finely chopped parsley.

Serves 6–8

GRAVETYE MANOR
Creamy Beetroot

1½ lb (675g) fresh raw
   beetroot
salt and pepper

freshly chopped chives to
   garnish

Sauce
½ pint (275ml) double
   cream
pinch of finely chopped
   fresh basil
juice of ½ a lemon
salt and freshly ground
   black pepper
2 oz (50g) unsalted butter

Peel the beetroot and slice thinly into baton shapes. Cook
in a small amount of water until soft. Drain well, season

with salt and black pepper and keep warm.

To make the sauce, pour the double cream into a saucepan and simmer gently, stirring occasionally, until reduced by a third. Blend in the basil and lemon juice, then season to taste with salt and pepper. Just before serving, whisk in the butter. Pour the sauce over the beetroot and sprinkle with chopped chives.

Serves 4–6

MILLER HOWE

Fried Brussels Sprouts with Chestnuts

---

1 lb (450g) Brussels sprouts $\frac{1}{2}$ lb (225g) fresh chestnuts
4 tablespoons bacon fat

Remove any wilting outer leaves from the Brussels sprouts. Slice off their bases, and cut a small criss-cross on their bottoms with a sharp, stainless steel knife. Add them to boiling, salted water, bring back to the boil and simmer for 3–6 minutes according to their size – but do *not* overcook. When you want to serve them, have some bacon fat melted in a small frying pan and toss the sprouts in it until they are browned on the outside.

Meanwhile, place the chestnuts in a bowl and cover them with boiling water. Remove two at a time and, using a small sharp knife, remove the outer shell and the inner skin. It's quite a simple process, really, provided you work quickly and don't let the water go cold (otherwise you have to throw out the water and repeat the process).

Chop the chestnuts and mix them in with the browned sprouts and bacon fat. Serve as soon as possible.

Serves 4

MILLER HOWE

Baked Cabbage
with Garlic and Juniper

2 lb (900g) white cabbage
8 juniper berries
2 large cloves of garlic,
   peeled

½ teaspoon sea salt
2 tablespoons olive oil

Preheat the oven to gas mark 7, 425°F (220°C). Remove the outer leaves and cut the cabbage into four. Cut out the firm, hard stalk from each quarter and slice the cabbage very finely with a sharp stainless-steel knife. In a pestle and mortar (or liquidizer) pound (or blend) the berries with the garlic and sea salt until you get a smooth paste.

Just cover the bottom of a 9-pint (5-litre) saucepan or ovenproof casserole with the olive oil and heat through. Put in the juniper-garlic mixture and stir sharply with a wooden spoon. Add the finely sliced cabbage and stir-fry for 3–5 minutes until the cabbage is well coated with oil, then bake in the preheated oven for about 15 minutes. (If you like very crisp vegetables, just stir-fry in the sauce-pan for about 3 minutes – the flavour is by then imparted to the cabbage and as the vegetable is so finely chopped, it will have heated through.)

A firm white cabbage of this size will give you quite a generous serving and this dish is delicious warmed through the next day and served with French dressing.

Serves 4–6

KINCH'S

Red Cabbage

½ red cabbage
½ large onion
2 dessert apples
handful of raisins
2 tablespoons red wine
    vinegar

4 tablespoons water
1 tablespoon brown sugar
salt and pepper

Shred the cabbage, then peel the onion and slice thinly. Peel and core the apples and cut into thick slices. Put the cabbage, onion, apple and raisins into a large heavy saucepan and sprinkle the wine vinegar, water and brown sugar over them. Shake the pan to distribute evenly, then cover and cook rapidly, stirring from time to time, until the cabbage is just tender (this will take about 1½ hours, but the cabbage should be *al dente*, not soggy). Season to taste with salt and pepper and keep warm until needed.

Serves 6

THE PLOUGH INN

Carrots with Lemon and Nutmeg Glaze

1 lb (450g) carrots
1 tablespoon salt
2 tablespoons finely
    chopped onion

1 oz (25g) butter
1 scant teaspoon sugar
1 scant teaspoon salt

freshly ground black
  pepper
1 teaspoon lemon juice

freshly grated nutmeg
plenty of finely chopped
  parsley

Wash and trim the carrots. If using small new ones, leave them whole. Otherwise cut into halves or quarters to resemble the size of new ones. Place in a steamer over a saucepan half full of boiling water to which 1 tablespoon of salt has been added. Steam for 10–15 minutes until just tender. Meanwhile, in another wide saucepan, gently fry the onion in the butter until soft and translucent but not coloured. Add the sugar and stir to dissolve, maintaining a gentle heat throughout. Add the scant teaspoon salt, several turns of black pepper, the lemon juice, a sprinkling of freshly grated nutmeg and chopped parsley. Mix together well, then add the carrots, turning gently until evenly coated with the butter mixture.

Serves 4

HOUSTOUN HOUSE

Hot Cauliflower Salad

1 large firm cauliflower
6 tablespoons olive oil
clove of garlic, finely
  chopped
$\frac{1}{2}$ teaspoon French mustard

2 tablespoons wine vinegar
2 egg yolks
1 teaspoon finely chopped
  parsley
salt and pepper

Trim a firm white cauliflower and soak it in cold water for 30 minutes. Divide it into florets and cook in boiling salted water (enough almost to cover them), taking care not to overcook or break the pieces. Drain them well and reassemble in the semblance of a whole cauliflower.

While the cauliflower cooks, heat the oil in a pan and steep the garlic in it, being careful not to let it brown. Whisk in the mustard, vinegar, egg yolks, parsley and a good seasoning of salt and pepper. Continue whisking until thick and hot, then pour over the cauliflower and serve.

Serves 4–6 (depending on size of cauliflower)

THE CARVED ANGEL

Celeriac Croquettes

1 lb (450g) celeriac
½ lb (225g) potato
salt
1 egg yolk
pepper

egg wash
dried breadcrumbs
fat for frying

Peel and cut the celeriac and potato. Put into a saucepan with a sprinkling of salt and a small amount of water. Cook until tender, then drain well and put through the fine plate of a mouli or sieve. Mix in the yolk and check the seasoning, adding a little pepper. Shape into neat croquettes on a floured board.

Make an egg wash by mixing one or two eggs together and seasoning with salt and pepper. Dip the croquettes into the egg wash, then roll in the dried breadcrumbs. Allow them to set for 1 hour before frying them in deep fat until they are golden brown.

Makes approximately 12 croquettes

ROTHAY MANOR

Dressed Cucumber

1 large cucumber
½ onion, finely chopped
1 oz (25g) cooked ham,
 finely chopped
salt and pepper
½ oz (15g) butter

several tablespoons chicken
 stock
1 egg
2 tablespoons cream *or* top
 of the milk
½ teaspoon lemon juice

large casserole with lid

Preheat the oven to gas mark 4, 350°F (180°C). Rinse the cucumber and wipe dry. Trim the ends off, then chop (no need to peel) into medium dice. Put into a bowl and mix in the onion and ham. Season well with salt and pepper. Generously butter a large casserole dish and put the vegetables and ham in it, moistened with several table-spoons of stock. Cover and cook in the preheated oven for 30–45 minutes.

Lightly beat the egg and mix together with the cream and lemon juice. Pour over the cooked cucumber and return to the oven for 10–15 minutes or until lightly set. Serve at once.

Excellent with roast gammon, pork or beef.

Serves 4

JOCKEY HALL

Cucumber à la Crème

1 large cucumber
2 oz (50g) butter
½ oz (15g) flour

¼ pint (150ml) single cream
salt and white pepper

Peel the cucumber and cut into 1-inch (2·5cm) cubes. Put in a saucepan with half the butter. Cover with a piece of buttered paper and cook gently until the cucumber is tender.

In another saucepan, melt the remaining butter. Stir in the flour to make a roux and cook for 1 minute. Blend in the cream and cook for another minute. Add the cucumber with all the pan juices. Mix thoroughly with a wooden spoon and season well with salt and white pepper, then serve.

Serves 4

ROTHAY MANOR

Creamed Parsnips and Cheese

2 lb (900g) parsnips
2 oz (50g) butter
good pinch of freshly
  grated nutmeg
pinch of dry mustard

salt and pepper
2 tablespoons cream
¼ lb (100g) grated cheese

Peel and slice the parsnips and boil in a small amount of water until soft. Drain completely, then mash well with the butter. Add the nutmeg and mustard, then season with salt and lots of freshly ground black pepper. Just before serving, mix in the cream and the grated cheese. Put over a low heat until the cheese has melted completely and then serve when piping hot.

Serves 6

WHITE'S

Paysanne

4 sticks of celery	2 oz (50g) streaky, rindless
½ lb (225g) carrots	bacon
½ lb (225g) courgettes	a little olive oil
½ lb (225g) leeks	salt and pepper
½ lb (225g) tomatoes	chopped parsley

Wash the celery and peel the carrots, then chop them both into thin finger-lengths. Wash the courgettes and leeks, then chop into rounds. Rinse the tomatoes and chop roughly.

Cook the celery separately in lightly salted boiling water, then lift out, drain well, and put to one side. Dice the bacon and put into a frying pan. Heat until the fat runs, then add a little olive oil and the carrots. Cover with a lid and leave on gentle heat until the carrots are half-cooked. Add the courgettes and leeks and continue cooking (with a lid), shaking the pan frequently, until they are almost cooked. Remove the lid, add the tomatoes and cook briskly for a further 5 minutes. Add the celery (well drained) and season well with salt and freshly ground black pepper. Sprinkle generously with choppped parsley and serve.

Serves 4

MALLORY COURT

Gratin Dauphinois

---

1 oz (25g) butter
2 lb (900g) potatoes
  (Desirée for preference)
salt and freshly ground
  black pepper
3 oz (75g) finely grated
  Cheddar *or* Swiss cheese

large clove of garlic, finely
  chopped
½ pint (275ml) double
  cream *or* ¼ pint (150ml)
  single, ¼ pint (150ml)
  double

10-inch (25cm) oval gratin *or* ovenproof dish

Preheat the oven to gas mark 1, 250°F (130°C). Use half the butter to grease the gratin dish well. Peel the potatoes and cut into ⅛-inch (·25cm) slices.

Arrange layers of the potato in the dish, seasoning each layer with salt and black pepper, cheese and garlic. End with a sprinkling of cheese and the remaining butter, dotted over the top. Pour over the cream and bake in the preheated oven for about 1½ hours or until tender and golden.

Serves 6

BOWLISH HOUSE

Rosti

---

4 medium-sized old
  potatoes
1 onion, peeled

salt and pepper
a little olive oil
knob of butter

Boil the potatoes (without washing them) by covering with cold water, bringing to the boil and simmering until cooked through. Drain and allow to cool. Peel the potatoes, then grate them, using a coarse grater. Chop the onion finely and mix in with the potato and a good seasoning of salt and pepper.

Put a thin layer of olive oil into a heavy 6-inch (15cm) frying pan and, when smoking, add a good knob of butter and the potato mixture (this must be done quickly before the butter burns). Trim the sides of the 'cake' but do not press down. When the underside is nicely browned, turn over and brown the other side. Then reduce the heat and cook gently for 5 minutes. Turn out on to a plate and serve at once.

Particularly delicious with roast meats.

Serves 4

TULLICH LODGE

Stovies

A marvellous dish for a cold day. Much better than the lowly ingredients would indicate.

3 oz (75g) roast beef dripping, with sediment	3 lb (1·5 kilos) potatoes
	7 oz (200ml) water
2 medium onions	1 teaspoon salt
2 oz (50g) roast trimmings (scrapings from the bones etc.) *or* if unavailable, streaky bacon	freshly ground black pepper

Melt the dripping in a large heavy frying pan. Peel and chop the onions finely. Add to the pan and cook until golden. Add the trimmings from the roast and continue cooking for a minute or two. Peel the potatoes and cube roughly. Put into the pan and toss well in the fat. Pour in the water (a little gravy may be included) and season well with salt and black pepper. Cover and cook slowly for about 30 minutes, turning occasionally.

Serves 8

BALLYMALOE

Swedes and Bacon

2 large swedes, about 4 lb
   (1·8 kilos) total weight
salt and pepper
3 oz (75g) butter

6 thick smoked rindless
   bacon rashers

Peel the swedes and discard the root end. Chop roughly. Put into a saucepan with several inches of water and a good sprinkling of salt. Cover and cook until soft (adding more water if necessary). Drain, then season to taste with salt and freshly ground black pepper. Add the butter and mash until smooth.

Cut the bacon rashers into small dice. Fry in a large sauté pan until coloured, then lift out and keep warm. Add the swedes to the same pan and fry them until they brown, turning frequently. (The flavour will improve enormously as they cook.) Return the bacon to the pan and mix into the swedes well. Keep warm until needed, then serve with meat or poultry.

Serves 6–8

Desserts

... Or take the abundance of sweet trolleys. It is
in adverse proportion to the quality of desserts. It
reflects the British customer as a gastronomic voyeur
rather than a discerning eater. But the best sweets
are often to be found where trolleys are absent ...

from The Egon Ronay Guide 1980,
Egon Ronay

One of the most vociferous battles amongst country
restaurateurs is fought over the sweet trolley. To be
with or without one is a delicate question.

Those in favour claim that it is rolling dynamite:
no one, not even the most invincible weight-watcher,
has the power to resist it. Loaded with Black Forest
cake, Crème caramel and Hazelnut meringue, it leaves
few calorie counters in its wake. Even those determined
to have only coffee are bound to have second thoughts

when the chocolate mousse and fresh figs are wheeled by. Equally popular with the chefs, it means they can hand the trolley over to the waiters early in the evening, abdicating all further responsibility. It also keeps the accountants happy as customers are far more likely to have a sweet if confronted with a selection than if they had to order one from the menu.

Those in the opposing camp feel that it is impossible to keep a sweet trolley from looking like something a dog-tired waiter dragged in by the end of the evening. Once the mousse has collapsed, the flan is half gone and the meringue has crumbled, resurrection requires a miracle. They insist that being without a trolley means greater flexibility, enabling them to serve steaming hot or chilled puddings straight from the oven or cold room.

The diplomats take the middle road by offering a modest sweet trolley, backed up by a few hot and cold desserts served from the kitchen. Paul McCluskey at Jockey Hall produces one of the most devastating sweet trolleys ever, yet it has only four dishes on it. They are all small masterpieces, each looking more tempting than the next. But if you happen to be short-sighted or feverish, he also provides homemade rum and raisin ice-cream and a selection of sorbets. At No. 3 in Glastonbury, everything is removed from the trolley when not in use, but as quality is far greater than quantity, this doesn't entail an endless parade of sweets from the kitchen. Another trolley to confound the critics is the one at Ballymaloe from which Mrs Allen serves her famous Irish Mist soufflé in a bowl made completely of ice (she also manages to keep both from melting).

On the whole, the majority of country restaurants (certainly those in this book) seem to be veering away from the sweet trolley and plumping instead for a smallish, frequently changing list of desserts. The standard favourites like profiteroles, meringues and lemon mousse are being supplemented with more daring alternatives: Iced cherry soufflé, *Fromage à la crème*, Grapefruit and Pernod syllabub. At the same time, there has been a revival of interest in old-fashioned 'puds' with 'Can't Leave Me Alone', Norfolk treacle tart and Sticky toffee pudding all making frequent appearances. The quality of homemade ice-creams and sorbets has improved dramatically and a selection has been included in this chapter to illustrate their range and the ease with which they can be made.

WELLS STORES

The cheeseboard at many restaurants would be a shadow of its present size were it not for Major Pat Rance and his Wells Stores. This tiny shop, ostensibly a 'family grocer' in Streatley-on-Thames, houses a small mountain of cheese. Considered by many to be the finest cheese shop in the British Isles, it stocks over 150 varieties. Amongst them are at least thirty British ones, collected from all parts of the country. A sign on the counter advising customers to 'taste before they buy' encourages the timid and the curious. Major Rance is passionate about his subject and as well as running the shop he gives lectures on cheese, caters for private parties and supplies various restaurants. He also bakes huge hams for the shop. ('He's very good at it,' claims his wife; 'He had no lessons. We ate the mistakes.') For any cheese-lover, a visit to the Wells Stores is a must.

SHARROW BAY

Ullswater, Cumbria

To mark the publication of his twenty-first guide, Egon Ronay took five British chefs to Paris, to cook a celebratory dinner at Maxim's.

The dinner became famous for many reasons. One was the arrival of Sonia Stevenson (*chef-patronne* of The Horn of Plenty), the first woman ever to cook in this bastion of male-dominated gastronomy. Another, and no less important event, was the appearance of Francis Coulson's Regency syllabub. With polished simplicity, it brought international gourmets to their feet.

Though delighted by this culinary *coup*, patrons of Sharrow Bay were somewhat relieved that Sticky toffee pudding had not crossed the Channel and was consequently safe from Gallic imitators. Had it been the one unveiled that evening, Sharrow Bay car park would, undoubtedly, be jammed with French number-plates today.

Though sophisticates may scorn, the flavour of this pudding is demoralizingly delicious. Once tasted, it will occupy your dreams for days afterwards.

Sticky Toffee Pudding

2 oz (50g) butter, at room
  temperature
6 oz (175g) granulated
  sugar
½ lb (225g) plain flour
1 teaspoon baking powder
1 egg, lightly beaten
6 oz (175g) stoned dates
½ pint (275ml) boiling
  water

1 teaspoon bicarbonate of
  soda
1 teaspoon vanilla essence

Toffee Sauce

1½ oz (40g) butter
2½ oz (65g) brown sugar
2 tablespoons double cream

1 cake tin, 11 × 7 inches (27·5 × 17·5cm), lightly greased

Preheat oven to gas mark 4, 350°F (180°C). Soften the
butter in a large mixing bowl, then add the sugar; cream
them until pale and light. Sift the flour and baking powder
on to a plate. Beat the egg, with a little flour, into the
creamed mixture. Continue beating for a few minutes
before mixing in the rest of the flour.

Flour the dates lightly and chop finely. Put into a
bowl and pour the boiling water over them. Mix in the
bicarbonate of soda and the vanilla. Gradually blend this
mixture into the batter, mixing in well. Transfer to the
prepared tin, spreading out evenly. Bake in the preheated
oven for 40 minutes.

To make the toffee sauce, melt the butter in a small
saucepan and add the sugar and the cream. Simmer gently
for 3 minutes. Cut the hot pudding into squares and cover
with the sauce. Place under a hot grill until it bubbles
(take care as it burns easily), then serve at once.

Serves 6–8

Chef: Francis Coulson
Proprietors: Francis Coulson and Brian Sack

TULLYTHWAITE HOUSE

Underbarrow, Cumbria

When many restaurants are still going overboard with *Crêpes Suzette* and producing enough *Bombe Alaska* to keep a polar bear afloat, it is a welcome change to find a restaurant which specializes in good old-fashioned 'puds'. For over thirty years Mrs Johnson (now in her eighties) has been delighting visitors to the Lake District, as well as locals, with her inimitable brand of home cooking.

Victorian favourites like Queen's pudding, Spotted Dick, Roly-poly and Marmalade Pudding feature on her menus as often as the Cumberland specialities: Caraway seed cake, Goosnargh cakes (page 371) and Rum butter. According to Mrs Johnson, most things are improved by a 'drop of rum' and her mincemeat pies, fruit cakes and other delicacies get a discreet dosage in the kitchen. (This fondness for rum is a well-known characteristic of Cumbrian cooking, dating back to smuggling days, and does not betray a weakness by Mrs Johnson for the bottle. Quite the opposite, as she is virtually teetotal and the restaurant is unlicensed!)

Mrs Johnson is regarded as the *grande dame* of the Lakes,

and other restaurateurs eat with her on their days off, enjoying a type of food which they love but rarely get a chance to eat. It is home cooking at its best, each dish prepared with care and individual attention.

Pineapple Meringue Pudding

15-oz (425g) tin
  unsweetened pineapple
  chunks
pineapple juice from the
  tin made up to 1 pint
  (575ml) with milk

2 oz (50g) butter, at room
  temperature
2 oz (50g) castor sugar
2 large eggs, separated
2 oz (50g) plain flour
2 tablespoons castor sugar

1 small pudding dish

Preheat the oven to gas mark 2, 300°F (150°C). Put the pineapple chunks into the pudding dish. Pour the pineapple juice into a measuring jug and make up to 1 pint (575ml) with milk. Cream the butter and sugar together, then gradually blend in the egg yolks, flour and liquid. Return to the pan and slowly bring to the boil, stirring all the time. Take off the heat and pour over the pineapple chunks.

Whisk the egg whites until stiff, then lightly fold in 2 tablespoons of sugar. Spread over the custard mixture. Bake in the preheated oven until the meringue is lightly browned and crisp (15–20 minutes). Take out and serve at once, or when cooled.

Serves 4

Chefs: Mary Johnson and Barbara Johnson
Proprietor: Mary Johnson

WHITE MOSS HOUSE

Rydal Water, Cumbria

First impressions can be misleading and though White
Moss House and Miller Howe may seem worlds apart, they
do have much in common. Their owners, Jean Butterworth (White Moss) and John Tovey (Miller Howe) have,
over the last decade, developed a unique style of country
house cooking.

Impossible to categorize, it is essentially an Edwardian
meal in modern dress. By taking dinner back to five
courses, they have restored its leisurely pace. But at the
same time, the dishes contain no hint of pre-war stodge.
They are light, well balanced and full of imaginative flair.
Their progression is effortless; from starter to soup or fish,
then the entrée, pudding and cheese. Vegetables receive
unprecedented attention and at least four (but usually six
at Miller Howe) accompany the main course. There is no
choice until the pudding stage but here profusion reigns.

Menus in both establishments are a congenial blend of
sophisticated and simple, country dishes. At White Moss,
Jean Butterworth might start with a complicated *Ballotine*
of guinea fowl with crab apple jelly followed by a simple
Tuna and sweetcorn bisque. (The juxtaposition may be
unorthodox but the result is staggeringly good.) The main
course could be Hunter's pot with herb scones and Lyth
valley damsons, then a selection of four different puddings.
These combine traditional favourites like Sussex pond

pudding and Raspberry shortcake with more unusual specialities: Apricot brandy flan, Walnut shortbread or this gorgeous Autumn glory.

Autumn Glory

Meringue
2 egg whites
¼ lb (100g) castor sugar

Filling
¾ lb (350g) cooking
    apples
¾ lb (350g) fresh
    blackberries
sugar to taste
2½ fl oz (40ml) brandy
¼ pint (150ml) double cream

1 baking tray lined with non-stick silicon paper *or* lightly oiled foil

Preheat oven to gas mark 2, 300°F (150°C). Whisk the egg whites until they stand in soft peaks, then gradually whisk in half the sugar. When stiff and glossy, fold in the remaining sugar. Pipe or shape into nests on the prepared tray and bake in the cool oven for 1½–2 hours, until crisp and dry.

Peel, core and slice the apples. Put into a large saucepan with the blackberries. Add several tablespoons of sugar but no water. Cover and cook over a low heat until soft. Blend in the brandy and add more sugar if necessary. When ready to serve, put the hot fruit mixture into the meringue nests and top with a ring of double cream, whipped fairly thickly. Take to the table just as it begins to melt.

Serves 8

Chef: Jean Butterworth
Proprietors: Jean and Arthur Butterworth

THE LLWYNDERW HOTEL

Llanwrtyd Wells, Powys, Wales

I often wonder how teachers of catering and hotel management account for the disturbing number of successful restaurateurs who have never seen the inside of a catering college. These renegades, on the whole, seem to have started off with experience totally unrelated to food or the restaurant business.

The route taken by Michael Yates to reach his present position as proprietor of The Llwynderw Hotel defies all textbook specifications and was, at best, circuitous. His first job after graduating from Oxford was with the *Oxford Times* as a sub-editor. From there he moved in a north-westerly direction, over to the Cotswolds to run the new Broadway Hotel.

Then the Second World War intervened, the hotel changed hands and for the next twenty years Mr Yates did various jobs connected with the arts but none related to food, hotels or restaurants. Then after a few years of seclusion, living and writing in Radnorshire, he bought Llwynderw and opened it as a hotel in 1969. (The previous owners, who had been running it as a guest house, were a sprightly eighty-one and eighty-three!)

Michael Yates was fortunate in having a friend who was an excellent cook and she provided glorious meals 'in the manner of Mrs Beeton' at Llwynderw for ten years. When she retired, Mr Yates began doing most of the cooking himself. He has continued in the same style, with roots firmly in Victorian and Edwardian cookery. Recipes like Lemon Molly, Lord John Russell's pudding and the one below have been, and still are, pillars of the menu.

Molly's Bread and Butter Pudding

4 very thin slices of white bread
1 oz (25g) butter
2–3 tablespoons sultanas
3 eggs
½ pint (275ml) milk (approx.)

1–2 tablespoons sifted brown sugar
ground cinnamon
castor sugar

cream to serve

oval pudding dish, lightly buttered

Butter the bread generously and trim off the crusts. Cut each slice in half so that you now have 8 pieces. Put a layer of sultanas in the bottom of the pudding dish and cover with 4 pieces of bread and butter. Scatter more sultanas on top and cover these with the remaining pieces of bread. Beat the eggs well and mix with enough milk to cover the contents of the dish. Sprinkle the top generously with brown sugar and cinnamon. Put to one side and leave for 1 hour.

Preheat the oven to gas mark 6, 400°F (200°C). Cover the dish with foil and stand in a shallow tray with water in it. Bake in the preheated oven for 1 hour, removing the foil for the final 10 minutes. Dust lightly with castor sugar and serve warm with icy cold cream.

Serves 4

Chef and proprietor: Michael Yates

THE CARVED ANGEL

Dartmouth, Devon

Pears *Savoyardes* illustrate beautifully how Joyce Molyneux, *chef-patronne* of The Carved Angel, can produce spectacular results from the simplest ingredients.

Even after several mouthfuls it is still difficult to believe how effortless they are to make. Miss Molyneux is also well known for her version of the classic Provençal sweet, Apples sautéed in butter and flamed in Calvados. Again, a simple but inspired blend of flavours. Her homemade ice-creams and sorbets get similar acclaim, with unusual flavours like apricot, Chinese gooseberry, pineapple, redcurrant and quince. For a more bracing finale, there is Grapefruit sorbet, Clementines in brandy, Iced lime soufflé or Claret wine jelly.

Pears Savoyardes

1 lb (450g) fresh pears
1 oz (25g) unsalted butter
1 tablespoon vanilla sugar
¼ pint (150ml) double
cream

toasted flaked almonds to
garnish
langues de chat biscuits to
serve

Peel, quarter and core the pears. Cut each quarter into
three or four slices, lengthwise. Melt the butter in a shallow
pan, put in the pears and sprinkle with the vanilla sugar.
Cook them gently until tender (about 5 minutes), turning
occasionally. Add the cream and boil briskly to reduce to
a coating sauce. Serve warm with a sprinkling of toasted
flaked almonds and crisp *langues de chat* biscuits.

Serves 4

Chef: Joyce Molyneux
Proprietors: Joyce Molyneux and Tom Jaine

THE LITTLE DAIRY

On the way to Devon, stop off at The Little Dairy
in Lyme Regis. On a sloping corner of Broad Street,
this doll's-house-sized shop is crammed with edible
delights. Because of the sixteenth-century proportions, its contents are wisely limited to speciality
foods: a wide range of cheeses, sugar-cured hams,
pâtes and sausages. There is also a good selection of
local produce: honeys, jams, clotted cream, pasties
and spiced apple pies.

BALLYMALOE

Shanagarry, Co. Cork, Eire

The menu at Ballymaloe changes three times a day. In the morning it is recited by enthusiastic waitresses who bring relays of hot porridge, cold cereals or fresh fruit (in the summer, huge bowls of succulent berries) and then any combination of eggs, ham or bacon (all from the farm), homemade sausages or freshly caught fish. Baskets of freshly made bread arrive with creamy butter and pots of Ballymaloe jam and honey.

At lunch the menu is purely visual with a hearty buffet of hot and cold dishes laid out in the dining-room. Dinner is a four-course *table d'hôte* with choice at every stage. Despite a strong leaning towards traditional Irish recipes, Mrs Allen's cooking shows distinct English and French influences. Her chunky terrines, smooth pâtés, herbed hollandaise and *gratin* of crab appear as frequently as the soda bread, Irish stew and famous Carigeen moss. A trolley wheels in the puddings and despite a tempting array, the favourite is usually Irish Mist soufflé. This light, lemon sorbet is flavoured with the leaves of sweet geraniums and a dash of Irish Mist liqueur.

As *Pelargonium Graveolens* (sweet geranium leaves) are not always readily to hand (nor is the Irish Mist), Pears in Port Wine make a delicious alternative.

Pears in Port Wine

6 good-sized pears
¼ lb (100g) sugar
8 fl oz (225ml) water

rind of ½ lemon
pinch of ground cinnamon
8 fl oz (225ml) port

Peel, core and quarter the pears. Put the sugar and water into a large saucepan and over gentle heat until the sugar has dissolved. Peel the lemon rind off thinly (using a vegetable peeler) and add to the pan with a pinch of cinnamon and the port. Bring up to simmering point, then carefully place the pears in the liquid. Cover and poach them gently, basting occasionally with the juices, until tender (20–30 minutes). Lift out with a slotted spoon and place in a serving dish. Take out the strips of lemon rind and discard. Boil down the liquid in the saucepan until thick and syrupy. Pour over the pears and serve warm or cold.

Serves 6

Chef: Myrtle Allen *Proprietors:* Myrtle and Ivan Allen

BALLYMALOE SHOP

Almost as tempting as Mrs Allen's lunchtime buffet is the array of goodies in her daughter's shop at the bottom of the garden. It is filled with the best of Irish 'homemade': from wicker picnic baskets to long fisherman's socks in oiled wool and hand-knitted sweaters. The earthenware comes from the Shanagarry pottery, the most outstanding in Ireland (and the only one to use Irish clay). Patchwork, period postcards and tweeds are also on sale.

NO. 3

Glastonbury, Somerset

The sweet trolley at No. 3 is virtually impossible to resist. It has a limited but mouth-watering selection of desserts, with a back-up of several hot and very cold ones which come straight from the kitchen.

To ensure that they are always at their best, the puddings are removed from the trolley when not being used and then brought back again just before serving. A rich Chocolate truffle, shaped like a gold bar and dusted lightly with cocoa, is a *specialité de la maison*. It is as light as a feather and as rich as a thousand profiteroles. (The recipe is also a dark secret and no amount of persuasion would procure it.) If you manage somehow to pass this by, then the alternatives of Lemon cheesecake, Strawberry *mille-feuille* and Hazelnut meringue look equally tempting. Though natural cooking links are with France, a certain Italian influence is detected in the fresh fruit *Zucotta* and the ice-cream with Amaretto. A trace of the Caribbean can also be found in these bananas, liberally laced with rum and brown sugar.

The joy of this recipe is that it can be made quickly at the last minute, with quantities which barely need to be measured.

Rum Baked Bananas

8 large bananas
½ lemon
6–7 tablespoons thin marmalade
4–5 tablespoons dark Navy rum

4–6 tablespoons grapenuts cereal
2 oz (50g) butter

whipped cream to serve

large, shallow ovenproof dish (a gratin dish is best), lightly buttered

Preheat the oven to gas mark 4, 350°F (180°C). Peel the bananas, then slice them in half lengthwise and arrange, rounded side up, in the buttered dish. Rub lightly with the cut side of the lemon to prevent browning. Cover with a thin layer of marmalade and sprinkle well with dark rum. Top with a layer of grapenuts, then dot the surface with butter. (If making in advance, chill until needed.) Bake in the oven for about 20 minutes, or until the grapenuts are crisp and lightly browned (taking care not to overcook as the bananas will become mushy). Take out and serve warm with lightly whipped cream.

Serves 8

Chef: George Atkinson
Proprietors: George Atkinson and Charles Foden

THE OLD BAKEHOUSE

Colyton, Devon

Simplicity is one of the hallmarks of French provincial cooking and Susan Keen uses it to great advantage at The Old Bakehouse.

She insists on only the best ingredients and now has a reliable team of country suppliers: the baker in Colyton provides the bread, as well as fresh croissants; a local farmer grows all the vegetables including the elusive *mange-touts*; the meat comes from the butcher up the road; and the fish from a shop in Brixham. Trips to France fill any gaps in the shopping list and the Keens bring back litre cans of walnut oil (an essential part of the dressing for *Salade périgourdine*), bottles of aged Calvados and cheeses too smelly for any shop to stock.

Mrs Keen has tried to follow the French tradition of serving a light, refreshing sweet after a rich meal. But her *Tarte aux pommes*, Red berry salad and Blackcurrant sorbet have become obvious wallflowers. Her customers unquestionably prefer a creamy Dacquoise or a gooey Chocolate gâteau. The *Ile flottante* is the only exception, yet it seems to be chosen more often for its exotic shape than for its simple taste.

Ile Flottante

4 egg whites
¼ lb (100g) castor sugar
4 egg yolks

2 oz (50g) castor sugar
few drops of vanilla essence
¾ pint (425ml) milk

2-pint (1·1-litre) charlotte tin, lightly buttered and dusted with castor sugar

Preheat the oven to gas mark 4, 350°F (180°C). Whisk the egg whites until stiff but not dry. Add 4 teaspoons of sugar and whisk until stiff and shiny. Fold in the remaining sugar. Turn the mixture into the prepared tin, pushing down well. Cover with a piece of foil and place in a baking tin filled with warm water. Bake in the preheated oven for 30–40 minutes or until firm. Take the tin out of the water and remove the lid. Leave to cool.

Beat the egg yolks, castor sugar and vanilla until smooth. Stir in the milk, then place the bowl in a bain-marie over gentle heat (or transfer the mixture to the top of a double saucepan). Stir constantly until the custard coats the back of the spoon. Put to one side and leave to cool (whisking from time to time to prevent a skin forming on top).

When ready to serve, turn the 'island' out on to a large shallow serving dish. Pour the vanilla cream all around the island.

Serves 6

Chef: Susan Keen *Proprietors:* Susan and Stephen Keen

PENLAN OLEU

Llanychaer Bridge, Dyfed, Wales

Ann Carr will be well known to many Londoners as the *chef-patronne* of the Peacock restaurant in Islington. Several years ago she and her designer-husband Martin Mac-Keown looked for and found an isolated farmhouse in Wales which they could convert to a miniature *auberge*. Though seemingly remote, it is only two miles from Fishguard and now provides an oasis for travellers en route to Ireland.

Ann Carr has long had an interest in regional cooking and the recipes used at Penlan Oleu are based on gleanings from old manuscripts and cookery books, as well as her extensive travels in the Middle East, Africa and Europe. It is a brave restaurateur who puts exotic dishes like Kashmir soup (page 105), Chicken *tagine* and Bulgur on a set menu in the depths of Wales. But this is exactly what she does and the only complaint from residents is of a certain *aggrandisement* during their stay.

It is not only the high standard of cooking but the small touches that make the difference: the crisp wholemeal bread which accompanies the soup, the immaculate presentation of the main course and vegetables, the whole Stilton in its linen napkin, offered to you before the temptation of pudding. It is essential to find an excuse to stay for breakfast, otherwise you will miss out on freshly baked

298

croissants, homemade crunchy muesli, bread and jams, fruit compote and fresh fish.

This recipe is Ann's own interpretation of an old English recipe which seems, from all reports, to be true to its name.

'Can't Leave Me Alone'

2 level teaspoons gelatine
4 tablespoons cold water
3 large egg yolks
2 oz (50g) castor sugar
   (scant)
few drops vanilla essence
3 large egg whites
several tablespoons
   homemade raspberry
   jam

8 fl oz (225ml) double
   cream, whipped

grated chocolate *or* toasted
   almonds to decorate
lacey biscuits to serve
   (page 371)

Sprinkle the gelatine on the cold water in a small cup and leave to soak until completely absorbed. Then put into a pan of hot water until the gelatine has dissolved completely. Whisk the egg yolks and sugar together (using an electric whisk makes this easier) until light and frothy. Add the vanilla essence and pour in the gelatine in a steady stream, whisking all the time. Whisk the egg whites until stiff but not too dry. Fold into the yolk mixture, then transfer to a glass bowl or serving dish. Chill for several hours until set. Just before serving, spread a thin layer of jam on top and cover with whipped cream. Decorate with a sprinkling of grated chocolate or toasted almonds. Serve with Lacey biscuits.

Serves 4

Chef: Ann Carr
Proprietors: Ann Carr and Martin MacKeown

MALLORY COURT

Tachbrook Mallory, Warwickshire

It is not unusual to find a traditional English dessert like 'burnt cream' in a restaurant which has shades of Elizabethan grandeur. But to find it at Mallory Court, with a hint of orange and wafer-thin biscuits, is more than a pleasant surprise. It keeps good company on the menu with Chocolate rum roulade, hot apple tarts, *Crème de menthe* ice-cream and Lemon, brandy and sauterne syllabub. They provide a fitting conclusion to Allan Holland's stylish dinners, with starters and main courses to bring on a rash of *gourmandise*.

Crème Brûlée à l'Orange

1 pint (575ml) double
cream
8 egg yolks
2 oz (50g) castor sugar
2 tablespoons orange
liqueur

1 tablespoon orange rind,
finely grated
soft light brown sugar

6–8 ramekin dishes (depending on their size)

Rinse out a heavy saucepan with cold water and leave wet. Pour in the double cream and heat to just below simmering point over a low heat.

Meanwhile beat the egg yolks and sugar together until thick and pale in colour. Slowly pour the hot cream on to the yolk and sugar mixture, stirring slowly. Then blend in the orange liqueur and orange rind.

Rinse out the saucepan and again leave wet. Pour in the custard mixture and over a very low heat, or a pan of simmering water, cook the custard, stirring continuously with a wooden spoon. (Make sure, as you stir, that you scrape the entire bottom of the pan.) Continue stirring until the mixture thickens sufficiently (until it leaves a trail when you lift the spoon out) but on no account must it boil.

Sieve the custard into the ramekin dishes and allow to cool. Refrigerate for 5–6 hours or overnight.

An hour before you are ready to serve, preheat the grill and sprinkle an even layer ¼-inch (·50cm) thick of soft brown sugar over the top of the custard. Place the ramekins in a shallow tin filled with ice cubes and place under the grill until the sugar melts and caramelizes. (This only takes a few moments so watch carefully.) Remove from the grill and allow to cool but not in the refrigerator.

Serves 6–8

Chef: Allan Holland
Proprietors: Allan Holland and Jeremy Mort

THE PLOUGH

Fadmoor, North Yorkshire

French cookery is filled with ingenious ways of combining fruit and soft cheese but our only attempt in this country seems to be lemon cheesecake.

The Plough is hardly next door to France, yet it still manages to produce an authentic *Fromage à la crème*. Served with its own cherry conserve and shortbread fingers, it provides a subtle contrast of sweet and sour flavours. It is a veteran favourite on The Plough menu and though new desserts threaten to supersede it, its popularity remains unchallenged. Even the chef, Kath Brown, admits a weakness for it, claiming this to be another reason for its frequent appearance on the menu. This is only one of many dessert specialities at The Plough; others include Boozy prunes, Redcurrant sorbet, *Bombe favorite* and Bilberry tart.

Fromage à la Crème

1 level tablespoon vanilla
sugar
¾ lb (350g) cream cheese
(homemade *or* bought
loose; the packet variety
is too firm)
a little cream *or* top of the
milk

shortbread fingers (page
374)

Conserve
4 rounded tablespoons best
quality pitted Morello
cherry jam
brandy to taste
1 level dessertspoon finely
chopped walnuts

First prepare the conserve. If the jam is homemade or
made from pure cane sugar, it will probably not be solid
in texture. But if this quality is not available, beat in some
boiling water to soften the jam. Add sufficient brandy for
the taste to be recognizable. Stir in the chopped walnuts.

Add the vanilla sugar to the cream cheese and beat
together with a fork until the mixture softens. If too firm,
add a little cream or top of the milk to give the consistency
of a homemade cream cheese.

Serve the cheese and conserve separately, in two small
dishes for each person, accompanied by shortbread fingers.

Serves 4

Chef: Kath Brown *Proprietors:* Kath and Don Brown

TULLICH LODGE

Ballater, Aberdeenshire, Scotland

As the focal point of dinner at Tullich Lodge may be a
magnificent haunch of venison, rib of beef or well-hung
pheasant, the sweets tend to be, in contrast, much lighter.
They frequently have a fruit base, using locally grown
berries or more exotic imports like chinese gooseberries.
Their simplicity is a far cry from the days when Tullich's
chef-patron, Neil Bannister, worked at the Tour d'Argent
restaurant in Paris. The culinary extravagances practised
there would hardly suit a Scottish castle in a far corner of
Aberdeenshire.

Cranachan, sometimes known as Cream-crowdie, is an
age-old Scottish pudding. It is traditionally made with
oatmeal, toasted in front of the fire, then combined with
fresh raspberries, brambles or 'blaeberries'. It is a gorgeous
blend of colour, taste and texture and, more to its credit,
takes only a minute to make.

Raspberry Cranachan

2 oz (50g) coarse oatmeal
½ pint (275ml) double
  cream

castor sugar to taste
1 lb (450g) fresh raspberries

Put the oatmeal on to a baking tray and under a hot grill. Toast until golden brown. Whisk the cream until thick and sweeten to taste. Fold in the oatmeal gently.

Divide the raspberries among four wine glasses. Spoon the cream over and chill slightly before serving. (But only for a short time; if left too long, the oatmeal will lose its crispness).

Serves 4

Chef: Neil Bannister
Proprietors: Neil Bannister and Hector Macdonald

LEITH'S

The bread and biscuits served with cheese at Tullich Lodge come from Leith's Bakery in Ballater. An old family business, they bake all the bread on the premises from 'recipes of old'. They make white, brown, bran and special 'Balmoral' loaves, as well as pure butter shortbread, black bun and ginger 'Perkins'. Their cheese biscuits are a speciality: one type resembles a slightly thicker Bath Oliver, another is a rich 'butter puff'. They hold royal warrants from H.M. The Queen and H.M. The Queen Mother.

McCOY'S

Staddle Bridge, North Yorkshire

The customary image of a restaurateur, amply proportioned and dressed in discreet fashion, is liable to fall flat on its face when it reaches McCoy's. For one thing, the McCoy brothers are all tall and skinny and, for another, they are about as traditional as Mick Jagger. Their usual restaurant gear is far from orthodox: jeans, plimsolls, T-shirts and striped aprons. A colourful feast for the eyes, if not for the fashion columns.

Their unaffected style is also evident in the way they run the restaurant. There is no grovel, grovel to important customers; everyone is welcomed with the same enthusiasm. But members of the public don't always reciprocate in the same democratic spirit and some prefer their restaurateurs cast in a more conventional (or at least recognizable) mould. On the rare occasions when demands have been made to 'see the manager', the arrival of T-shirted Eugene McCoy has been met with frank astonishment.

Though the McCoys have simple taste in clothes, their preferences in the kitchen are a good deal more sophisticated. Their famous Champagne sorbet, made with the finest champagne cognac, almost breaks the bank every time they make it. And this Raspberry charlotte is, they claim, a pale shadow without a liberal dose of *framboise*.

Raspberry Charlotte

½ lb (225g) castor sugar
½ lb (225g) unsalted butter
½ lb (225g) ground almonds
2 liqueur glasses Cointreau
   or other orange-
   flavoured liqueur
24 sponge fingers
1 lb (450g) fresh or frozen
   raspberries

Raspberry Sauce

1 lb (450) fresh or frozen
   raspberries
5 tablespoons castor sugar
1 liqueur glass *framboise*
   or any fruit liqueur

charlotte mould, lightly buttered

Cream the sugar, butter, almonds and most of the Cointreau together to make a light, frothy cream (this is easiest done in a food processor or with an electric hand whisk). Soak the sponge fingers in the remaining Cointreau. Use most of them to line the bottom and sides of the charlotte mould.

Fill the mould with alternate layers of almond cream, sponge fingers and raspberries (if using frozen, make sure they are completely thawed first). Finish off with a layer of sponge fingers which will form the base when the charlotte is turned out. Cover with foil and put a small weight – about 4 lb (2 kilos) – on top. Chill in the refrigerator for 3 hours.

To make the raspberry sauce: heat the raspberries in a saucepan with the sugar and fruit liqueur. Simmer together for about 3 minutes, then press through a sieve to remove the pips and allow to cool.

When ready to serve, turn out the charlotte on to a plate and hand round the sauce separately.

Serves 8

Chefs: Tom and Peter McCoy
Proprietors: Eugene, Tom and Peter McCoy

WHITE'S

Lincoln, Lincolnshire

Though White's in Lincoln has only been open for eighteen months, it has already set tongues wagging in gastronomic circles.

To reach it, you must climb the cobbled streets towards the cathedral until you come to No. 15 The Strait. Here you will find the Jew's House, a twelfth-century building thought to be one of the oldest dwelling houses in Europe. Until Colin and Gwen White bought it in 1978, it had been used as an antique shop. Its potential was spotted by Colin's father, a local builder who lives round the corner. Once the sale was complete, the Whites Elder and Younger worked together to restore it to the original; stripping plaster off the oak beams, uncovering the fireplaces and putting in a new wood floor.

The result is well worth the hours of hard labour. Though tiny, it is full of character. On entering, you step down into a room flanked on one side by large windows and on the other by a pearly grey stone wall. A pine mantelpiece frames the old fireplace which now holds an alluring display of vintage bottles. The rough beams, polished wood tables and watercolours dotted round the room strike the right note between cosiness and bold good looks.

White's is open for lunch and dinner and the menu (which changes weekly) is the same for both. Guests are encouraged, if a three-course meal seems too daunting, to eat two starters or simply starter and pud. If this were done (though apparently few are willing to pass up Colin's main courses), one could feast on a meal of Piperade with Fennel and apple salad or *Soupe verte* and Fresh salmon mousse. If combining starter and pud, then Barbecued spare ribs (spiced spare ribs of pork with honey and soy sauce – page 227) could be followed by homemade Mango ice-cream or *Fraises Escoffier*.

Fraises Escoffier

2 lb (900g) fresh
   strawberries
4–5 oz (100–150g) castor
   sugar
juice of 2 oranges
zest of 1 orange, finely
   grated

2 fl oz (50ml) orange
   Curaçao *or* Grand
   Marnier
½ pint (275ml) double
   cream
castor sugar

langue de chat biscuits to
   serve

4 tall wine glasses

Hull the strawberries and put into a large bowl (giving them lots of room so they don't bruise). Sprinkle the castor sugar, orange juice and zest on top. Finally pour over the orange liqueur. Cover the bowl with cling film and leave for 2 hours, basting the strawberries with the juices from time to time.

When ready to serve, whisk the cream until thick and add sugar to taste. Divide the strawberries and their juice amongst the wine glasses, then top each one with a dollop of the whipped cream. Serve with crisp *langue de chat* biscuits.

Serves 4

Chef: Colin White *Proprietors:* Gwen and Colin White

MILLER HOWE

Windermere, Cumbria

Miller Howe is not a place to go to with a preconceived idea of what you want to eat. Or when you want to eat it; for as the gong sounds at 8.30 there will be a mass exodus into the dining-room.

When the last napkin is tucked into place, the lights dim and the first of five courses is put before you. Whether it is Savoury cheese peach or Utter bliss, it will certainly bear no resemblance to any starter you have had before or since (and it will not be remotely like any starter you thought of while lying in the bath two hours earlier). If hoping for Prawn cocktail or *Pâté maison*, your disappointment will fade with the first forkful.

The second course will be equally novel: a soup made of Apricot and marrow, Carrot and coriander or Pea, pear and watercress. The third course might be Grilled river trout with hazelnuts and grapefruit.

By the time the sweet course arrives, you wish passionately that John Tovey had chosen this as well. Trying to decide between 'My Nan's tipsy trifle', Chocolate rum squidgy gâteau and Banana walnut farmhouse pie almost proves too much. Especially when the Calvados apple mousse and Kiwi Pavlovas look equally good.

Kiwi Pavlovas

¼ lb (100g) egg whites
½ lb (225g) sieved castor
  sugar
1½ level teaspoons cornflour
¾ teaspoon white wine
  vinegar

Filling
½ pint (275ml) double
  cream
castor sugar to taste
4–6 kiwi fruits
several tablespoons brandy
  (optional)

Preheat the oven to gas mark 3, 325°F (170°C). Whisk the egg whites until white, foamy and light. Add gently (while still whisking) a quarter of the sugar. When it forms a soft peak, add another quarter of the sugar and so on, until it has all been used up. Sprinkle on (while still whisking merrily) the cornflour and white wine vinegar (whatever you do, don't use malt vinegar). The mixture will be quite firm and all you have to do is scoop tablespoon-sized dollops out of the bowl and plonk them on to good silicone-treated greaseproof paper on a baking tray. Bake in the preheated oven for 1¼ hours, then turn the oven off. Wedge the door slightly open with a wooden spoon, and leave the Pavlovas in the oven for a further 3 hours at least. (When the Pavlovas have been in the oven for 20 minutes, take the trays out and carefully scatter lightly toasted flaked almonds on top of each one, before returning them to the oven.) After 3 hours, take the trays out and remove the Pavlovas. Use straight away or store.

When ready to serve the Pavlovas, whisk the cream until just stiff, adding castor sugar to taste. Peel and slice the kiwis and, if adding brandy, macerate them in it for 15–30 minutes before using. Whisk several tablespoons of the kiwi/brandy juices into the whipped cream and put a dollop on each Pavlova. Top with a few slices of kiwi and, if room, a tiny snowdrop of cream. Serve at once.

Makes about 12 Pavlovas

Chef and proprietor: John Tovey

THE TOASTMASTER'S INN

Burham, Kent

Tim Daglish has the contented air of a man who knows what he's doing and enjoying every minute of it. He has done catering on a large scale and was for a while general manager of the Cockney Pride in Piccadilly Circus. But this was not for him and now at The Toastmaster's, where he has been since 1974, he can cook without pressure and outside constraints (no portion control here). He is a complete devoté of the *nouvelle cuisine* and *cuisine minceur*, Guérard, Bocuse and Vergé being the chefs whose ideas he uses most.

Dishes like *Carré d'agneau cuit dans le foin* (rack of lamb, cooked in hay with fresh herbs and lavender, served with a fresh herbed tomato sauce) and *Faisan truffée au persil* show the influence of Guérard, while *Steak de canard aux poivres verts* and *Petits crèmes de brochet, sauce nantua* lean more towards the classical. His own invention is more obvious in the *Civet de lapin aux deux moutardes*, Veal olives with Stilton and pickled walnuts, Chicken and salsify pie. Throughout the menu one senses, simply by the way the dishes are described, that they will be done to perfection. One is rarely disappointed and the starters as well, particularly the Baked clams with oregano, *Terrine de trois poissons* and

Potted chicken with tarragon sauce, more than exceed one's expectations.

It may be the aphrodisiac qualities attributed to Pernod or it may simply be the unusual flavour, but this syllabub is by far the most popular sweet served at The Toastmaster's.

Grapefruit and Pernod Syllabub

1½ tablespoons castor sugar
juice of 1 grapefruit (pink
   if possible)
2 tablespoons Pernod
¾ pint (425ml) double
   cream

grapefruit segments for
   decoration
shortbread fingers to serve
   (page 374)

Dissolve the sugar in the grapefruit juice and Pernod. Pour the cream into a large bowl, then whisk until it is just starting to thicken. Gradually pour in the liquid, whisking all the time until it has all been incorporated. When quite thick, spoon the syllabub into a piping bag and pipe into tall glasses. Decorate with grapefruit segments and serve with shortbread fingers.

Serves 4–6

Chefs: Tim Daglish and Paul Duval
Proprietors: Judith and Gregory Ward

FINDON MANOR

Findon, West Sussex

The trouble with manor houses is they're usually too draughty for comfort or so comfortable that you wonder if the bill will be as big as the four-poster bed.

At Findon Manor, a mini-manor house built about five hundred years ago, it may come as a surprise to find that there are no brass chandeliers, no gilt-edged ancestors on the stairs, no heavy oak furniture and no crossed swords on the landing. In a manner quite uncharacteristic of its type, the house has been decorated with a light hand: in muted shades of pink and green, William Morris fabrics and buff-coloured beams overhead. The Bannisters, a young husband and wife team (she runs the front of the house, he cooks) have done the house exactly as they would have liked it, for comfort rather than effect.

Though the standards are high, they have still managed to keep the style informal. Mary Bannister hardly fits the traditional image of a *patronne* and delights guests with her disarming candour. Her husband Adrian performs a double act by cooking *and* serving dinner, giving guests a rare glimpse of the man 'behind the scenes'. While Mary takes the orders, delivers starters and clears the plates, Adrian is usually able to serve the main course, with his young *sous-chef* as back-up in the kitchen.

Iced Black Cherry Soufflé

6 oz (175g) vanilla sugar
  or castor sugar flavoured
  with a few drops of
  vanilla essence
4 fl oz (100ml) water
1 lb (450g) fresh black
  cherries
2½ fl oz (65ml) Kirsch

5 eggs, separated
½ pint (275ml) double
  cream

fresh black cherries to
  garnish

8–12 ramekin dishes, depending on size

Start by preparing the ramekin dishes. Put a folded piece of greaseproof paper, around the outside of each dish, extending about ½ inch(1cm) above the rim, and tie with a piece of string.

Put the sugar and water into a saucepan and heat gently until the sugar has dissolved. Then boil rapidly for 4 minutes. Take off the heat and put to one side. Stone but do not peel the cherries and liquidize them with most of the Kirsch. Put the egg yolks into a pudding basin and pour in the sugar syrup, whisking all the time. Continue whisking until the mixture is quite cold. Whisk the cream until thick, then fold in carefully with the remaining kirsch. Whisk the egg whites until stiff and fold in. Use the mixture to fill the ramekins three-quarters full. Finish by pouring the cherry mix into each ramekin from a height sufficient to make it sink into the creamy mixture. Put into the freezer and leave overnight.

Just before serving, remove the greaseproof paper collars and decorate each soufflé with a small cluster of black cherries. (Be sure to take the soufflés out of the freezer 10–15 minutes before serving so that they are not frozen solid.)

Serves 8–12

Chef: Adrian Bannister
Proprietors: Mary and Adrian Bannister

POPJOY'S

Bath, Avon

I would like to meet the person who has room for pudding after revelling in Popjoy's *Soupe de poisson, Poulet vallée d'Auge, mange-touts* and *Gratin dauphinois*.

Rum and coffee bavarois, Hazelnut meringue with fruit purée and Walnut tart with lemon cream sound tempting but wicked. Popjoy's hot chocolate soufflé could only be more sinful yet few people, however replete, seem able to resist it. Like a cushion of melting chocolate, it is so light that it surely couldn't get anywhere near the waistline. The taste is nothing short of sensational and would provide, for anyone with a penchant for sweets, a perfect finish to the meal.

Popjoy's Hot Chocolate Soufflé

6 oz (175g) plain chocolate	3 egg yolks
(Meunier is ideal)	1 tablespoon rum
1 oz (25g) butter	5 egg whites

6 straight-sided ramekin dishes, buttered and dusted lightly with flour

Preheat the oven to gas mark 4, 350°F (180°C). Put the prepared ramekins into the refrigerator and leave to chill.

Melt the chocolate in the top half of a double saucepan, then stir in the butter. When well blended, whisk in the egg yolks and rum. Take off the heat and leave to cool (but don't let the mixture set). Whisk the egg whites until stiff and fold into the chocolate. Take the ramekins out of the refrigerator and fill each to within ½ inch (1cm) of the top with the soufflé mixture. Bake in the preheated oven for 8–10 minutes. Take out and serve at once.

Serves 6

Chef: Stephen Ross
Proprietors: Stephen and Penny Ross

SHIPDHAM PLACE

Shipdham, Norfolk

The flatness of the Norfolk countryside gives the outline of
Shipdham Place a dramatic prominence. Its classical proportions make it look from the front like the archetypal
doll's house, created for a giant child.

A sweeping drive brings you to the front door and a first
glimpse of Melanie de Blank's menu, sellotaped un-
ceremoniously to the windowpane. If you can resist the
urge to rush straight into the dining-room, you will be
confronted with a magnificent pine staircase which curves
round to the bedrooms upstairs. It has, like all the pine in
the house, been stripped and restored to its original flaxen
hue. Across the hall, a sitting-room decorated in spring
colours is furnished with generous sofas and chunky pieces
of pine and oak.

The kitchens are wonderfully old-fashioned and one,
now used as a family dining-room, has the old iron range
still in place, complete with bread oven. The main kitchen
at the back of the house, with the original stone flags, has
in the middle an enormous miller's table. It is five feet
square with drawers which stretch from one side to the
other! All the cooking is done here by Melanie de Blank
and her Cordon Bleu trained assistant. A smaller kitchen
off the dining-room, dominated by a large Aga, is used to
serve the food and keep it warm. The scullery between the

two kitchens and the back pantry make it seem distinctly Edwardian and one expects a bustling Mrs Bridges to sweep through at any moment. (The slim and lovely Mrs de Blank hardly fits the traditional image but she runs her kitchen with the same efficiency.) At the back door, a pathway leads to a large kitchen garden, filled with vegetables, fruit and herbs.

Iced Lemon Mousse

4 large egg yolks
$\frac{1}{4}$ pint (150ml) water
6 oz (175g) sugar
grated rind of $1\frac{1}{2}$ lemons
juice of $2\frac{1}{2}$ lemons

$\frac{1}{2}$ pint (275ml) double cream
4 large egg whites

lemon twists for garnish

Beat the egg yolks until light in colour and fluffy. Combine the water, sugar, lemon rind and juice in a saucepan. Bring slowly to the boil, stir and boil for 7 minutes. Beat the boiling syrup into the yolks and continue to beat until frothy. Chill this mixture for 30 minutes or until cold. Whisk the cream until thick and whisk the egg whites until stiff. Lightly fold the cream, then the egg whites, into the lemon mixture. Pour into a plastic container with a lid and freeze for 2 hours. Take out, stir well and put back into the freezer. Leave until quite firm. When ready to serve, scoop out and serve decorated with lemon twists.

NB. If you prefer to serve the mousse unfrozen, soak $\frac{1}{2}$ oz (15g) gelatine in 4 tablespoons cold water then dissolve over hot water. Stir into the lemon mixture after you have added the boiling syrup. Continue to follow the recipe as above but chill in the refrigerator instead of the freezer.

This can also be made in half the time by using a food processor.

Serves 6–8

Chef: Melanie de Blank
Proprietors: Melanie and Justin de Blank

CHURCHE'S MANSION

Nantwich, Cheshire

When Mrs Clowes, the cook at Churche's Mansion for twenty years, retired in 1972, Mrs Richard Myott (the *patronne*) donned an apron and took over. She has continued the tradition of providing outstanding home cooking at a price that even you and I can afford.

The restaurant is open every day for lunch and dinner (with the exception of Sunday dinner) and also serves morning coffee and afternoon tea to those who are visiting the house (a striking example of Tudor architecture, lovingly restored by two generations of the Myott family). In keeping with the 'homey' atmosphere, dishes on the daily menu offer a good range of traditional favourites like homemade soup, Roast beef and Yorkshire pudding, Steak and mushroom pie or Grilled halibut with garlic butter. But for the more adventurous, there is also Avocado and tomato ice, Smokie with whisky butter, Beef Trevarrick, Rabbit casserole and Guinea fowl casserole with cranberries.

The sweets are a speciality and offer an abundance of homemade goodies. Edwardian stand-bys like Junket with nutmeg and Apple amber pudding feature, as well as the more international Chocolate marguerite, Walnut fudge flan, *Crème blanche* with poached apricots and Lime soufflé. There is a mouth-watering selection of ice-creams and sorbets, all made from Mrs Myott's recipes, with flavours ranging from damson, gooseberry, black cherry and melon to peppermint, rum and raisin, coffee and walnut. For those wanting only 'a little something' to finish with, dessert grapes and fresh fruit are always available.

The Ginger syllabub and Coffee soufflé can be eaten separately, but together they are food for the gods.

Ginger Syllabub and Coffee Soufflé

Ginger Syllabub

2 tablespoons medium sherry
1½ oz (40g) castor sugar
large pinch of ground nutmeg
large pinch of ground ginger
juice of ½ lemon
½ pint (275ml) double cream
2–3 pieces stem ginger, finely chopped

Coffee Soufflé

3 large eggs
3 oz (75g) castor sugar
½ oz (15g) gelatine
4–5 tablespoons strong black coffee *or*
2 tablespoons Camp coffee essence
1 tablespoon Tia Maria (optional)
¼ pint (150ml) double cream

Ginger syllabub. Put the sherry, sugar, spices and lemon juice into a large mixing bowl. Stir until well blended, then leave to soak for at least 30 minutes. Pour in the cream and whisk until stiff. Fold in the chopped ginger, reserving a few pieces for decoration. Chill thoroughly.

Coffee soufflé. Separate the eggs and beat the yolks with the sugar until thick and light in colour. Dissolve the gelatine in the black coffee (or soak in coffee essence, then dissolve over hot water) and whisk into the yolks with the Tia Maria (if used). Whisk the cream until it holds its shape, then fold into the coffee mixture lightly. Finally whisk the whites until stiff and fold in.

To combine the two sweets, take 8 tall wine glasses and fill with alternate layers of syllabub and soufflé. Chill for at least 4 hours, then just before serving top with a dollop of cream and a sliver of stem ginger.

If serving the sweets separately (each serves 4), they both need to be well chilled before taking to the table (the soufflé needs several hours to set).

Serves 8

Chefs: Mrs Richard Myott and Ian Allan
Proprietors: Mr and Mrs Richard Myott

SHARROW BAY

Ullswater, Cumbria

Fernand Point, *patron* of La Pyramide restaurant in Vienne and acclaimed as one of this century's greatest chefs, shared with others in his profession a profound distrust of any chef who looked under-nourished. A larger-than-life character himself, he was once heard to say, 'Whenever I go into a restaurant I don't know, I always ask to meet the chef before I eat. For I know that if he is thin, I won't eat well. And if he is thin and sad, there is nothing for it but to run.'

Though Point was the teacher and mentor of many of the chefs now practising the *nouvelle cuisine*, he didn't live long enough to see the popularization of *cuisine minceur*. He would certainly have had second thoughts upon meeting Francis Coulson who, despite matchstick proportions, is a chef of remarkable talent. For thirty years, he has maintained a standard of cooking rarely found in this country. His enthusiasm remains undimmed and the dishes at Sharrow are still characterized by their innovativeness and unerring flair. Yearly trips to France provide a regenerative source of inspiration and recipes provide diners with a privileged tasting of the best regional French cuisine.

Cadet Mathieu Auvergnate

(*French Apple Tart*)

½ lb (225g) plain flour
pinch of salt
6 oz (175g) butter, at room
   temperature
1 rounded dessertspoon
   castor sugar
1 egg yolk
2–3 tablespoons cold water
few drops of any liqueur

1 egg, lightly beaten
castor sugar

Filling
2 oz (50g) butter
2 oz (50g) plain flour
½ pint (275ml) single cream
3 egg yolks
3 oz (75g) castor sugar
1–2 teaspoons of liqueur
   (preferably the same
   used for pastry)
¾ lb (350g) dessert apples,
   cored and thinly sliced

8-inch (20cm) flan ring *or* dish

Start by making the pastry. Sift the flour and salt into a large bowl and rub in the butter. Mix in the castor sugar, then tip in the egg yolk, mixed with 2 tablespoons of water and a few drops of liqueur. Mix quickly, adding more water if necessary to make a firm dough. Put into a polythene bag and chill for at least 30 minutes. Then bring to room temperature and use to line the flan ring, reserving about a third of the dough for the top. Chill until needed.

Preheat the oven to gas mark 5, 375°F (190°C). Melt the butter in a saucepan and stir in the flour. Cook for 1 minute, then gradually stir in the cream. Heat until it just comes to the boil, then take off the stove and whisk in the egg yolks, sugar and chosen liqueur (to taste). Put to one side and leave to cool completely, whisking from time to time to prevent a skin forming. When cold, pour into the lined flan ring. Arrange the apple slices on top. Roll out the remaining pastry, cut a small hole in the centre and fit over the flan. Trim off any excess and pinch the edges to seal. Brush the top with lightly beaten egg and dust with castor sugar. Bake in the preheated oven for 20–30 minutes or until crisp and golden brown. Take out and serve warm or cold with thick cream.

Serves 8

Chef: Francis Coulson
Proprietors: Francis Coulson and Brian Sack

THE TOFFEE SHOP

If Francis Coulson's Sticky toffee pudding leaves you craving for more of the same, then stop off on your way home at The Toffee Shop in Penrith. This tiny shop, lined with blue and white china, is extremely modest but sells fabulous homemade fudge and toffee. It is all made on the premises and Mrs Fearon, who has owned the shop since 1964, produces four different kinds: plain fudge, chocolate fudge, butter toffee and treacle toffee. Beautifully wrapped in waxed paper and their own white and gold box, both fudge and toffee can be ordered and sent by post.

LONGUEVILLE HOUSE

Mallow, Co. Cork, Eire

With fields of raspberries, blackberries, strawberries and gooseberries growing right up to the back door of Longueville, it's not surprising they find their way on to both the breakfast and sweet trollies. A boon to any cook but the bane of her existence when every bowl in the kitchen is filled with the day's pickings.

When the deluge of fruit becomes overwhelming, Jane O'Callaghan tips half of it into the food processor to make purées for the freezer and the remainder goes straight into the preserving pan. Every conceivable type of jam, jelly and chutney is made at Longueville and there is rarely a day that doesn't include at least one taste of the summer harvest. Greenage jam is served with soda bread at breakfast; gooseberry chutney with the *terrine maison*; redcurrant jelly with the lamb; and a selection of loganberry, blackberry and raspberry ice-creams.

Though the kitchen itself is tiny, a stairway leads from it to a labyrinth of storage cellars below. It is an Aladdin's cave of food and wine. A magnificent cellar holds Michael O'Callaghan's impressive wine collection, with room to hold the first bottles from his own vineyard this year. A small larder beside it holds shelves of homemade preserves, farm butter and cheeses, with a larger room next door for basic supplies. Next to this, in an order which doesn't quite follow, is a room with an enormous Victorian billiard table!

If Jane had her way, the menu at Longueville would be much more adventurous than it is now. There would be hints of John Tovey and Robert Carrier and a good range of classical French dishes. But she finds that her guests, especially those staying for several weeks, prefer simpler food. Consequently, she always has one or two modest dishes like Irish stew or Steak and kidney pie on the dinner menu. The sweet trolley allows her greater scope and her Blackberry *mille-feuille* is as devastating as her Sticky chocolate gâteau (her version of a Miller Howe speciality) and double crust fruit pie, served with generous dollops of homemade vanilla ice-cream.

Blackberry Tart

¾ lb (350g) plain flour
pinch of salt
¼ lb (100g) castor sugar
6 oz (175g) butter, at room
   temperature
drop of vanilla essence
3 egg yolks

Filling
1 lb (450g) fresh
   blackberries *or* half
   blackberries, half apples
1 oz (25g) plain flour
several tablespoons of
   brown sugar

milk and castor sugar
vanilla ice-cream (page
   356) *or* thick cream to
   serve

8-inch (20cm) flan ring

Sift the flour and salt on to a pastry board or marble slab. Make a well in the centre and add the sugar, butter, vanilla and egg yolks. Work together with the fingers of one hand

327

until soft and pliable. Gradually draw in the flour from around the sides and knead lightly until smooth. Wrap in cling film and leave for several hours (or overnight) to chill.

Let the pastry come to room temperature then roll out just over half of it and use to line the base and sides of the flan tin. Pack the berries fairly tightly into the flan case. Scatter the flour, then brown sugar liberally over the top (you will have to judge the quantity by how sweet the fruit is). Roll out the remaining pastry and place on top, dampening the edges and pinching together to seal. Decorate the top with pastry trimmings, and prick the surface lightly with a fork. Put back into the refrigerator and chill for a further 15–20 minutes.

Preheat the oven to gas mark 4, 350°F (180°C). Take out, brush with milk and dust with castor sugar. Bake in the preheated oven for 20–30 minutes or until golden brown. Dust lightly with castor or icing sugar and serve warm with Jane O'Callaghan's homemade vanilla ice-cream or thick cream.

Serves 8

Chef: Jane O'Callaghan
Proprietors: Jane and Michael O'Callaghan

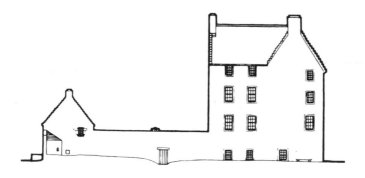

HOUSTOUN HOUSE

Uphall, West Lothian, Scotland

Keith Knight, *chef-patron* of Houstoun House, got his first
taste of the hotel business when he started work, soon after
graduating with a degree in architecture, at the Fortingall
Hotel in 1956. Run by the legendary Willie Heptinstall, it
was reputed to have the finest food of any hotel outside
London. Earning the dazzling sum of £3 a week (with no
days off) Keith became a jack of all trades, working in
the front of the house his first year and in the kitchen the
second. His tasks during the former included manning the
cocktail bar, serving wine in the dining-room and regular
stock taking. The necessity for frequent visits to the cellar
and an introduction to its contents generated an interest
in wine which has grown stronger over the years.

When Keith and Penny Knight bought Houstoun
House in 1967, it took almost two years to get a licence
for the restaurant. Due to an archaic quirk in a local law,
it was necessary to canvas 11,000 people before a poll
could be taken to change the licensing laws. (The licence
finally came through, with hair-breadth timing, on the day
the hotel opened.) The wine list at Houstoun, with its
175 vintages and 12,000 bottles in the cellar, now has few
rivals in Scotland. While you sit in the stone-flagged bar,
contemplating a La Tâche '62 or Le Montrachet

'70, you can sample any one of twenty different malt whiskies – including Houstoun's own eight-year blend, called enigmatically 'Himselfs'.

With such an extensive store so close at hand, it is hardly surprising that wine is put to good use in the Houstoun kitchen. Spirits are used less often but just as effectively, as witnessed by the following Rum sauce.

Virgin Island Fruit Pie with Rum Sauce

¼ lb (100g) soft brown sugar
¼ teaspoon salt
1 oz (25g) flour
2 bananas, peeled and sliced
2 ripe pears, cored and quartered
2 large rings of pineapple, cubed
5 dried figs, roughly chopped
juice and zest of 2 limes (if unavailable use 1 small lemon)
10 oz (275g) shortcrust pastry
milk *or* egg

9-inch (23cm) pie plate *or* dish

Sift the brown sugar, salt and flour together into a large mixing bowl. Add the fruit and toss carefully until well coated with the mixture. Pour over the juice and zest of the limes and mix again.

Preheat the oven to gas mark 6, 400°F (200°C). Roll out the pastry and use just over half to line the pie dish. Fill with the fruit mixture, pouring over any juices that remain in the bowl. Top with the remaining pastry, pinching the edges to seal. Make slits or an opening for the steam to escape, then brush with milk or egg and bake in the hot oven until golden brown (25–30 minutes). Serve warm with rum sauce.

Rum Sauce

4 tablespoons brown sugar
2 teaspoons arrowroot *or*
  cornflour
½ teaspoon ground
  cinnamon

6 tablespoons rum
8 tablespoons orange *or*
  pineapple juice

Mix the sugar, arrowroot and cinnamon together in a small saucepan. Gradually blend in the liquids. Put over a gentle heat and cook slowly until it thickens, allowing it to boil no longer than 1 minute. Pour into a warmed jug and serve with the Virgin Island pie.

Serves 6–8

Chef: Keith Knight *Proprietors:* Penny and Keith Knight

BOWLISH HOUSE

Shepton Mallet, Somerset

The sweets at Bowlish House are Martin Schwaller's strong point, and consequently everyone else's weakness. It is impossible to even talk to him about them without feeling an overwhelming urge to attack the luscious *Buntnertorte* or at least get a sniff of the newly baked Lemon and gooseberry pie.

His kitchen, dominated by a scrubbed pine table, is the scene of frequent sweet-creation schemes. He is a compulsive inventor, drawing inspiration from French provincial, European and English sources. But he comes by it honestly and perhaps his culinary precociousness (he is only twenty-four) is partly due to the experience gained in the kitchen of his father's restaurant (The Old Manor House at Knaresborough).

The menu changes frequently and dishes are rarely repeated (such is the pressure of new inventions). It is small and carefully thought out with four starters and the same number of main courses and desserts. To begin, there is hot garlic or herb bread or wholemeal rolls from the local baker. Most of the vegetables come straight from the garden, others from neighbouring farms. Connoisseurs now come to this 'restaurant with rooms' as much for the breakfasts as for the dinners since the former feature home-made croissants, meaty rashers of Somerset bacon, buttery field mushrooms and lots of Carwardine's delicious coffee.

Lemon and Gooseberry Meringue Pie

6 oz (175g) rich shortcrust pastry (page 385) *or* pâte sucrée (page 327)

Filling
2 ripe lemons
7 oz (200g) granulated sugar

½ lb (225g) gooseberries, topped and tailed
8 fl oz (225ml) water
1½ oz (40g) cornflour
2 large eggs
4 oz (100g) castor sugar

8-inch (20cm) flan ring and a baking tray

Preheat the oven to gas mark 5, 375°F (190°C). Bring the pastry to room temperature and roll out thinly. Use to line the flan ring, then prick the base lightly and cover with a circle of greaseproof paper. Fill with baking beans and bake in the preheated oven for 15 minutes. Remove the paper and beans and bake for a further 5–7 minutes or until golden brown. Remove the flan ring and cool on a cold surface or on a wire rack. Turn down the oven to gas mark 2, 300°F (150°C).

Grate the rind of both lemons and squeeze all their juice. Strain the juice into a saucepan and add the rind, sugar, gooseberries and water. Bring to the boil and stir in the cornflour, mixed first with a little water. Reduce the heat and simmer gently for 3 minutes. Allow to cool slightly.

Put the pastry case on a baking tray. Separate the eggs and whisk the yolks, one at a time, into the gooseberry mixture. Press the mixture through a sieve into the pastry case. Whisk the egg whites until stiff, then whisk in half the sugar. Fold in the remainder and pile the meringue on top of the filling. Bake in the cool oven until crisp and lightly browned. Take out and leave to cool before serving.

Serves 8

Chef: Martin Schwaller *Proprietors:* Pat and Brian Jordan

ROTHAY MANOR

Ambleside, Cumbria

Rum crops up suspiciously often in Cumbrian cooking and is, no doubt, a legacy from the days when smugglers from the Caribbean delivered cases of contraband to the ports on the west coast.

Rum butter must have dated from then, being used to accompany rich, steamed puddings and pies or spread thickly on crusty bread. Traditionally, it has always been served with bread and mulled ale or wine at a feast to celebrate the birth of a new baby. A delicious concoction, it is made by creaming together butter, demerara sugar, rum, cinnamon and nutmeg until smooth.

Cumberland Rum. Nicky is a lesser known but equally popular favourite. Once in the oven, it fills the kitchen with a heady aroma of fruit, spice and sugar. The amount of rum used to anoint it depends entirely on personal taste (if the bottle slips, the flavour will certainly not suffer). Serve it warm (not hot) with dollops of thick cream.

Cumberland Rum Nicky

6 oz (175g) plain flour
pinch of salt
1½ oz (40g) lard
1½ oz (40g) butter
1 oz (25g) sugar
½ egg

Filling
¾ lb (350g) dried dates
2 knobs of stem ginger
2 oz (50g) butter
2 oz (50g) demerara sugar
1 tablespoon rum

egg *or* milk

6-inch (15cm) flan ring *or* tin

First remove the stones from the dates and chop roughly. Put into a bowl and cover with about 2 tablespoons of boiling water. Leave to soak for at least 30 minutes.

Now make the pastry. Sift the flour with a pinch of salt into a mixing bowl. Rub in the lard and butter until the mixture resembles breadcrumbs. Blend in the sugar. Lightly beat the egg, pour over the dry ingredients and mix to a firm dough. Knead lightly, then leave to rest in a cool place for 20–30 minutes.

Preheat the oven to gas mark 4, 350°F (180°C). Allow the pastry to come to room temperature, then roll out two-thirds of it and use to line the flan ring. Drain the dates and mash well, then spread an even layer over the pastry base. Chop the ginger roughly and arrange on top of the dates. Put the butter and sugar into a bowl and cream until light. Dot this mixture over the dates and ginger. Roll out the remaining pastry thinly and make a lattice over the top. Brush with lightly beaten egg or milk. Bake in the centre of the preheated oven for 30 minutes. Take out and leave to cool on a wire rack, then pour over 1 tablespoon of rum (or more if you like).

Serves 6

Chef and proprietor: **Bronwen Nixon**

SHIPDHAM PLACE

Shipdham, Norfolk

Inspiration for the cooking at Shipdham Place is drawn mainly from English and French provincial sources. It combines the techniques and recipes of both countries to make the most of top quality country produce.

The owners, Justin and Melanie de Blank, soon realized that to offer an *à la carte* menu in the middle of Norfolk, where there might be two or twenty-two for dinner, would be suicidal. Instead, they provide four courses with no choice at all. Though seemingly restrictive, this does guarantee a high standard and minimum wastage. It also means that the meals are modest in price and continually different. The *table d'hôte* changes daily and is determined by seasonal ingredients. On an autumn evening, dinner might be Soupe de Crécy, Baked hake with prawn sauce and several fresh vegetables, followed by Profiteroles with chocolate sauce and the cheeseboard.

However simple the dish, great care is taken to see that it is perfectly cooked and presented. If soup is being served, each table is given its own tureen with enough in it for generous second helpings.

As the name suggests, this recipe represents the English provincial side of the Shipdham Place repertoire. It is Melanie de Blank's own interpretation of a classic favourite. Moist, rich and crumbly, it is served with a jug of thick Jersey cream.

Norfolk Treacle Tart

¾ lb (350g) plain flour
pinch of salt
5 oz (150g) butter
1 egg, lightly beaten
iced water

Filling
4 thick slices of white bread
2 crisp apples

8 level tablespoons golden
   syrup
grated rind of 1 lemon
juice of 2 lemons
2 eggs, lightly beaten
¼ pint (150ml) double
   cream

1 egg, lightly beaten

10-inch (25cm) flan dish *or* tin

Make the pastry first by sifting the flour and salt into a large bowl. Rub in the butter until the mixture resembles coarse breadcrumbs. Make a well in the centre and tip in the egg. Blend in, adding just enough iced water to bind the mixture lightly together (it should be as short as possible). Wrap and chill for at least 30 minutes.

Preheat the oven to gas mark 5, 375°F (190°C). Bring the pastry to room temperature, then roll out thinly and use to line the flan dish or tin. Reserve any remaining pastry for the lattice work. Bake blind for 10 minutes.

Grate the bread to make breadcrumbs, then peel and core the apples and grate them as well. Mix together in a large bowl. Heat the syrup to lukewarm and mix into the breadcrumbs with the lemon rind and juice, lightly beaten eggs and the cream. When well blended, pour into the flan case and decorate with interweaving lattice work. Brush the pastry with a little beaten egg. Bake in a hot oven – gas mark 6, 400°F (200°C) for 10 minutes, then decrease the heat to gas mark 4, 350°F (180°C) and bake for a further 20–25 minutes. Serve warm or cold with cream.

Serves 8–10

Chef: Melanie de Blank
Proprietors: Melanie and Justin de Blank

THE HUNGRY MONK

Jevington, Sussex

If I could take one sweet thing off to a desert island it would
be (failing Roy Plomley) Banoffi pie. A devastating combination, its secret will confound even the most sophisticated gastronome. I use it unashamedly to seduce those
who claim never to eat (or not to like) puddings and pies
of any description. One bite and they are yours for second
and third helpings.

Banoffi pie is an Ian Dowding creation and has been on
the menu at The Hungry Monk for as long as he has been
in the kitchen (ten years at the last count). If eager to taste
it as made by the master's hand, request it when you book
a table and he will try to have it on the menu (if it isn't
already). The restaurant now has so many veteran
'favourites' that it must involve a Herculean squeeze to get
them all on but they do promise, with ample warning, to
indulge your gastronomic whims.

With this recipe, the Banoffi is practically foolproof but
you must make sure that the tin is completely immersed in
water and keep it topped up for the full four hours. Its
flavour actually improves if made the day before serving.

Banoffi Pie

14-oz (397g) tin
  sweetened condensed
  milk
6 oz (175g) rich shortcrust
  pastry (page 385)
½ pint (275ml) double
  cream

1 rounded teaspoon
  powdered instant coffee
1 oz (25g) castor sugar
1 large banana, peeled and
  chopped

8-inch (20cm) flan tin

The secret of this delicious pudding lies in the condensed milk. Immerse the can *unopened* in boiling water. Cover and boil for 4 hours. Remove from the water and allow to cool completely before opening. Inside you will find the soft toffee filling.

Butter the flan tin and line with a thin layer of short-crust pastry. Bake blind at gas mark 5, 375°F (190°C) for about 20 minutes or until crisp and golden brown.

Whisk the cream with the coffee and sugar until thick. Now empty the toffee mixture into the flan case. Spread evenly with the back of a spoon. Put the banana in an even layer on top. Finish by spooning or piping on the cream.

Serves 8

Chefs: Ian Dowding and Kent Austin
Proprietors: Susan and Nigel Mackenzie

MARLFIELD HOUSE

Gorey, Co. Wexford, Eire

Bailey's Irish Cream, according to the vintners who launched it recently, has become an overnight sensation and is now the most popular liqueur in Ireland. A creamy, cocoa-coloured drink with a rich chocolate taste, it takes over where crème de menthe left off. Designed with the ladies in mind, it provides a light post-prandial drink with a relatively harmless alcoholic content. The formula seems to have worked like magic and now, instead of eating After-eights, everyone drinks them.

At Marlfield House, there seems to be as much Bailey's Irish Cream in the kitchen as there is in the bar. It finds its way into homemade ice-creams, chocolate mousse, the cream filling for the meringues and this deliciously rich cheesecake. It's a dream of a pudding but a dieter's nightmare!

Bailey's Irish Cream Cheesecake

Crumb Crust
½ lb (225g) biscuits, coconut
  or digestive
¼ lb (100g) butter

Filling
½ lb (225g) cottage cheese
½ lb (225g) cream cheese
2 tablespoons cold water
1 dessertspoon gelatine

juice and rind of 2 lemons
6 tablespoons Bailey's Irish
  Cream (if unavailable
  use chocolate-flavoured
  liqueur)
½ pint (275ml) double
  cream
2 egg whites
¼ lb (100g) castor sugar
2 oz (50g) melted chocolate

8-inch (20cm) spring-form cake tin

To make the crust, crush the biscuits to crumbs with a rolling pin or in a liquidizer. Melt the butter, add the crumbs and mix well. Press the mixture on to the base and sides of the tin. Chill in the refrigerator while preparing the filling.

Push the cottage cheese through a sieve, then combine in a mixing bowl with the cream cheese. Beat together well. Put the cold water into a small cup and sprinkle the gelatine on top. Leave for about 5 minutes to soak, then put the cup over or in a small amount of hot water until the gelatine has dissolved completely. Blend into the creamed mixture with the lemon rind and juice. Continue beating until the mixture is very smooth. Beat in the liqueur. Whip the cream until thick and fold into the creamed mixture. Whisk the egg whites until stiff, then gradually whisk in the sugar. Fold them carefully into the cake batter. Pour into the prepared crumb crust. Refrigerate for 6 hours or overnight. Just before serving, drizzle the melted chocolate over the surface of the cheesecake.

Serves 8

Chef and proprietor: Mary Bowe

341

ISLE OF ERISKA HOTEL

Ledaig, Connel, Scotland

The West of Scotland would be an obvious choice for a walking, shooting or sailing holiday but not, alas, a gastronomic tour. Despite bountiful natural resources, few restaurateurs have done full justice to them. Tradition appears to have dealt a death-blow to innovation, with most Scottish menus distinguished only by their predictability. But in the last five years, a small number of enterprising establishments have begun to reverse the trend.

One of the best to be found is the Isle of Eriska Hotel, about ten miles north of Oban. This towering Victorian edifice, virtually the only house on the island, enjoys unrivalled privacy and quiet. The owners, Sheena and Robin Buchanan-Smith, are rapidly dispelling the clichéd myth that in Scotland draughts, lumpy porridge and anti-social eating hours are *de rigueur*. While Sheena supervises the kitchen, assisted by a Cordon Bleu cook, Robin runs the front of the house. His relaxed manner puts guests immediately at their ease and his obvious interest in their welfare promotes a general feeling of well-being.

Dinner is five courses, with little choice until the pudding. As much as possible is gleaned from their own land or local suppliers, with the emphasis always on top-quality ingredients. The meal might begin with Haddock Montrose, a creamy blend of smoked haddock, tomato and cheese, then a homemade vegetable or game soup. Main

342

courses tend to be simply done, a joint carved from a Victorian trolley or a poached salmon with hollandaise sauce. The puddings range from an exceptional trifle to a rich chocolate or chestnut and orange roulade. Breakfasts are not to be missed as steaming dishes of eggs, bacon, sausages and fish are arrayed, under domed silver covers, on a magnificent sideboard.

Chestnut and Orange Roulade

3 large eggs
$\frac{1}{4}$ lb (100g) castor sugar
1 orange
$\frac{1}{2}$ lb (225g) unsweetened
   chestnut purée

$\frac{1}{2}$ pint (275ml) double
   cream
1–2 tablespoons orange
   liqueur

Swiss roll tin, lined with greaseproof paper

Preheat the oven to gas mark 4, 350°F (180°C). Separate the eggs and put the yolks in a large pudding basin with the sugar. Beat until light and pale in colour. Finely grate the orange rind and blend in with the chestnut purée. Whisk the whites until stiff, then fold in lightly. Transfer the mixture to the prepared tin, levelling out carefully. Bake in the preheated oven for 12–15 minutes or until firm to the touch. Take out, cover with a damp tea towel and leave for several hours or overnight.

When ready to serve the roulade, turn out on to a sheet of greaseproof paper dusted lightly with castor or icing sugar. Whisk the cream until thick, then blend in the orange liqueur. Spread this over the cake then roll up (like a Swiss roll). Dust lightly with sifted icing or castor sugar and decorate with the orange, cut into thin slices.

Serves 8

Chef: Sheena Buchanan-Smith
Proprietors: Sheena and Robin Buchanan-Smith

LOWER BROOK HOUSE*

Blockley, Gloucestershire

All the sweets at Lower Brook House come under Gill Greenstock's culinary umbrella. She attributes its scope to the fact that she is allowed to specialize in this area while her husband Bob looks after the rest of the menu. Besides the traditional Cotswold apple cake and Syrup tart, she also makes a number of Continental specialities and a few of her own invention: Banana and ginger meringue, Chocolate praline pudding and Apple and hazelnut galette.

---

* As this book went to press, Lower Brook House changed hands.

Cotswold Apple Cake

¼ lb (100g) butter
1 medium egg
¼ lb (100g) sugar
½ lb (225g) self-raising
 flour
¾ lb (350g) apples
2 oz (50g) sultanas
1 level teaspoon ground
 ginger

1 level teaspoon ground
 cinnamon
several tablespoons sugar

castor *or* icing sugar to finish
lightly whipped cream to
 serve

8-inch (20cm) loose-bottomed cake tin, well greased

Preheat the oven to gas mark 4, 350°F (180°C). Melt the butter in a saucepan. Scrape out with a rubber spatula into a large mixing bowl. Lightly beat the egg and blend into the butter with the sugar. Sift the flour and mix in gradually. Place half this mixture in the bottom of the prepared tin.

Peel, core and slice the apples thinly. Put into a bowl and mix with the sultanas, spices and several tablespoons of sugar (depending on the tartness of the fruit). Arrange the apple mixture on top of the dough in the tin, then cover with the remaining dough.

Place the tin in the centre of the preheated oven and bake until the apples are cooked and the top is a nice golden brown. Take out, carefully remove from the tin and cool slightly on a wire rack. Dust lightly with castor or icing sugar. Serve warm or cold with a dollop of lightly whipped cream.

Serves 6–8

Chef: Robert Greenstock
Proprietors: Robert and Gillian Greenstock

JOCKEY HALL

Curragh, Co. Kildare, Eire

Paul McCluskey's culinary links with France become even more obvious when one glimpses the sweet trolley. It looks as if it could have been wheeled in from any starred restaurant in the French Michelin guide.

A case of delicious understatement, it may only have four sweets on it but they will all be exquisite. The 'Chocolate Box' catches your eye the minute you enter the room: a mass of brilliant fruits (kiwi, strawberries, oranges and grapes) with snowdrops of cream and a palisade of chocolate squares round the sides. It shares the top of the trolley with a huge snowball of fluffy Pavlova, while on the shelf below, there sits a glistening Caramel bavarois and a Fresh peach tart, with crisp pastry and a golden centre of crème patissière. As a further temptation there is also homemade Rum and raisin ice-cream (page 355) and a selection of sorbets.

Chocolate Box Gâteau

Chocolate Squares
½ lb (225g) dessert
  chocolate (Meunier is
  ideal)
Sponge Base
3 large eggs, separated
¼ lb (100g) castor sugar
1 tablespoon boiling water
3 oz (75g) plain flour

Decoration
3 tablespoons kirsch
½ pint (275ml) double
  cream
¾–1 lb (350–450g) fresh
  fruits
½ lb (225g) sugar
½ pint (275ml) water

8-inch (20cm) square cake tin, greased and lightly floured

Start by making the chocolate squares. Break the chocolate into small pieces and melt in a basin over hot water, then spread the thickness of a 50p piece on a sheet of greaseproof paper. When just set, cut into squares measuring approximately 1½ inches (3·5cm), using a long, sharp knife and leave to set completely. Peel off the paper and put on a plate. (If making in advance, store the squares in a covered container with greaseproof paper between the layers.)

Preheat the oven to gas mark 4, 350°F (180°C). Put the egg yolks, half the sugar and the boiling water in a basin and set over a pan of hot water on a low heat. Whisk until thick and mousse-like, then remove from the heat and transfer to a large mixing bowl. In another bowl, whisk the egg whites until white and opaque, then whisk in the remaining sugar until peaks form. Gently fold this mixture into the egg yolks, sifting the flour in gradually as you work. Transfer to the prepared tin and bake in the preheated oven for about 25 minutes or until golden brown and springy to the touch. Turn out on to a wire rack and leave to cool.

To assemble: sprinkle the cake with the kirsch, whip the cream and spread some of it around the sides of the cake. Set the cake on a serving dish and press the chocolate squares all the way round the sides, overlapping slightly. Pipe a border round the top edge of the cake with the remaining cream, then pile the fresh fruit on top of the cake. Make a syrup glaze by dissolving the sugar in the water then boiling rapidly until thick and syrupy. Cool, then spoon a small amount over the fruit.

Serves 8–10

Chef: Paul McCluskey
Proprietors: Monica and Paul McCluskey

MOORES DORSET SHOP

Close to the Devon/Dorset border is Moores Dorset Shop, renowned for its 'Dorset Knobs'. These round, rusk-like biscuits were traditionally served with early morning tea to local farm workers. Now they are more often partnered with cheese, though not, alas, with the almost extinct Blue Vinny. Each biscuit is moulded by hand and has three separate bakings, lasting a total of eight to ten hours. The bakery has been run by the Moores family since 1880 and in addition to the 'Knobs', they make Dorset Shortbread, Dorset Gingers, Walnut Crunch and Butter Biscuits. In the shop itself, West Country produce (jams, honey, fudge, doughcakes and stone ground wholemeal flour) is also sold. Visitors are welcome to watch the biscuits being made in the bakery next door.

THE HORN OF PLENTY

Gulworthy, Devon

You have a choice at The Horn of Plenty of eating either *à la carte* or *régionale*. There are two menus: one offering a wide range of international recipes, the other a regional *table d'hôte* – matching dishes and wines of a particular region in France.

If it is a Côte d'Azur week, there might be *Pataffia*, a croûte of French bread stuffed with onion, pimento, capers, tomato and olives; a *Marmite des pêcheurs* with *rouille*; *Grillade provençale au feu de bois*; Banon cheese and fruit. The *à la carte* menu has a limited number of exquisitely prepared specialities. Under a section headed 'St Peter's Possibilities' is a listing of several fish dishes (these are all dependent on 'supply' which, in the country, is not always one hundred per cent). Foreign flavours are represented by the Peruvian duck, Poitrine of pork with juniper berries and *Hut B'Camoun*, a Moroccan recipe.

The presentation of Sonia Stevenson's dishes is as flawless as their execution. The Duck pâté, for instance, is often pressed into the cavity of a boned duck and then sliced, giving a striking contrast of texture and flavour. Her rich chocolate cake, glistening with hot sauce, is so seductive that most diners find some excuse to try it.

Rich Chocolate Cake

three 3½-oz (90g) bars of
  Meunier chocolate
½ lb (225g) unsalted butter
zest of 1 orange
3 tablespoons Grand
  Marnier
5 whole eggs
½ lb (225g) castor sugar
1 teaspoon vanilla essence
¼ lb (100g) cornflour, sifted

Chocolate Covering
5 oz (150g) butter
two 3½-oz (90g) bars of
  Meunier chocolate
3 tablespoons Grand
  Marnier

two 8-inch (20cm) cake tins, preferably with removable bases, lined with a circle of silicon non-stick paper.

Preheat the oven to gas mark 4, 350°F (180°C). Put the 3 bars of chocolate, butter, orange zest and Grand Marnier into a pudding basin. Place over a saucepan filled with a small amount of hot water. Leave until melted, then blend until smooth. Put to one side.

Put the eggs, sugar and vanilla essence into a mixing bowl and beat with an electric whisk until light and fluffy (5–10 minutes). Lightly fold in the chocolate mixture. Sift the cornflour on top and fold in lightly. Divide equally between the prepared tins, smoothing out evenly. Place just above the centre of the oven, turning it down as you put them in to gas mark 3, 325°F (170°C). Bake for 35–40 minutes or until the cakes have shrunk slightly from the edge of the tins and feel springy to the touch. (If the cakes get too brown, move them down a shelf.) Take out, turn the cakes upside down on to wire racks and leave for a few minutes to 'set'. Remove the tins and bases and leave the cakes to cool completely (then remove the paper bases).

Shortly before serving, put the butter, 2 bars of chocolate and Grand Marnier into a basin and melt as before.

Remove from the heat, blend well and allow to cool slightly. Then beat hard before using. Place the cakes on a serving dish and coat with the warm chocolate sauce.

Serves 10–12

Chef: Sonia Stevenson
Proprietors: Sonia and Patrick Stevenson

Ice-creams and Sorbets

Ice-cream and sorbet making have taken a churn for the better with the advent in most hotel and restaurant kitchens of the French *sorbetières* and English or Italian ice-cream machines.

No longer does one get the crunch of pebble-sized crystals while spooning down the strawberry 'ice', nor does the sorbet taste like flavoured snow. Now it is possible to produce, at the flick of a switch, velvety smooth ice-cream or sorbet and in quantities large enough to be practical for the professional caterer. No more mixing, whipping and beating again during freezing. All energies can now be directed towards devising the most delicious and unusual concoctions.

THORNBURY CASTLE

Banana Ice-cream

3 egg yolks
2½ oz (65g) sugar
½ pint (275ml) double
   cream

2 large bananas
tot of rum

Beat the egg yolks with the sugar in a large mixing bowl. Heat the cream to boiling point, then whisk into the yolks. Return the mixture to the saucepan and reheat carefully, stirring all the time, until it is thick enough to coat the back of a spoon. (If you heat it too quickly, the eggs will scramble; if this happens, add cold milk or cream at once and beat vigorously.) Remove from the heat and leave until almost cold. Then put it into a liquidizer with the peeled bananas and a tot of rum. Blend until smooth.

Put into a churn, electric ice-cream machine or a plastic container. Freeze until just solid. Serve with crisp tuiles biscuits (page 373).

Serves 4

WHITE MOSS HOUSE

Blackcurrant Ice-cream

1 lb (450g) blackcurrants
castor sugar to taste
4 eggs
¼ lb (100g) sifted icing
   sugar

½ pint (275ml) double
   cream

Put the blackcurrants into a large saucepan with a small amount of water and several tablespoons of castor sugar. Cover and cook over a low heat until soft. Taste and add more sugar if necessary. Put through a sieve or mouli to get a thick, smooth purée. Put to one side and leave until completely cold.

Separate the eggs. Whisk the whites until stiff, then whisk in the icing sugar, 1 tablespoon at a time. Whisk in the egg yolks until evenly blended. Whip the cream until it will just hold on to the whisk, then fold it gently into the meringue, followed by the blackcurrant purée. Pour into a ½-gallon (2·25 litre) container, cover with a lid or double layer of foil and freeze.

NB. This ice-cream does not set hard and can be used straight from the freezer.

Serves 6–8

WELL HOUSE

Brown Bread Ice-cream

2 thick slices of granary *or* wholemeal bread	¾ pint (425ml) double cream
1½ rounded tablespoons demerara sugar	¼ lb (100g) sifted icing sugar
4 large eggs	

Preheat the oven to gas mark 4, 350°F (180°C). Pull the bread into small pieces and place close together on a shallow baking tray. Sprinkle the demerara sugar evenly over the top and put the tray into the oven. Bake for about 1 hour or until the sugar has caramelized slightly and the bread is crisp and lightly browned. Cool, then tip the contents of the tray into a polythene bag and, using a rolling pin, crush to coarse crumbs (it gives a crunchier texture to the ice-cream if the crumbs are not too fine).

Separate the eggs. Half-whip the cream, then whisk in the egg yolks (being careful not to let the mixture get too thick). Whisk the egg whites until just stiff, then whisk in half the icing sugar. Fold in the remainder carefully. Sprinkle the crumbs and demerara sugar over the cream mixture, add the egg whites and fold in lightly. Transfer to a large plastic container, cover with a lid and freeze until firm.

Serves 10

LOAVES AND FISHES

Caramel and Orange Ice-cream

9 oz (250g) castor sugar
1 pint (575ml) whipping
  cream
4 large eggs
juice and finely grated rind
  of 5 large oranges

juice of 1 large lemon
2 heaped dessertspoons
  cornflour
½ pint (275ml) double
  cream

Put 5 oz (150g) of castor sugar into a large heavy saucepan and, over a gentle heat, caramelize it until a deep golden colour (it needs to be a good strong colour, otherwise its flavour will be lost in the freezing). In another saucepan, heat the whipping cream, without boiling.

When the caramel is the right colour, remove from the heat and stir in the hot whipping cream. (This must be done with great care as the caramel will bubble furiously and may splatter.) Return the caramel and cream to a low heat until the caramel has completely melted again, stirring until it is thoroughly blended with the cream. Keep warm until needed.

354

Whisk the eggs with the remaining sugar until thick and mousse-like, then blend in the grated orange rind and the lemon juice. Put the cornflour in a small bowl and gradually mix in the orange juice. Pour this mixture into the caramel and cook over a gentle heat until you have a custard, stirring constantly. Pour the hot custard into the egg mixture, whisking all the time. Taste and, if too sweet, add more lemon juice. (The lemon juice will also bring out the flavour of the caramel and orange which needs to be quite strong.) Put to one side and leave to cool.

Whisk the double cream until thick, then fold carefully into the caramel mixture. Transfer to a plastic container and freeze until firm (no need to beat again during freezing).

Serves 12

JOCKEY HALL

Rum and Raisin Ice-cream

6 oz (175g) raisins
2 pints (1·1 litres) rich milk
   or single cream

8 egg yolks
9 oz (250g) castor sugar
6 dessertspoons dark rum

Put the raisins into a bowl, cover with boiling water and leave to soak for 1 hour. Then drain very well and put to one side.

Pour the milk into a saucepan, bring to scalding point, then remove from the heat. Mix the egg yolks and sugar together in a basin over hot water. Gradually blend in half the hot milk or cream and continue whisking until the mixture thickens slightly (this is much quicker if an electric hand whisk is used). Take off the heat and carefully stir in the remaining milk or cream and the rum. Transfer to a large plastic container, cover with a lid and freeze until there is 1 inch (2·5cm) of solid ice-cream around the sides. Beat the mixture well to remove any large ice crystals, then freeze for a further 1–2 hours. Take out, beat well with a fork, then mix in the raisins. Return to the freezer and freeze until firm. (If an ice-cream machine is used, beating during the freezing will not be necessary.)

Serves 10

LONGUEVILLE HOUSE

Vanilla Ice-cream

6 egg yolks
½ lb (225g) castor sugar

2 pints (1·1 litres) double cream
1 teaspoon vanilla essence

Beat the egg yolks and sugar together until very creamy. In another bowl, whip the cream until thick. Add the vanilla essence to the yolks and lightly fold in the cream. Transfer to a large plastic container, cover with a lid and freeze until firm.

NB. Any purée of fresh fruit and sugar can be added to the above to make a flavoured ice-cream. (You will need about ½ pint (275ml) good, thick purée, sweetened to taste, for the above quantity.)

Serves 10–12

LA POTINIÈRE

Tortoni

½ pint (275ml) double cream

2 tablespoons Bacardi rum

2 oz (50g) crushed macaroons

3 oz (75g) castor sugar

2 large egg whites

toasted almond nibs *or* flakes for garnish

8 ramekin dishes

Whisk the cream until it is just beginning to thicken. Add the Bacardi, crushed macaroons and 1½ oz (40g) sugar. Continue to whisk until the mixture will stand in soft peaks.

In another bowl (preferably a copper one), whisk the egg whites until stiff. Whisk in 2 teaspoons of sugar, then fold in the remainder. Using a metal spoon, fold the meringue into the cream mixture, gently but thoroughly. Spoon the mixture into the ramekin dishes, then freeze for several hours.

Take the ramekins out of the freezer about 5 minutes before serving. Top with toasted almonds and serve.

Serves 8

KINCH'S

Blackcurrant and Cassis Sorbet

1 lb (450g) fresh *or* frozen
  blackcurrants
½ pint (275ml) water
¼ lb (100g) castor sugar

juice of ½ lemon
3 fl oz (75ml) Cassis
2 egg whites

Remove the stalks from the blackcurrants, then put into a large saucepan with the water. Boil rapidly until almost all the water has dissolved, leaving a thick purée. Stir in the sugar and continue stirring over moderate heat until it has dissolved completely. Remove from the heat and blend in the lemon juice and Cassis. Transfer to a large bowl. Whisk the egg whites until stiff, then add a spoonful to the purée to loosen it slightly. Fold in the remaining whites lightly. Pour the mixture into a plastic container, cover with a lid and freeze until firm. (Or freeze in a *sorbetière* or ice-cream machine.)

Serves 4

THE WIFE OF BATH

Elderflower Sorbet

This sorbet is only possible in early summer when the elderflowers are in full bloom and heavy with pollen.

¼ pint (150ml) fresh lemon
  juice
zest of 1 lemon
7 oz (200g) sugar

1¼ pints (700ml) cold
  water
6 large elderflower heads
2 egg whites

Put the lemon juice, zest, sugar and water into a large saucepan. Submerge the elderflower heads in the liquid and slowly heat to just below boiling point. Remove from the heat and leave to cool, then strain off the flowers.

Churn the mixture in an ice-cream maker or put into a plastic container and then into the freezer (if using the latter method, the mixture must be stirred frequently during the freezing). Whisk the egg whites until stiff, and fold into the sorbet just before it becomes completely solid.

Serves 4

THE BEAR

Loganberry Sorbet

½ lb (225g) fresh *or* frozen loganberries (if unavailable use raspberries)
2–3 oz (50–75g) icing sugar, sifted

juice of 1 lemon
¾ pint (425ml) fizzy lemonade
1 egg white

Put the loganberries into a covered saucepan and cook extremely slowly over a low heat. When just softened, remove from the heat and sieve very carefully, leaving out all the pips. Put to one side and leave to cool.

Add the icing sugar, lemon juice and fizzy lemonade to the loganberries and blend in well. Taste and add more sugar if necessary. Pour into a plastic container and freeze. Remove just before the mixture gets too solid. Whisk the egg white until stiff with an electric mixer and, with the mixer still going, add the loganberry mixture slowly, in smallish pieces, until it has all been incorporated. Pour back into the plastic container and freeze until firm.

Serves 6–8

POPJOY'S

Popjoy's Pear Sorbet

2½ lb (1 kilo) ripe pears
11 oz (300g) castor sugar
9 oz (250ml) water
rind and juice of 1 lemon

3 fl oz (75ml) *eau de vie*
'Poire William' (or
failing that, brandy)
3 egg whites (optional)

Peel, core and quarter the pears. Put the sugar and water into a large heavy saucepan and heat gently until the sugar has completely dissolved. Increase the heat until the liquid is simmering gently and add the pears. Poach them over low heat until soft, basting frequently with the pan juices. Take off the heat and leave to cool completely. Reserve 1–2 pear quarters for decoration.

When cool, purée the mixture with the syrup, lemon juice, rind, and the *eau de vie* in a liquidizer (or pass the mixture through a sieve). Put into a *sorbetière* or in a plastic container and into the freezer. Freeze for 3–4 hours (or overnight) until firm. Serve in tall chilled glasses and decorate with slices of the reserved poached pear.

NB. Egg whites (whisked until stiff) may be added to the mixture when partially frozen to give a lighter, more crumbly effect (3 egg whites for the above quantity).

Serves 6–8

Breads and Biscuits

Perhaps four or five courses for luncheon ...
in case the set menu of that meal failed to
satisfy, there were always cheese and biscuits,
'luncheon cake' and port, followed by coffee, to
make good any deficiency.

from Architect Errant, *Clough Williams-Ellis*

Though normally of calm and equitable disposition,
there is one thing which is guaranteed to send me
screaming from any restaurant. It is the appearance,
with great pomp but little circumstance, of bread which
resembles toasted marshmallow. In restaurants with
swanky décor and expensive-looking waiters, this false
economy seems ludicrous. With lobster, caviar and
melon flown in from all parts of the globe, surely
they can bring in bread from a good local baker?
However smooth and brandied their pâtés may be, a
slice of spongy cardboard cannot possibly do them
justice; whereas a wedge of nutty granary bread or
toasted wholemeal will do them (and their customers)

361

untold good. No establishment which purports to serve 'the finest food' could seriously think that the polythene-wrapped variety falls into this category.

A respect for natural ingredients is shared by all the restaurateurs in this book and they are staunch defenders of 'real bread'. Some bake their own, others get it from a local baker still producing old-fashioned loaves with distinctive flavour and texture. The butter which accompanies it is not in toffee wrappers of aluminium foil but in generous earthenware pots. The unsalted version appears frequently, providing a divine complement to crusty French bread.

There has been a major *coup* at the cheeseboard and the long-serving cream cracker has finally been ousted. Thick chunks of farmhouse Cheddar, Cheshire and Stilton are now partnered with homemade rolls or crisp oat biscuits.

CHURCHE'S MANSION

Granary Rolls

½ lb (225g) wholemeal
   flour
½ lb (225g) granary flour
1½ teaspoons salt
1 oz (25g) butter

4 fl oz (100ml) milk
¼ pint (150ml) water
1 oz (25g) fresh yeast
1 teaspoon sugar

baking tray *or* 2-lb (900g) loaf tin, lightly greased

In a warm bowl, mix the flours and salt together, then rub in the butter. Put the milk and water into a saucepan and over a low flame until the liquid reaches blood heat. Cream the yeast and sugar together in a small bowl. Gradually blend the lukewarm milk and water into the yeast and sugar. Make a well in the centre of the flours and pour in the liquid. Blend in the flour from around the sides to make a sticky (but not sloppy) dough, adding a little more water – but no more than 2 fl oz (50ml) – if needed. Cover the bowl with a damp cloth and leave the dough to rise in a warm place for 40–60 minutes or until it has almost doubled in bulk.

    Take the dough out of the bowl and punch down on a lightly floured board. Knead well, then divide into 2-oz (50g) portions and place quite close together on the baking tray (for soft-sided rolls) or well apart (for a crisp crust). Preheat the oven to gas mark 6, 400°F (200°C). Cover and allow to rise again in a warm place for about 20 minutes. Brush the tops lightly with milk or lightly salted water and bake in the oven just above the centre of the oven until nicely browned (about 15–20 minutes). Take out and leave to cool on a wire rack, away from draughts.

NB. The same dough can be used to make a large loaf instead. Place it after knocking back into a greased 2-lb (900g) loaf tin, allow to rise again until it almost reaches

the top of the tin and then bake at the same temperature
for about 40 minutes (when done, it should sound hollow
when rapped with knuckles on its base). Cool in the same
way.

Makes about 14 rolls or 1 large loaf

THE TOASTMASTER'S INN

The Toastmaster's Wholemeal Rolls

½ lb (225g) strong white
  flour
1 lb (450g) wholemeal
  flour
1½ teaspoons salt
1 oz (25g) fresh yeast

1 teaspoon castor sugar
1½ oz (40g) unsalted
  butter
¾ pint (425ml) milk
¼ pint (150ml) water
1 egg, lightly beaten

2 large baking trays, well greased

Start by warming a large mixing bowl. Sift the flours and
the salt into the bowl, tipping in at the end the bran that
remains. Put in a warm place for 15–20 minutes.

Cream the yeast with the sugar. Melt the butter and
warm the milk and water to hand-hot temperature. Add
a little of the liquid to the yeast mixture and sprinkle a little
flour on top. Leave in a warm place until it becomes
'spongy'. Make a well in the remaining flour and pour in
the yeast, the butter (make sure that this is hand-hot) and
all but about 2½ fl oz (65ml) of the liquid. Gradually mix

in the flour from around the sides, using one hand with the fingers fanned out (this incorporates more air during the mixing). The dough must be pliable; if it feels dry, add some more of the remaining liquid. Knead the dough for 10 minutes until resilient to the touch. Put back into the bowl and cover with a warm damp cloth. Leave to prove in a warm place until doubled in size.

Take out and knock down the proved dough. Knead into shape, then divide into 2 oz (50g) pieces and shape into rolls. Place on the greased trays (close together if you like soft-sided rolls, further apart if you like them with a crisp crust). Leave in a warm place until doubled in size, then brush lightly with beaten egg and bake on the top shelf of a preheated oven – gas mark 7, 425°F (220°C) – for 10 minutes until set. Then move down to the middle of the oven and bake for a further 10–15 minutes. Tap the bottom of the rolls to test if ready; if done they will sound hollow. Cool on a wire rack or serve straight from the oven.

Makes about 22 rolls

POOL COURT

White Bread

1 oz (25g) fresh yeast
1 level teaspoon castor
  sugar
¾ pint (425ml) water
1¾ lb (800g) strong white
  flour

1½ teaspoons salt
¾ oz (20g) milk powder
  (full cream)
½ oz (15g) butter

1 egg, lightly beaten

1–2 baking trays, lightly floured, *or* a 1-lb (450g) loaf tin, lightly greased and a baking tray

Put the yeast and sugar into a small bowl and blend in $\frac{1}{4}$ pint (150ml) of water, warmed to blood heat. Cover and leave in a warm place until it becomes frothy.

Sift the flour and salt into a large warmed mixing bowl, then mix in the milk powder and rub in the butter. Make a well in the centre, then pour in the frothy yeast mixture and enough of the remaining water (warmed to blood heat) to make a soft, but not sticky dough. Turn out on to a lightly floured counter and knead for about 7 minutes or until smooth and elastic. Put into a large plastic container with a lid (or back into the mixing bowl and cover with cling film) and leave in a warm place until the dough has doubled in size. Take the dough out and knock back (punch down firmly with your fist), then knead for a further 5 minutes. Cut off pieces of dough – about 2 oz (50g) in weight – and shape into rolls (or cut off 1 lb (450g) of dough and place in the prepared bread tin and use the remaining dough for rolls). Place on the floured tray (keeping well apart for crusty rolls, close together for soft-sided ones). Place the tray inside a large lightly oiled polythene bag or put a slightly dampened cloth over it. Leave the tray in a warm place for a further 45 minutes. Remove the bag or cloth, brush the tops of the rolls with lightly beaten egg and bake in a hot oven (just above the centre), gas mark 8, 475°F (240°C) for 15–20 minutes or until golden brown. Take out and cool on a wire rack.

Makes 27 rolls or 1 1-lb (450g) loaf and 19 rolls

DUNDERRY LODGE

Wheaten Soda Bread

1½ lb (675g)
  coarse-ground
  wholemeal flour
¼ lb (100g) strong white
  flour

1 teaspoon salt
1 pint (575ml) buttermilk
  (scant)
2 teaspoons bread soda,
  sifted, *or* bicarbonate
  of soda

two 1-lb (450g) loaf tins *or* one 2-lb (900g) tin, greased and
dusted lightly with flour

Preheat the oven to gas mark 7, 425°F (220°C). Sift the
flours, soda and salt into a large mixing bowl, tipping in
at the end the bran that remains. Make a well in the
centre and pour in almost all the buttermilk. Mix to a
stiff but not sticky dough, adding more buttermilk if
necessary.

Turn out the dough on to a lightly floured counter and
knead for several minutes. Then divide in two and press
each half into a loaf tin. Level off the top and press the
dough well into the corners. Bake in the preheated oven
for 25 minutes, then remove the loaves from their tins and
return them to the oven for a further 10–15 minutes. (The
bread is ready when the bottom of the loaf sounds hollow
when tapped.)

Makes 1 large or 2 small loaves

WHITE MOSS HOUSE

White Moss Oatcakes

½ lb (225g) plain flour
½ teaspoon salt
½ teaspoon bicarbonate of
  soda
½ lb (225g) porridge oats

3 oz (75g) margarine
3 oz (75g) lard
3 oz (75g) castor sugar
milk to mix

baking tray, well greased

Preheat the oven to gas mark 6, 400°F (200°C). Sift the flour, salt and bicarbonate of soda into a large bowl. Add the porridge oats, then rub in the margarine and lard. Mix in the sugar. Make a well in the centre and pour in a little milk. Gradually blend in the dry ingredients to make a firm dough, adding more milk if necessary.

Turn out on to a lightly floured counter and roll out to an ⅛-inch (·25cm) thickness. Cut out into rounds with a lightly floured glass or a biscuit cutter. Transfer to the prepared tray, keeping the oatcakes at least an inch apart. Bake in the preheated oven until light golden (about 10 minutes). Lift off with a spatula and cool on a wire rack. Store in an airtight tin.

Makes 3½ dozen oatcakes

Ballymaloe Cheese Biscuits

2 oz (50g) wholemeal
  flour
2 oz (50g) plain white
  flour
½ teaspoon baking
  powder

½ teaspoon salt
1 oz (25g) butter
2 dessertspoons cream
cold water as needed

large baking tray, greased

Preheat the oven to gas mark 4, 350°F (180°C). Sift the flours, baking powder and salt into a large bowl, tipping in at the end the bran that remains. Rub in the butter. Moisten with cream and enough water to make a stiff paste. Roll out very thinly and stamp out into rounds. Transfer to the prepared tray, leaving about 1 inch (2·5cm) between each one. Prick the tops lightly with a fork and bake on the second shelf from the top of the pre-heated oven for approximately 10 minutes. Lift off with a palette knife and serve warm or leave to cool on a wire rack. Store in a tin with a close-fitting lid. Delicious with all types of cheese, particularly Cheddar.

Makes about 18 biscuits

ROTHAY MANOR

Grasmere Gingerbread

½ lb (225g) plain flour
1 rounded teaspoon
  baking powder
1 level teaspoon ground
  ginger
¼ lb (100g) butter
¼ lb (100g) demerara
  sugar

1 tablespoon golden syrup
1 oz (25g) sultanas
1 oz (25g) crystallized *or*
  stem ginger, coarsely
  chopped
1–2 teaspoons granulated
  sugar

8-inch (20cm) sandwich *or* square tin, greased

Preheat the oven to gas mark 2, 300°F (150°C). Sift the flour, baking powder and ginger into a large mixing bowl. Rub in the butter until the mixture resembles fine breadcrumbs. Blend in the demerara sugar. Heat the syrup slightly (just enough to melt it) and mix into the dry ingredients with the sultanas and the stem ginger to make a dryish dough. Press into the prepared tin and level off with the back of a spoon, pressing well in the corners. Dust the top lightly with granulated sugar and bake in the centre of the oven until golden brown (approximately 40–50 minutes). Cool in the tin, then cut into finger lengths or squares.

NB. The original recipe for this gingerbread belongs to 'The Original, Celebrated Gingerbread Shop' in Grasmere. From premises the size of a biscuit tin, it has been producing and selling this famous sweetmeat for over 125 years. Sarah Nelson baked the first batch in 1855 and sold to the passing trade until she died, aged eighty-eight. The recipe (still a closely guarded secret) produces oblong biscuits with a brittle centre and crumbly crust.

Makes 16 squares

TULLYTHWAITE HOUSE

Goosnargh Cakes

6 oz (175g) plain flour
¼ lb (100g) butter
1 oz (25g) castor sugar
1 level teaspoon caraway
   seeds

a little extra castor sugar
   for topping

Sift the flour into a large mixing bowl and rub in the butter. Mix in the sugar and caraway seeds. Knead together until smooth, then roll out to a ¼-inch (·50cm) thickness. Cut into rounds with a medium cutter and spread about a teaspoonful of castor sugar on each cake, pressing smoothly over the top. Leave to stand on a baking sheet for a few hours or overnight. Bake in a very slow oven – gas mark 2, 300°F (150°C) – until tinted a deep cream colour (about 25 minutes). Lift off with a palette knife and leave to cool on wire racks (or eat when still warm).

Makes 16 biscuits

PENLAN OLEU

Lacey Biscuits

2 oz (50g) butter
2 oz (50ml) golden syrup
1 level tablespoon castor
   sugar

2 oz (50g) plain flour, sifted
2 oz (50g) nibbed *or*
   toasted almonds

baking sheet, lightly buttered

Preheat the oven to gas mark 6, 400°F (200°C). Melt the butter in a saucepan over low heat. Take off the heat and blend in the golden syrup. Stir in the sugar, sifted flour and almonds. When well blended, drop by salt-spoonfuls on to the baking sheet – space well apart as they spread! Bake in the preheated oven until pale golden (6–10 minutes approximately). Allow to cool slightly before lifting carefully off the tray with a palette knife. Cool on a wire rack. Delicious with sorbets and ice-creams.

Makes about 20 biscuits

LE TALBOOTH

Brandy 'Baskets'

8 fl oz (225ml) golden
  syrup
7 oz (200g) butter
6 oz (175g) sugar

juice of ½ lemon
6 oz (175g) plain flour
1 level tablespoon ground
  ginger

baking tray, greased

Put the first four ingredients into a saucepan and bring slowly to the boil, stirring frequently. Take off the heat and stir in the flour and ginger. Beat until smooth, then put to one side and leave until cool.

Preheat the oven to gas mark 6, 400°F (200°C). Shape the dough into small balls and flatten, well apart, on the baking tray. Bake just above the centre of the oven for 5–10 minutes. When golden brown, take out of the oven and allow to cool for a minute or two. Lift off with a palette knife and place each one over an inverted, greased teacup. Leave until hardened and quite cold, then turn upright and fill with scoops of ice-cream.

Makes 10 brandy 'baskets'

THORNBURY CASTLE

Tuiles

2 egg whites
¼ lb (100g) castor sugar
2 oz (50g) plain flour, sifted
2 oz (50g) butter, melted

few drops vanilla essence
chopped almonds to
    decorate

baking tray lined with silicon paper or well greased

Preheat the oven to gas mark 4, 350°F (180°C). Put the egg whites into a large mixing bowl. Whisk in the castor sugar, then the flour, followed by the melted (but not hot) butter and a few drops of vanilla essence (or better still, use vanilla-flavoured castor sugar instead).

When the mixture is well blended, drop rounded tea-spoonfuls on to the lined baking tray, keeping the drops well apart. Sprinkle a little finely chopped almond on top of each one. Bake just above the centre of the preheated oven for 7–9 minutes, or until crisp and golden brown around the edges. Lift off the baking tray with a palette knife and leave to cool on a wire rack or over horizontal wine bottles (as they cool they will take the shape of the bottle). Store in an air-tight tin.

If you have the patience, the biscuits can be rolled around a pencil to make cigar shapes; in this case, don't add the almonds and don't be surprised if you end up with slightly burned fingers.

Makes about 2 dozen biscuits

THE TOASTMASTER'S INN

Shortbread Fingers

$\frac{1}{2}$ lb (225g) plain flour
$\frac{1}{4}$ lb (100g) cornflour
$\frac{1}{2}$ lb (225g) unsalted butter

$\frac{1}{4}$ lb (100g) castor sugar
1 teaspoon rose water

baking tray, well greased

Preheat the oven to gas mark 2, 300°F (150°C). Sift the flour and cornflour into a large bowl and rub in the butter finely. Mix in the sugar, then add the rose water and press together to make a firm dough (or mix together in a food processor). Knead lightly, then press on to the prepared tray, mark into finger lengths and prick lightly. Bake in the preheated oven until the shortbread is golden. Lift off with a palette knife and cool on a wire rack.

Makes about 24 'fingers'

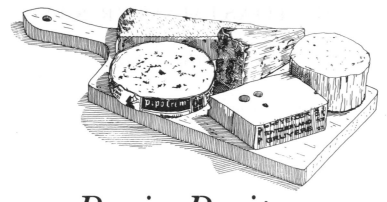

Basic Recipes

Basic White Sauce

1¾ oz (45g) butter
¾ pint (425ml) milk
pinch of salt

1½ oz (40g) plain flour,
   sifted

Melt the butter in a saucepan (preferably deep and narrow), and in another pan, warm the milk with a pinch of salt. When the butter is bubbling, add all the sifted flour in one go and using a wooden spoon, stir vigorously until the mixture is smooth. Gradually stir the warm milk into the basic roux, allowing the milk to be absorbed little by little. When the sauce is thick and smooth, pass it through a fine sieve before adding the flavouring.

Makes about ¾ pint (425ml)

VARIATIONS:

White Wine Sauce

Put half a bottle of good white wine into a saucepan with four black peppercorns and, over a low heat, reduce it to a couple of tablespoons. Fish out the peppercorns, then sieve in the basic white sauce and whisk together until creamy. Season to taste with salt and white pepper.

Curry Sauce

Heat a tablespoon of good olive oil in a fry pan, then add 1 oz (25g) of finely chopped onion. Sauté until soft and transparent. Add 1 dessertspoon of curry powder, 1 teaspoon of tomato purée, 2½ oz (65ml) red wine and 1 tablespoon apricot jam and blend in well. Simmer slowly for 30 minutes, then pass through a strainer. Whisk this mixture into the basic white sauce and heat gently. Season to taste.

MILLER HOWE

Basic Béchamel

large slice of onion	6 peppercorns
sprig of parsley *or*	½ pint (275ml) milk
½ teaspoon dried	1 oz (25g) butter
blade of mace	1 oz (25g) plain flour
small bay leaf	salt and white pepper

Put the onion, parsley, mace, bay leaf, peppercorns and milk into a saucepan and, over gentle heat, bring up to simmering point. Remove from the heat, cover with a lid and leave to infuse for 10–15 minutes.

Melt the butter in another saucepan and stir in the flour. Cook for 1 minute, then remove from the heat. Using a wooden spoon, gradually beat in the strained infused milk. Return to the heat and slowly bring to the boil, stirring all the time. Season to taste with salt and white pepper.

Makes about ½ pint (275ml)

'No. 3' Béchamel

1 onion, peeled and diced	bouquet garni
1 carrot, peeled and diced	pinch of ground mace *or*
2 sticks of celery, diced	blade of mace
2 oz (50g) butter	salt and pepper
1 oz (25g) flour	1–2 tablespoons double
1 pint (575ml) milk	cream (optional)

Melt half the butter in a saucepan, add the vegetables and cook over gentle heat until soft but not coloured. Turn the contents of the pan on to a plate and melt the remaining butter in the pan. Add the flour and stir until smooth. Blend in the milk and whisk by hand over a gentle heat until thick. Add the vegetables to this sauce with the bouquet garni, mace and a good sprinkling of salt and pepper. Simmer gently for 40 minutes, then sieve and add a little double cream if you like. Check for seasoning and adjust if necessary.

Makes about ¾ pint (425 ml)

NO. 3

Sage and Onion Sauce

1 onion	8 fresh sage leaves *or*
2 oz (50g) butter	1 level teaspoon dried
1 level tablespoon flour	sage
½ pint (275ml) milk	salt and pepper to taste

Peel and chop the onion finely. Melt the butter in a medium saucepan and toss the onion in it. Cook over a moderate heat until the onion is soft but not coloured. Stir in the flour and cook for 1–2 minutes. Gradually blend in the milk and continue cooking, stirring constantly, until the mixture thickens. Put into a liquidizer with the sage leaves and blend until smooth. Season to taste with salt and pepper. Keep warm until needed.

Makes about ½ pint (275ml)

WHITE MOSS

---

*Hollandaise Sauce**

6 oz (175g) unsalted
  butter
3 egg yolks
1 tablespoon lemon juice
1 tablespoon of water *or*
  dry white wine

good pinch of salt
1 oz (25g) cold butter
salt, pepper and lemon
  juice to taste

Cut the unsalted butter into small pieces. Let it melt *slowly* in any small pan, over a gentle heat, but take it off as soon as it's melted; don't let it get oily.

Meanwhile, put the egg yolks into a small heavy pan and beat them up well, using a wire balloon whisk. Add the lemon juice, the water or white wine and a good pinch of salt. Beat again. Now add ½ oz (15g) of cold butter, set the pan over a *very* low heat and cook, stirring steadily with the whisk, till the egg yolks are creamy and beginning to thicken and to coat the wires of the whisk. Take the pan off the heat and beat in another ½ oz (15g) of cold butter. Add the melted butter to the eggs just as if you were using oil to make a mayonnaise – drop by drop at first and then, when the mixture is beginning to get really thick, more rapidly.

When it is the consistency that mayonnaise should be before you add the lemon juice or vinegar, your sauce is ready. Now you add salt, pepper and lemon juice to taste. If it's too thick, thin it with a couple of spoonfuls of water or cream.

378

Although hollandaise is such a delicate sauce, it is good-tempered. It can be kept warm over a pan of hot water for as long as an hour. It can be stored in the refrigerator for a couple of days – or even deep-frozen and reheated. Treat it very gently, though. Heat just 2 tablespoons first over a very low heat, and then add the rest of the sauce, a little at a time, stirring constantly. If anything should go wrong at any stage and the mixture shows signs of curdling, snatch the pan from the heat and quickly stir in a tablespoon of cold water. Blend it in gently and quickly, and you should be able to 'bring back' the sauce.

Makes about ¼ pint (150ml)

* Taken from the *Four Seasons Cookery Book* by Margaret Costa, herself a restaurateur (she runs Lacey's in London with her husband Bill Lacey). It is one of the cook books most frequently used by country chefs (second only to Elizabeth David's).

Hollandaise Sauce *(using a liquidizer)*

4 egg yolks
2 teaspoons warm water
1 lb (450g) unsalted butter, melted

squeeze of lemon juice
salt and pepper

Put the yolks into a liquidizer with the water. Place the lid on firmly, removing the centre cap. Whiz for several seconds, then *slowly* pour in the hot butter. When it has all been incorporated, switch the liquidizer off. Season to taste with a squeeze of lemon juice, salt and pepper. Give a final whiz and serve at once (or transfer to a pudding basin and keep warm in a bain-marie until needed).

Makes about ¾ pint (425ml)

THE HORN OF PLENTY

379

Sauce Messine

½ onion, finely chopped
juice of 1 lemon
¼ lb (100g) butter
2 teaspoons flour
2 teaspoons French
  mustard

2 egg yolks
1 pint (575ml) single
  cream
large pinch each of
  tarragon, parsley,
  chervil

Put all ingredients into a blender and whiz thoroughly until smooth. Transfer to a pudding dish and place in a bain-marie. Cook very gently for about 15 minutes until it thickens.

Makes 1¾ pints (1 litre)

Béarnaise Sauce

2 teaspoons finely
  chopped shallots
4 tablespoons tarragon
  vinegar
4 tablespoons dry white
  wine
pinch of ground black
  pepper

1 tablespoon cold water
2 egg yolks
4–6 oz (100–175g) butter
1 tablespoon freshly
  chopped tarragon *or*
  ½ tablespoon dried
  tarragon

Put the first four ingredients into a saucepan. Boil until completely reduced and the pan is almost dry but not browned. Add 1 tablespoon of cold water immediately and mix in, scraping the bottom of the pan well. Transfer to a pudding basin (or keep in the same saucepan) and stand in a bain-marie over gentle heat. Add the egg yolks. Whisk in thoroughly, then add the butter bit by bit. As it

becomes hot and thick, remove from the heat. If it is slow
to thicken, increase the heat. Do not leave the pan or stop
beating until the sauce is made. Finally add the chopped
tarragon. (If the sauce gets too hot, it will separate. This
can sometimes be stopped in time by plunging the pan or
bowl into cold water. Then put a tablespoon of iced water
into another bowl and gradually whisk in the sauce by tea-
spoonfuls.) Keep warm until needed. Serve with grilled
and roast meat and fish.

Makes about ¼ pint (150ml)

BALLYMALOE

Espagnole Sauce (*quick method*)

2 oz (50g) good
  dripping
2 oz (50g) finely diced
  carrot
2 oz (50g) finely diced
  onion
2 oz (50g) finely diced
  celery
some mushroom stalks,
  finely chopped
1 oz finely diced streaky
  bacon

2 oz (50g) plain flour
1½ pints (850ml) good
  brown meat stock
1 level tablespoon
  tomato purée
1 teaspoon Worcestershire
  sauce
bouquet garni
1 bay leaf
salt and pepper

Melt the dripping in a saucepan and fry the carrot, onion,
celery, mushroom stalks and bacon until golden brown.
Then tip in the flour and continue to cook for 2–3 minutes,
stirring briskly. Gradually pour in the stock, bring to the
boil and simmer for 10 minutes. Now add the tomato
purée, Worcestershire sauce, bouquet garni and bay leaf.

Allow to bubble gently for a further 10 minutes. Season to taste with salt and freshly ground black pepper. Reduce the sauce by half by boiling rapidly (uncovered) over a low flame for 30–45 minutes. Pour through a sieve into a warmed jug and use as required.

Makes about ¾ pint (425ml)

THE HUNGRY MONK

Cumberland Sauce

1 large orange	pinch of ground ginger
1 large lemon	pinch of cayenne
½ small onion, peeled and finely diced	½ teaspoon dry *or* French mustard
½ lb (225g) redcurrant jelly	1 teaspoon red wine vinegar
	1 dessertspoon port

Use a vegetable peeler to remove the rind from the orange and lemon. Then shred it finely and put into a saucepan with the onion. Barely cover with water and blanch quickly for 5 minutes. Strain and put to one side.

Squeeze and strain the orange and lemon juice. Put into a saucepan with the redcurrant jelly, ginger, cayenne, mustard, vinegar and port. Heat gently, stirring all the time, until completely blended. (If using the sauce hot, you might like to thicken it slightly with a small amount of arrowroot. You will need 1–2 teaspoons slaked with a little water.) Strain and add the orange and lemon zest and the onion. Cover and refrigerate until needed.

Makes about ½ pint (275ml)

LAMB'S

Mayonnaise

3 egg yolks
½ teaspoon salt
½ teaspoon dry *or* prepared mustard
large pinch cayenne pepper

1 tablespoon wine vinegar *or* lemon juice
¾ pint (425ml) corn *or* olive oil (or a mixture of both)

Before starting to make the mayonnaise, make sure that all the ingredients are at room temperature. Rinse out the mixing bowl in hot water and dry carefully. With an electric or hand whisk beat the egg yolks in the bowl for 1–2 minutes until thick and sticky. Add the seasonings and all but a few drops of the wine vinegar or lemon juice and beat for a further 1–2 minutes.

Begin adding the oil in drops, whisking continuously. Continue adding the oil very slowly until the mayonnaise begins to thicken. Once the mayonnaise has thickened, you may add the oil a little faster. When the mayonnaise becomes too stiff to whisk add a few drops of lemon juice or vinegar and then continue adding the oil until it has all been absorbed. Check the seasoning and adjust if necessary.

Should the mayonnaise curdle, warm and dry a fresh basin and put in 1 teaspoon of prepared mustard. Add 1 tablespoon of the curdled mayonnaise and whisk together until creamy. Continue adding the curdled mayonnaise by tablespoons.

Makes ¾ pint (425ml)

MALLORY COURT

Pesto Sauce

2 cloves of garlic, peeled
8 small sprigs of fresh basil
2 tablespoons pine nuts
5 tablespoons grated
   Parmesan cheese

4–6 tablespoons olive oil
salt and pepper

Put all the ingredients into a liquidizer or food processor and blend until smooth. Season to taste with salt and pepper. Store in a jar with a tightly fitting lid in the refrigerator. (Once the jar has been opened, seal the pesto sauce with a layer of olive oil.)

PLUMBER MANOR

Basic Shortcrust Pastry (for Savoury Dishes)

½ lb (225g) plain flour
large pinch of salt
2 oz (50g) butter

2 oz (50g) lard
4 tablespoons iced water

Sift the flour and salt into a large mixing bowl. Rub in the fats until the mixture resembles breadcrumbs. Add the iced water and mix with a knife or fork until the dough leaves the sides of the bowl clean. Shape into a ball, put into a polythene bag (or wrap in cling film) and chill for at least 30 minutes. Bring to room temperature before rolling out.

Rich Shortcrust Pastry *(for Savoury Dishes)*

6 oz (175g) plain flour
pinch of salt
3 oz (75g) butter

1 oz (25g) lard
1 egg yolk
2–3 tablespoons iced water

Sift the flour and salt into a large mixing bowl. Rub in the fats until the mixture resembles breadcrumbs. Mix the egg yolk with the water and tip over the dry ingredients. Mix quickly with a knife or fork until the dough leaves the sides of the bowl clean. Shape into a ball, put into a polythene bag or wrap in cling film and chill for at least 30 minutes. Bring to room temperature before rolling.

For other savoury shortcrust pastry recipes, see pages 65, 254 and 263

Rich Shortcrust Pastry *(for Sweet Dishes)*

6 oz (175g) plain flour
pinch of salt
3 oz (75g) butter
1½ oz (40g) castor *or* icing sugar

1 egg yolk
2 tablespoons iced water

Sift the flour and salt into a large mixing bowl. Rub in the butter until the mixture resembles breadcrumbs. Blend in the sugar. Mix the yolk and water together, then pour over the dry ingredients. Mix quickly with a knife or fork to a firm dough (adding more water if necessary). Put into a polythene bag or wrap in cling film and chill for at least 30 minutes. Bring to room temperature before rolling out.

For French pastry (pâte sucrée), see page 327.
For other sweet shortcrust pastry recipes, see pages 324, 335 and 337.

Puff Pastry

1½ lb (675g) plain flour 8 fl oz (225ml) water
1½ lb (675g) butter
2 oz (50ml) white wine
 vinegar

Sift the flour into a large bowl and rub in a third of the butter. Mix in the wine vinegar and water to achieve a soft, elastic paste. Roll out this paste so it forms an oblong about ½ inch (1cm) thick. Flatten the remaining butter between two sheets of greaseproof paper so that its shape is two-thirds the length of the oblong and a little less than the width. Place the butter at one end of the paste. Fold back the other end to cover the butter. Now fold the paste over again so that it completely encases the butter. The effect is of a flattened Swiss roll.

Flour the work surface lightly. Place the paste, folds towards you, with the bottom flap resting on the work surface. Roll out the paste until it is back to its original size. Fold in three. Rest for 15 minutes (the pastry, that is, not the cook). Repeat five times more. After each fold the Swiss roll should be facing you before rolling. Each rolling is called a 'turn' because the folded paste has to turn through 90 degrees each time in order to be facing you.

Makes 1½ lb (675g)

POPJOY'S

Beef Stock

3 lb (1·5 kilos) beef bones
a little butter *or* beef
    dripping
2 large onions, peeled and
    chopped
2 large leeks, roughly
    chopped
2 large carrots, peeled and
    chopped

2 stalks of celery,
    chopped
handful of mushroom
    stalks
bouquet garni (bayleaf,
    sprig of thyme, parsley)
8 peppercorns
salt
3–4 pints (1·7–2·3 litres)
    water

Put the beef bones in a very large deep saucepan and brown gently for 15–20 minutes. Then add a small amount of butter or beef dripping to the pan with all the chopped vegetables. Cook for a further 20 minutes or until the vegetables are soft and lightly coloured. Add the bouquet garni, peppercorns and a good sprinkling of salt. Pour in the water and bring up to the boil. Then reduce the heat and simmer for about 4 hours. Strain the stock, discarding the bones and vegetables, then return to the pan. Allow to cool, then skim off the fat. Taste for seasoning and adjust if necessary.

Makes about 1½ pints (850ml) stock

Chicken Stock

rasher of unsmoked bacon
½ oz (15g) butter
1 large onion, peeled and
    chopped
2 large carrots, peeled and
    sliced
1 large leek, roughly
    chopped

large stalk of celery, finely
    chopped
bouquet garni (bay leaf,
    sprig of thyme, parsley)
8 peppercorns
salt
1 chicken carcass
water

387

Remove the rind from the bacon, then chop into small pieces. Melt the butter in a large saucepan and add the bacon. Cook until the bacon fat begins to run, then stir in the chopped onion. Continue cooking until the onion is soft and transparent. Add the remaining vegetables, cover with a piece of buttered paper and 'sweat' for about 10 minutes. Remove the paper, add the bouquet garni, peppercorns and a good sprinkling of salt. Put the chicken carcass on top and just cover with water. Bring up to the boil, then reduce the heat and allow to simmer uncovered for 2–3 hours. Strain, discarding the carcass and vegetables, and pour the stock back into the pan. Allow to cool, then skim off the fat and adjust the seasoning.

Makes about 2 pints (1·1 litres) stock

Potted Stilton

½ lb (225g) unsalted
  butter

½ lb (225g) Stilton
2 tablespoons port

Put the butter into a large bowl and cream until soft. Grate the Stilton and beat into the softened butter (or better still, blend together in a Magimix). Gradually blend in the port. Transfer to an earthenware pot and seal tightly.

WHITE MOSS HOUSE

Gooseberry Chutney

4 lb (2 kilos) gooseberries
4 onions
1 oz (25g) salt
1½ lb (675g) brown sugar
½ lb (225g) sultanas

2 pints (1·1 litres) vinegar
1 teaspoon dry mustard
¼ teaspoon cayenne
  pepper

Top and tail the gooseberries. Chop the onions and put into a greased saucepan with all the other ingredients. Stir over a low heat until the sugar has completely dissolved. Bring up to the boil, then reduce the heat and simmer until thick and pulpy, stirring frequently. Pour into sterilized pots and close tightly.

LONGUEVILLE HOUSE

Pickled Red Cabbage

1 pint (575ml) malt
   vinegar
1 dessertspoon pickling
   spice

1 red cabbage
salt
½ lb (225g) onions
sugar

Start by making a spiced vinegar: put the malt vinegar and the pickling spice into a saucepan and simmer for 15 minutes. Strain then leave to cool completely.

Quarter the cabbage, remove the core, then shred finely. Put alternate layers of cabbage and salt in a bowl. Put a plate with a weight on top and leave overnight.

The next day, rinse the cabbage in a colander and drain. Slice the onions and pack in jars with alternate layers of cabbage. Press down, then add 1 teaspoon of sugar to each jar. Fill the jars with cold spiced vinegar (be sure that the vinegar completely covers the cabbage – top up as necessary).

ROTHAY MANOR

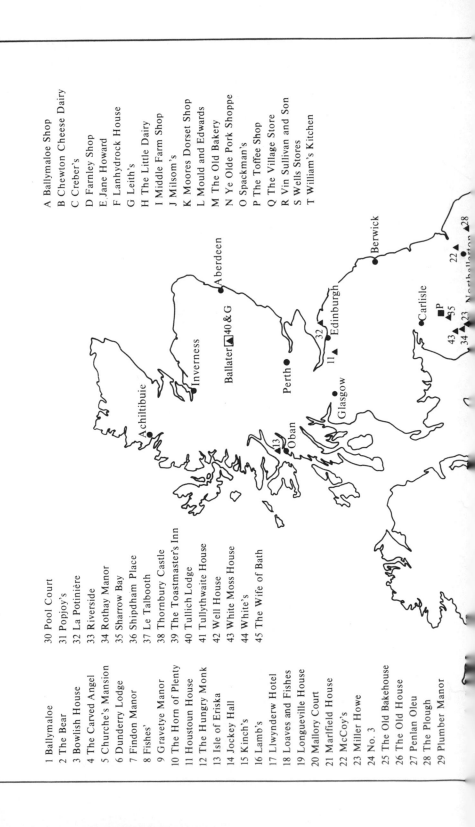

A Ballymaloe Shop
B Chewton Cheese Dairy
C Creber's
D Farnley Shop
E Jane Howard
F Lanhydrock House
G Leith's
H The Little Dairy
I Middle Farm Shop
J Milsom's
K Moores Dorset Shop
L Mould and Edwards
M The Old Bakery
N Ye Olde Pork Shoppe
O Spackman's
P The Toffee Shop
Q The Village Store
R Vin Sullivan and Son
S Wells Stores
T William's Kitchen

1 Ballymaloe
2 The Bear
3 Bowlish House
4 The Carved Angel
5 Churche's Mansion
6 Dunderry Lodge
7 Findon Manor
8 Fishes'
9 Gravetye Manor
10 The Horn of Plenty
11 Houstoun House
12 The Hungry Monk
13 Isle of Eriska
14 Jockey Hall
15 Kinch's
16 Lamb's
17 Llwynderw Hotel
18 Loaves and Fishes
19 Longueville House
20 Mallory Court
21 Marlfield House
22 McCoy's
23 Miller Howe
24 No. 3
25 The Old Bakehouse
26 The Old House
27 Penlan Oleu
28 The Plough
29 Plumber Manor

30 Pool Court
31 Popjoy's
32 La Potinière
33 Riverside
34 Rothay Manor
35 Sharrow Bay
36 Shipdham Place
37 Le Talbooth
38 Thornbury Castle
39 The Toastmaster's Inn
40 Tullich Lodge
41 Tullythwaite House
42 Well House
43 White Moss House
44 White's
45 The Wife of Bath

Achiltibuie
Inverness
Aberdeen
Ballater 40 & G
Perth
Oban
Glasgow
Edinburgh
Berwick
Carlisle
Northallerton

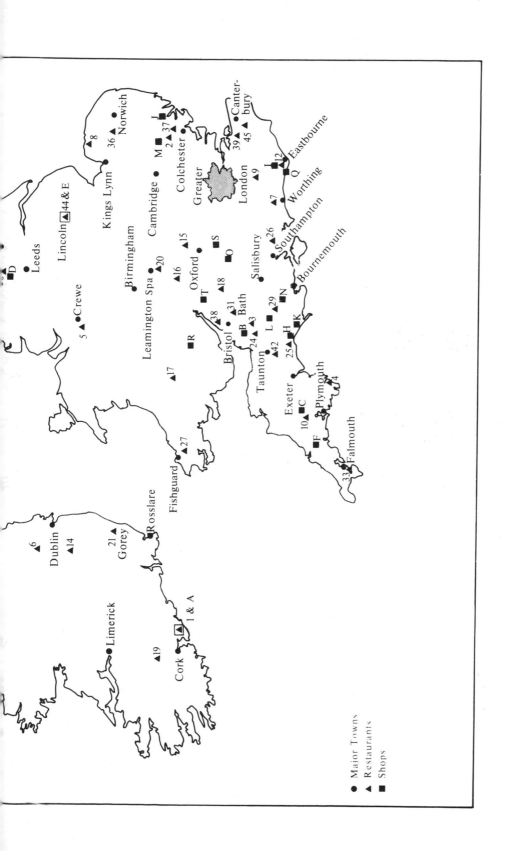

Complete Restaurant and Shop Listing

Restaurants

(Booking is advisable)

The South-East

THE TOASTMASTER'S INN
Church Street, Burnham, Kent. [0634] 61299.
Lunch 12–2pm. Dinner 7–9.30pm.
Closed Sunday, Monday, Saturday lunch, two weeks in August, one week at Christmas, 1 January.

THE WIFE OF BATH
4 Upper Bridge Street, Wye, Kent. [0233] 812540.
Lunch 12–2pm. Dinner 7–10pm.
Closed Sunday, Monday (except public holidays), 24–26 and 31 December.

GRAVETYE MANOR
East Grinstead, West Sussex. [0342] 810567.
Lunch 12.30–1.45pm. Dinner 7.30–8.45pm. 14 bedrooms.
Open every day.

THE HUNGRY MONK
Jevington, near Eastbourne, East Sussex. [03212] 2178.
Sunday lunch 12.15–2pm. Dinner 7–10pm.
Closed 24, 25 December and for lunch Monday–Saturday.

FINDON MANOR
Findon, near Worthing, West Sussex. [090671] 2269.
Bar lunches 12.30–2pm Tuesday–Sunday.
Dinner from 7.30pm. 5 bedrooms.
Closed Sunday and Monday dinner, public holidays.

Also recommended:

MALLET'S
Simon Mallet, another Perry-Smith protégé and previously at The Wife of Bath, has now opened his own restaurant in Ramsgate. He offers a short, frequently changing menu which has a distinct emphasis on French provincial cooking and includes, as well as superb *charcuterie*

(prepared by Mallet himself), dishes such as *Aillade*, Duck with green-
gages and rosé wine, Pork noisette with orange and ginger.
58 Queen Street, Ramsgate, Kent. [0843] 52854.
Dinner only, 7.30–10.30pm.
Closed Sunday, Monday, 25, 26 and 31 December, all January.

The South-West

THE OLD HOUSE
The Square, Wickham, Hampshire. [0329] 833049.
Lunch for residents only, or parties by arrangement.
Dinner 7.30–9.30pm. 10 bedrooms.
Closed Sunday, public holidays, two weeks at Christmas, one week at
Easter, two weeks July/August.

LOAVES AND FISHES
The Old Lime Kiln, Wootton Bassett, Wiltshire. [079370] 3597.
Lunch 12.30–1.30pm. Dinner 7.30–8.30pm.
Closed Saturday lunch, Sunday dinner, Monday, 24–26 and 31
December, 1 January.

PLUMBER MANOR
Sturminster Newton, Dorset. [0258] 72507.
Dinner 7.30–9.30pm. 6 bedrooms.
Closed for lunch (except 25 December), Sunday (except residents),
Monday, 1 January, February and the first two weeks of November.

BOWLISH HOUSE
Wells Road, Shepton Mallet, Somerset. [0749] 2022.
Dinner only 7–11pm. 5 bedrooms.
Closed Sunday, 25 and 26 December.

NO. 3
Magdalene Street, Glastonbury, Somerset. [0458] 32129.
Sunday Lunch 12.30–1.30pm. Dinner 7.30–9.30pm.
Closed Sunday dinner, 25 December dinner, Monday, May, Novem-
ber, lunch Monday–Saturday.

WELL HOUSE
Poundisford, Somerset. [082342] 566.
Sunday lunch 12.30–1.30pm. Dinner 7–9.30pm.
Closed Sunday dinner, Tuesday lunch, Monday, 25 December dinner,
weekday lunches (mid-September – mid-May).

Also recommended:

BLOSTIN'S

A small restaurant run with enthusiasm by its *chef-patron*, Bill Austin. As much as possible is gleaned locally (vegetables from his garden, game from local shoots) and the menu is based on seasonal produce. Specialities include Tomato and fresh thyme sorbet, Salmon and crab terrine, Pheasant and mushroom pie, homemade Coffee and walnut ice-cream.
29 Waterloo Road, Shepton Mallet, Somerset. [0749] 3648.
Dinner only 7–10pm.
Closed Sunday, 24–26 December and 1 January.

MILTON SANDFORD RESTAURANT

Church Lane, Shinfield, near Reading, Berkshire. [0734] 883783.
Lunch 12–2pm. Dinner 7–9.30pm.
Closed Sunday, Saturday lunch.

The West Country

THE OLD BAKEHOUSE

Colyton, Devon. [0297] 52518.
Dinner only, 7–9pm. 7 bedrooms.
Closed Sunday (except residents) November–February.

THE CARVED ANGEL

2 South Embankment, Dartmouth, Devon. [08043] 2465.
Lunch 12.30–1.45pm. Dinner 6.30–10.30pm.
Closed Sunday dinner, Monday, 24–26 December.

RIVERSIDE

Helford, Cornwall. [032623] 443.
Sunday lunch 12.45–2.15pm. Dinner 7.30–10pm. 4 bedrooms.
Closed for lunch (except Sunday), Sunday and Monday dinner (except residents), public holidays and 1 November–28 February.

THE HORN OF PLENTY

Gulworthy, near Tavistock, Devon. [0822] 832528.
Lunch 12.15–2pm. Dinner 7.15–9pm.
Closed all day Thursday, Friday lunch and 25 December.

Also recommended:

GIDLEIGH PARK

Run with great charm by an American couple, Gidleigh Park provides country house entertaining at its best. Kay Henderson cooks with the light touch of *nouvelle cuisine*, producing dishes of exquisite flavour

and style. Paul Henderson is an enthusiastic wine collector and his prodigious list includes an unrivalled selection of Californian vintages. An oasis for *bon viveurs*.
Chagford, Devon. [06473] 2367.
Open every day. Lunch 12–2.30pm. Dinner 7.30–9.30pm. 11 bedrooms.

The West and Wales

POPJOY'S
Beau Nash House, Saw Close, Bath, Avon. [0225] 60494.
Lunch 12–2pm. Dinner 6.45–10.30pm.
Closed Sunday, Monday lunch, lunch October–March, three weeks at Christmas, public holidays.

THORNBURY CASTLE
Thornbury, Avon. [0454] 412647.
Sunday lunch 12.30–2pm. Dinner 7.30–9.30pm.
Closed for lunch Monday–Saturday, Sunday dinner, Monday, 25, 26 December and 1 January.

LAMB'S
High Street, Moreton-in-Marsh, Gloucestershire. [0608] 50251.
Sunday lunch 12.30–2pm. Bar lunches Tuesday–Saturday. Dinner 7.30–10.30pm.
Closed Sunday dinner, Monday, dinner 25 December.

KINCH'S
Chesterton, Oxfordshire. [08692] 41444.
Sunday lunch 12–1.30pm. Dinner 7–9.30pm. Closed Sunday dinner, Monday, lunch Monday–Saturday, first week in January and public holidays.

MALLORY COURT
Harbury Lane, Tachbrook Mallory, Bishop's Tachbrook, Warwickshire. [0926] 30214.
Dinner only (except for Christmas Day lunch), 7.30–9.45pm. 6 bedrooms.
Closed Sunday dinner (except residents), 26 December, 1 January and the last fortnight in February.

LLWYNDERW HOTEL
Abergwesyn, Llanwrtyd Wells, Powys, Wales. [05913] 238.
Dinner only 7.45pm. Lunch by arrangement. 12 bedrooms.
Closed November–mid-March.

PENLAN OLEU
Llanychaer Bridge, near Fishguard, Dyfed, Wales. [034882] 314.

Dinner only, 8–9.30pm. Lunch by arrangement. 4 bedrooms.
Closed ten days in October, six weeks January–February.

Also recommended:

THE PRIORY
Made famous by John and Thea Dupays (see below), The Priory is now under the careful management of John Donnithorne. With Robert Harrison still in the kitchen, the standard of cooking remains high. The fish is exceptionally good and specialities include Terrine of scallops *au beurre blanc*, Sole soufflé and Seafood *pot au feu*.
Weston Road, Bath, Avon. [0225] 331922.
Lunch 12.30–1.30pm. Dinner 7.30–9.30pm. 15 bedrooms.
Closed 24–26 and 31 December, 1 January.

HUNSTRETE HOUSE
After sculpting The Priory to fine perfection, John and Thea Dupays have moved a few miles south-west to Hunstrete. Here they have created a retreat of equal elegance; with cuisine as stunning as the décor. Their chef, Alain Dubois, cooks for the discerning palate and habitués enthuse about his starters, game dishes, wonderful vegetables and puddings.
Hunstrete, near Bath, Avon. [07618] 570.
Lunch 12.30–1.45pm. Dinner 7.30–9.15pm. 19 bedrooms.
Closed Sunday dinner, 24 December–3 January.

COUNTRY ELEPHANT
This small dining-room of Cotswold stone, lit by fire and candlelight, cocoons the diner in an atmosphere of cosiness and warmth. Pamela Medforth cooks, using the best ingredients to produce excellent country dishes: Steak and red wine pie, Venison casserole, Mushroom and bacon pancakes. Her husband Michael acts as host and *sommelier*, with a list which offers European and American wines.
New Street, Painswick, Gloucestershire. [0452] 813564.
Sunday lunch 12.30–2pm. Dinner 7.15–10pm.
Closed Sunday dinner, Monday, 24–26 December, mid-October–mid-November. Open for lunch 31 December and 1 January.

CROQUE-EN-BOUCHE
Formerly at the Lavender Hill restaurant in London, Marion and Robin Jones are now delighting country *patrons* with their inimitable French provincial cooking. As well as the main menu, they offer a five-course set dinner which might feature unusual hors d'oeuvres, various *potages*, Turbot with sorrel sauce, perhaps *Poulet de Bresse en bourride*, followed by a homemade sorbet and an outstanding cheeseboard.
221 Wells Road, Malvern Wells, Hereford and Worcester. [06845] 65612.

Sunday lunch 12.45–1.45pm. Dinner 7.45–9.15pm.
Closed Sunday dinner, Monday, Tuesday, lunch Monday–Saturday, 25 and 26 December.

WALNUT TREE INN

For over a decade, the Taruschios have made this corner of Wales 'worthy of a detour'. Using only top quality ingredients, they provide outstanding Italian cooking. As well as the traditional favourites (e.g. home-cured *bresaola*, homemade lasagna, *brodetto*), unusual and delicious dishes like Duck with kumquats, Veal Benedictine or Trinidad curried prawns crop up frequently.
Llandewi Skirrid, near Abergavenny, Gwent, Wales. [0873] 2797.
Lunch 12.15–2.30pm. Dinner 7.30–10.30pm.
Closed Sunday, 25 and 26 December.

The Midlands and East of England

CHURCHE'S MANSION

150 Hospital Street, Nantwich, Cheshire. [0270] 65933.
Lunch 12–2pm. Dinner 7–8.30pm.
Closed Sunday dinner, 24 (dinner), 25 and 26 December, 1 January.

WHITE'S

The Jew's House, 15 The Strait, Lincoln, Lincolnshire. [0522] 24851.
Lunch 12.30–1.30pm. Dinner 7.30–10pm.
Closed Sunday, Monday lunch, public holidays, two weeks in August, two weeks in January.

Also recommended:

LAKE ISLE

After a spell of cooking with Kenneth Bell at Thornbury Castle, Roy Richards has now moved on to Uppingham to open his own restaurant. His enthusiasm for wine is well matched by the excellence of the five-course set dinners. Prepared with imagination and skill, dishes include superb homemade soups, Pork and spinach terrine, *Canard aux abricots*, *Poulet au citron*. Vegetables are treated with respect and the cheeseboard is varied and interesting.
16 High Street East, Uppingham, Leicestershire. [057282] 2951.
Dinner only, 7.30–9.30pm.
Closed Sunday, Monday, public holidays.

RESTAURANT BOSQUET

97a Warwick Road, Kenilworth, Warwickshire. [0926] 52463.
Dinner only, 7–10pm.
Closed Sunday, Monday, Good Friday, 25, 26 and 31 December, 1 January.

JEAN-PIERRE

Cauldon Lowe, Near Ashbourne, Staffordshire. [05386] 338.
Lunch 12–1.30pm. Dinner 7.30–9.30pm.
Closed Saturday lunch, Sunday, 25 December and 1 January.

FRENCH PARTRIDGE

Horton, near Northampton, Northamptonshire. [0604] 870033.
Dinner only, 7.30–9.30pm.
Closed Sunday, Monday, three weeks in the summer, two weeks at
Christmas.

East Anglia

THE BEAR

Bear Street, Nayland, Suffolk. [0206] 262204.
Sunday lunch 12.30–2pm. Dinner 7.30–9.30pm.
Closed Monday, Tuesday, Sunday dinner, one week at Easter,
25, 26 December and 1 January.

LE TALBOOTH

Gun Hill, Dedham, Essex. [0206] 323150.
Lunch 12.30–2pm. Dinner 7.30–9pm. Bedrooms (10) available at
nearby Maison Talbooth.
Closed one week at Christmas.

SHIPDHAM PLACE

Shipdham, near Thetford, Norfolk. [0362] 820303.
Sunday lunch 1–1.30pm. Dinner 7.30–8.30pm. 6 bedrooms.
Closed mid-December–Easter and first fortnight in October.

FISHES'

Market Place, Burnham Market, Norfolk. [032873] 588.
Lunch 12–1.45pm. Dinner 7–9.30pm.
Closed Monday (mid-September– mid-July), Sunday dinner (October
–June), 24 (dinner), 25 and 26 December.

Also recommended:

HINTLESHAM HALL

This is country cuisine 'par elegance'. Robert Carrier has converted his
stately sixteenth-century home to a sophisticated restaurant, with food
on the same elevated plane. Aided by a magnificent kitchen garden,
fully restored to its original proportions, he is able to offer dishes of
impeccable freshness and flavour. *Aiguillettes de canard aux herbes, Filet de
turbot aux poireaux*, crisp *mange-touts* and *Tulip d'été* are just a few of the
delicacies to be found on his generous *table d'hôte*.

Hintlesham, Suffolk. [047387] 227.
Lunch 12.30–2.30pm. Dinner 7.30–10.30pm.
Closed 1 January.

The Lake District and Yorkshire

SHARROW BAY
Ullswater, Cumbria. [08536] 301.
Lunch 1–1.30pm. Dinner 7.45–8.30pm. 28 bedrooms.
Closed December–February.

MILLER HOWE
Windermere, Cumbria. [09662] 2536.
Dinner only, 8 for 8.30pm (two sittings Saturday). 13 bedrooms.
Closed 14 December–early March.

WHITE MOSS HOUSE
Rydal Water, Grasmere, Cumbria. [09665] 295.
Dinner only, 7 for 7.30pm. 7 bedrooms.
Closed the end of October–mid-March.

ROTHAY MANOR
Rothay Bridge, Ambleside, Cumbria. [09663] 3605.
Lunch 12.30–2pm. Dinner 7.30–9pm.
Closed January and February.

TULLYTHWAITE HOUSE
Underbarrow, Cumbria. [04488] 397.
Sunday lunch 12.30pm. Dinner 7pm.
Closed for lunch (except Sunday), Sunday dinner, Monday, Friday,
public holidays, December–Easter.

POOL COURT
Pool Bank, Pool-in-Wharfedale, West Yorkshire. [0532] 842288.
Dinner only, 6.30–9.30pm.
Closed Sunday, Monday, 25, 26 and 31 December, 27 July–11 August,
first two weeks in January.

THE PLOUGH INN
Fadmoor, Kirkbymoorside, North Yorkshire. [0751] 31515.
Bar lunches on Sunday and public holidays. Dinner 7.30–8.30pm.
Closed Sunday dinner, Monday, first week in May, October and Feb-
ruary, 24–26 and 31 December, 1 January.

McCOY'S
Staddle Bridge, near Northallerton, North Yorkshire. [060982] 207.
Dinner only, 7.30–11pm.
Closed Sunday and public holidays.

Also recommended:

BOX TREE
(See Introduction for description.) Church Street, Ilkley, West York-
shire. [0943] 608484.
Dinner only, from 7.30pm.
Closed Sunday, Monday, 25, 26 December, 1 January, public holidays,
first week in February.

Scotland

LA POTINIERE
Gullane, East Lothian. [0620] 843214.
Lunch 12.45 for 1 pm. Saturday dinner 7.30 for 8pm.
Closed Wednesday, Saturday lunch, dinner Sunday–Friday, 25 and
26 December, October.

HOUSTOUN HOUSE
Uphall, West Lothian. [0506] 853831.
Lunch 12.30–2pm. Dinner 7.30–9pm. 29 bedrooms.
Open every day.

TULLICH LODGE
Ballater, Grampian. [03382] 406.
Lunch 1pm. Dinner 7.30–9pm. 10 bedrooms.
Closed January–March.

ISLE OF ERISKA
Eriska, Strathclyde. [063172] 371.
Lunch 1–1.30pm. High tea 5.45pm. Dinner 7.30–8.30pm. 24 bed-
rooms.
Closed the end of November–March.

Also recommended:

SUMMER ISLES HOTEL
Achiltibuie, Highland. [085482] 282.

In the Smokehouse restaurant lunch 12–2pm; dinner 7–9pm (May–September, by arrangement). In the main restaurant: dinner 7 for 7.30pm. 16 bedrooms.
Closed mid-October–Easter.

DUNAIN PARK
Inverness, Highland. [0463] 30512.
Lunch (snacks) 12.30–1.30pm. Dinner 7.30–9pm. 6 bedrooms.
Closed November–March.

KINLOCH LODGE HOTEL
Isle Ornsay, Skye, Highland. [04713] 214.
Lunch (bar) 12–2pm. High tea 6pm. Dinner 8pm. 12 bedrooms.
Closed November–February.

INVERLOUNIN HOUSE
Lochgoilhead, Strathclyde. [03013] 211.
Lunch 12.30–2pm. Dinner 7.30–9.30pm. 4 bedrooms.
Open every day.

Ireland

BALLYMALOE HOUSE
Shanagarry, Co. Cork, Eire. [Cork] 62531 and 62506.
Lunch 1–1.30pm. Dinner 7–9.30pm. 23 bedrooms.
Closed 24–26 December and two weeks mid-January.

DUNDERRY LODGE
Dunderry, near Navan, Co. Meath, Eire. [Navan] 31671.
Dinner only, 7.30–10.30pm.
Closed Sunday, Monday, most public holidays.

JOCKEY HALL
Curragh, near Kildare, Co. Kildare, Eire. [Naas] 41416 and 41401.
Dinner only, 6.30–10pm.
Closed Sunday, Good Friday, 24 and 25 December.

LONGUEVILLE HOUSE
Mallow, Co. Cork, Eire. [Mallow] 27156.
Dinner only, 7–9pm. 20 bedrooms.
Closed Sunday, Monday (except residents), mid-October–Easter.

MARLFIELD HOUSE
Courtown Road, Gorey, Co. Wexford, Eire. [Courtown Harbour] 21124.

Lunch 1–2.30pm. Dinner 7.30–8.30pm. 11 bedrooms.
Closed 24–26 and 31 December, 1 January.

Also recommended:

ARBUTUS LODGE

Nesting on a hilltop overlooking Cork, Arbutus Lodge is nothing short
of a gastronomic paradise. Its young and energetic owner, Declan
Ryan, trained with the Frères Troisgros in Roanne and a distinct
French influence is easily detected. The cooking is now closer to
haute cuisine than *cuisine bourgeoise* and though a few traditional Irish
dishes like Nettle soup and Drisheen are featured, they take second
place to the *Mosaïque de légumes*, *Côte de boeuf sauce Beaujolais à la moelle*,
Salmon with sorrel sauce. The dessert trolley will make gastronomes
weak with delight, as will the cheeseboard, with French and Irish offerings (including the rare Milleen variety) served with homemade soda
or walnut bread.
St Luke's Cross, Montenotte, Cork, Co. Cork, Eire. [Cork] 501237.
Lunch 1–2pm. Dinner 7–9.30pm. 20 bedrooms.
Closed Sunday lunch (except in the bar), Sunday dinner (except residents), 24–26 December.

DOYLE'S SEAFOOD BAR

A friendly atmosphere awaits diners who decide to try John and
Stella Doyle's seafood bar. As one would expect, the fish is excellent:
well cooked and imaginatively prepared. Dishes are chalked up on a
board beside the kitchen door and changed daily. As well as mussel
soup, crab bisque, fresh lobster, oysters, scallops and jumbo prawns,
there are various fish pies and stews, plus a good range of salads and
sweets. Children are made to feel welcome, as are visitors of any age.
John Street, Dingle, Co. Kerry, Eire. [Dingle] 144.
Lunch 12.30–2.15pm. Dinner 6–9pm.
Closed Sunday and November–February.

CROCNARAW

Wonderful home cooking, with vegetables from the garden, local fish
and lamb, this restaurant is a West coast treasure. Virtually everything
is made in the Crocnaraw kitchen with its owner, Joanne Fretwell, at
the stove every day. Fish dishes, particularly, are superb.
Moyard, Co. Galway, Eire. [Moyard] 9.
Lunch 1–2.15pm. Dinner 8–9.30pm. 10 bedrooms.
Closed Sunday dinner, Monday lunch, Good Friday and Easter,
24–26 December, 1 January.

Shops

BALLYMALOE
Shangarry, Co. Cork [62531], Eire.
Open 9am–6pm (or whenever you can find a member of the Allen
family with a key).

CREBER'S
48 Brook Street, Tavistock [2266], Devon. Open Monday–Saturday
9am–1pm, 2–5.30pm (early closing Wednesday).

CHEWTON CHEESE DAIRY
Priory Farm, Chewton Mendip [560], Bath, Somerset.
Open Monday–Saturday 8am–5pm, Sunday 9am–1pm.

FARNLEY SHOP
Farnley, Otley [56217], near Pool-in-Wharfedale, West Yorkshire.
Open Tuesday–Saturday 9.30am–5.30pm, Sunday (February–December) 10.30am–5.30pm.

JANE HOWARD
82–4 Bailgate, Lincoln [20010], Lincolnshire.
Open Monday–Friday 9am–5.30pm. Saturday 9am–3pm.

JUSTIN DE BLANK
42 Elizabeth Street, London S.W.1 [01-730-0605].
Open 9.30am–7.30pm, early closing Saturday (2pm).

LANHYDROCK HOUSE
Lanhydrock Park, near Bodmin [3320], Cornwall.
Open Monday–Sunday 11am–6pm April–October 31.

LEITH'S
Church Square, Ballater [474], Aberdeenshire.
Open Monday–Saturday 9am–5pm.

MIDDLE FARM SHOP
Firle, Ripe [303], Lewes, Sussex.
Open Monday–Saturday 10am–5pm.

MILSOM'S
63 St Matthews Street, Ipswich [53516], Suffolk.
Open Tuesday–Saturday 8.30am–5.30pm.

MOORES DORSET SHOP
Morcombelake, Chideock [253], Bridport, Dorset.
Open Monday–Friday 9am–5.30pm.

MOULD AND EDWARDS
19 Cheap Street, Sherborne [2412], Dorset.
Open Monday–Saturday 8.45am–1pm, 2–5pm (early closing Wednesday).

SPACKMAN'S
25 High Street, Hungerford [2593], Berkshire.
Open Monday–Saturday 8.30am–1pm, 2–5pm (early closing Thursday and Saturday).

THE OLD BAKERY
Woolpit, Bury St Edmunds [Elmswell 40255], Suffolk.
Open Tuesday–Saturday 10.30am–5pm (for coffee, lunch, teas and shop), Friday and Saturday evenings (for dinner in winter), Sunday (for lunch and tea), Tuesday–Saturday (dinner in summer).

THE VILLAGE STORE
Alfriston, Polegate [870201], East Sussex.
Open Monday–Saturday 9am–1pm, 2–5.30pm (early closing Wednesday).

VIN SULLIVAN AND SON
11 High Street, Abergavenny [2331], Gwent, Wales.
Open Monday–Saturday 9am–5.30pm (early closing Thursday).

WELLS STORES
Opposite The Bull, Streatley-on-Thames [Goring-on-Thames 2367], Berkshire.
Open Monday–Saturday 9am–1pm, 2.30–5pm.

WILLIAM'S KITCHEN
3 Fountain Street, Nailsworth [2240], Gloucestershire.
Open Monday 9am–1pm, Tuesday–Saturday 9am–5.30pm.

THE LITTLE DAIRY
4 Broad Street, Bell Cliff, Lyme Regis [2317], Dorset.
Open Monday–Sunday 9am–5.30pm (closed Sundays in the winter).

THE TOFFEE SHOP
7 Brunswick Road, Penrith [2008], Cumbria.
Open Monday–Saturday 9am–5pm (early closing Wednesday).

YE OLDE PORK SHOPPE
31 Salisbury Street, Blandford Forum [52828], Dorset.
Open Monday–Saturday 9am–5pm (early closing Wednesday and Saturday).

Bibliography

Allen, Myrtle, *The Ballymaloe Cookbook*. Cork: Agri Books, 1977

Bertholle, Louisette, *Secrets of the Great French Restaurants*. London: Sphere Books, 1975

Blake, Anthony, and Quentin Crewe, *Great Chefs of France*. London: Mitchell Beazley, 1978

Bocuse, Paul, *The New Cuisine*. London: Granada, 1978

Campbell, Susan, *Guide to Good Food Shops*. London: Macmillan, 1979

Cooper, Derek, *The Bad Food Guide*. London: Routledge and Kegan Paul, 1967

Costa, Margaret, *The Four Seasons Cookery Book*. London: Macdonald and Jane's, 1979

David, Elizabeth, *Mediterranean Food*. London: John Lehmann, 1950

David, Elizabeth, *French Country Cooking*. London: John Lehmann, 1951

David, Elizabeth, *French Provincial Cooking*. London: Michael Joseph, 1960

Dowding, Ian, and Nigel and Susan Mackenzie, *The Secrets of The Hungry Monk*. Jevington: Hungry Monk Publications, 1971

Dowding, Ian, and Kent Austin, *Deeper Secrets of The Hungry Monk*. Jevington: Hungry Monk Publications, 1974

Driver, Christopher, *The Good Food Guide 1979*. London: Consumers' Association and Hodder and Stoughton, 1979

Fothergill, John, *My Three Inns*. London: Chatto and Windus, 1949

Grigson, Jane, *English Food*. London: Macmillan, 1974

Guérard, Michel, *Cuisine Minceur*. London: Macmillan, 1977

Houston Bowden, Gregory, *British Gastronomy*. London: Chatto and Windus, 1975

Postgate, Raymond, *The Good Food Guide 1951–2*. London: Cassell, 1951

Robinson, Jancis, *The Wine Book*. London: Fontana, 1979

Ronay, Egon, *The Egon Ronay Guide 1980*. London: Penguin, 1980

Rubinstein, Hilary, *The Good Hotel Guide*. London: Jonathan Cape, 1979

Schloesser, Frank, *The Greedy Book*. London: Gay and Bird, 1906

Simon, André, *The Week-end Gourmet*. London: Seeley Service, 1942

Smith, Michael, *Posh Nosh*. London: BBC Publications, 1979

Tovey, John, *Entertaining with John Tovey*. London: Macdonald and Jane's, 1979

Williams-Ellis, Clough, *Architect Errant*. London: Constable, 1971

Index

Italicized entries refer to recipes

409

411

412

413